THEY CALL ME GEORGE

Also by Cecil Foster

Fiction
Independence
Dry Bone Memories
Slammin' Tar
Sleep On, Beloved
No Man in the House

Non-Fiction
Where Race Does Not Matter: The New Spirit of Modernity
Island Wings: A Memoir
A Place Called Heaven: The Meaning of Being Black in Canada
Caribana: The Greatest Celebration
Distorted Mirror: Canada's Racist Face

Academic Works
Blackness and Modernity: The Colour of Humanity and the Quest for Freedom
Genuine Multiculturalism: The Tragedy and Comedy of Diversity

THEY CALL ME GEORGE

*The Untold Story of Black Train Porters
and the Birth of Modern Canada*

CECIL FOSTER

BIBLIOASIS
WINDSOR, ONTARIO

FIRST EDITION, REVISED
SECOND PRINTING, MARCH 2019.

Library and Archives Canada Cataloguing in Publication

Foster, Cecil, 1954-, author
        They call me George : the untold story of black train porters and the birth of modern Canada / Cecil Foster.

(Untold lives)
Issued in print and electronic formats.
ISBN 978-1-77196-261-2 (softcover).--ISBN 978-1-77196-262-9 (ebook)

        1. Pullman porters--Canada--History. 2. Porters--Canada--History.
3. Train attendants--Canada--History. 4. Black Canadians--History.
I. Title.

HD6528.R362C25 2019   331.7'613852208996071   C2018-901743-0
                                                        C2018-901744-9

Edited by Janice Zawerbny
Copy-edited by Emily Donaldson and James Grainger
Cover designed by Michel Vrana
Typeset by Chris Andrechek

Quotations from new Canadian immigrants on front flap originated in the Permanent Collection of the Canadian Museum of Immigration at Pier 21 (www.pier21.ca).
Gloria Betty Brock, English War Bride, 1946. Canadian Museum of Immigration at Pier 21 (S2012.209.1).
Anna Silins, English Immigrant, 1951. Canadian Museum of Immigration at Pier 21 (S2012.768.1).
Martin Wydenes, Dutch Immigrant, 1952. Canadian Museum of Immigration at Pier 21 (S2012.1162.1).

Published with the generous assistance of the Canada Council for the Arts, which last year invested $153 million to bring the arts to Canadians throughout the country, and the Government of Canada. Biblioasis also acknowledges the support of the Ontario Arts Council (OAC), an agency of the Government of Ontario, which last year funded 1,709 individual artists and 1,078 organizations in 204 communities across Ontario, for a total of $52.1 million, and the contribution of the Government of Ontario through the Ontario Book Publishing Tax Credit and the Ontario Media Development Corporation. This is one of the 200 exceptional projects funded through the Canada Council for the Arts' New Chapter program. With this $35M investment, the Council supports the creation and sharing of the arts in communities across Canada.

PRINTED AND BOUND IN CANADA

MIX
Paper from
responsible sources
FSC® C004071
www.fsc.org

Dedicated to the Memory of
Billy Downie of Halifax
A sleeping car porter who became a dear friend
and whose spirit enlivens this book

For my grandchildren:
Akil, Markus, Michael, Liam, Amias, Armea, Ryan, Dominic ...

"*The members and officials of the Negro Citizenship Association and the Toronto C.P.R. Division of the Brotherhood of Sleeping Car Porters will continue to fight unremittingly for the right of all peoples of this planet to enter Canada and become its citizens without penalty or reward because of their race, colour, religion, national origin or ancestry. Yes, we take the uncompromising position that what appears to be premeditated discrimination in Canada's Immigration Laws and policy is utterly inconsistent with democratic principles and Christian ethics.*"

— Stanley Grizzle, president of the Toronto chapter of the
Brotherhood of Sleeping Car Porters, April 27, 1954

CONTENTS

INTRODUCTION

I WAS ON MY WAY to Windsor, Ontario, on VIA Rail Train 75, in late-summer 2018. A female voice, flawlessly bilingual in English and French, welcomed everybody on board. Everything seemed so routine. Settling into my aisle seat near the front of the car, I cracked open a book and started to read to help me get through the five-hour trip.

"Tickets, please," a gentle voice said over my head. I looked up to see a young woman with long, flowing black braids cascading down past her shoulders, in a navy uniform with an open-neck polo shirt, the corporation's insignia on her blazer; she was smiling at me, the traditional mile-wide smile historically associated with her job.

"Well, look at that," I said. "A Black train porter." Realizing how strange that statement might have sounded in our modern-day multicultural, diverse, and inclusive Canada, I felt compelled to explain why I was remarking on the obvious. "Do you know that I've been travelling a lot on the train in Canada and you are the first Black porter I've seen?"

This was true: train porter was once a job reserved exclusively for Black workers. I had recently been speaking to former train porters, and the old-timers were the first to draw my attention to this observation. You can hardly find any Black porters these days, they said wistfully. Nothing in my train travels had proven them wrong. Until now.

"No, man," she said laughing. "There are others."

"And you're a woman too," I said.

She laughed again.

"Do you know there was a time when the only porters you'd find on trains in Canada and the United States were Black men?" I asked her. "It was the only job they could get in Canada and the United States. Those porters fought to change all that so that Black workers could have greater employment opportunities."

She did not know any of this. The quizzical look remained on her face as she waited for me to produce my ticket. I thought about the time, three years earlier, when, following his election victory, Prime Minister Justin Trudeau was asked why he wanted gender parity in his cabinet and he replied simply, "Because it is 2015!" thereby ending the conversation. Canada has evolved over time, so that now issues such as gender—and presumably race, ethnicity, and religion too—do not matter in daily life. Or so was the implication in his statement.

At that point my wife, who was sitting next to me, entered the conversation and explained that I was an author and professor, and that my research into a book about the history of Black train porters in Canada was the very reason we were on the train.

"My name is Rokhaya Ndiaye," she answered when I asked. "I am Senegalese."

"And that's another thing," I blurted out. "It was the train porters who made it possible for people like you and me to be in this country. Indeed, they forced Canada to open up immigration to people from all parts of the world, including Africa and Asia."

"Oh," she said, sounding genuinely interested in the discussion. "I must find out more about that." After saying she was happy to have met me, she zapped the ticket barcode on my phone with a hand-held machine and posted two white card strips on the luggage container above our heads. She had a carload of other passengers waiting for her attention and could linger no more. She handed me her business card—which called her a manager in "customer experience" and not a "train porter"—and we promised to continue the conversation at another time.

As I travelled on the train, I thought of all the train porters who came before Rokhaya Ndiaye, and who left a legacy of social change in Canada as part of the Civil Rights Movement—and indeed the entire Black experience in the Americas and beyond. But nobody is more deserving of recognition than Stanley Grizzle, whose tireless efforts for change make him effectively the hero of this book.

Following the Second World War, Stanley Grizzle and his fellow porters fought to create a new Canada by embodying a citizenship that reflected the entire diversity and dignity of humanity itself. The train porters battled to make normal what is now socially routine, and even taken for granted, in our daily living: Black workers' ability to hold a wide range of jobs and to be hired and promoted in the civil service; and for Black people from Africa and the West Indies to immigrate and become citizens of Canada.

We should always remember this was not a fight they were guaranteed to win. We should also not forget that Canada wasn't originally intended to be a multicultural society. Official multiculturalism in Canada was a fluke of history. Some thought of multiculturalism as democracy gone wrong. Against great odds, the sleeping car porters sacrificed themselves and all that they had to put a stick in the wheels, figuratively speaking, that were driving Canada toward a different destination. The train porters turned Canada black, brown, and a host of other shades. Yet this important piece of Canadian history has yet to be fully told.

The last time I saw Stanley Grizzle, he was standing in the mid-afternoon sun at the corner of Toronto's Bathurst Street and St. Clair Avenue West, a few years before his death in 2016 at the age of ninety-eight years.

"There's Stan waiting for a bus," I said to my wife, Sharon, who was in the car beside me. "Let's give him a lift."

I pulled up to the bus stop. "Stan, where are you going?" I called to him.

The tall, slim man, his age showing in the slight droop of his shoulders, seemed momentarily surprised that someone was calling to him from a car. Under his broad-brim hat, his eyes flitted around until he recognized me. He smiled.

"I'm going home," he said.

"Get in," I replied. "We'll give you a ride."

In the car we chatted generally, about nothing of consequence that I can recall. A few blocks on, we arrived near the Bathurst Street subway station where Grizzle would have exited had he taken the bus. "I'll walk in from here," he said.

"No, man," I replied. "We'll take you right home." Guided by his backseat directions, we meandered through side streets in the Bloor and Bathurst area—historically one of the main neighbourhoods where Black people lived in Toronto—until we arrived at a detached home with a verandah on a tree-lined street.

At that time, I thought I knew Grizzle. I'd seen him around the Black and Caribbean communities at major Toronto events, for he was that kind of a presence: a respected community leader and activist who led protest demonstrations in the name of social justice at home and abroad; a speaker at

Black History Month events; a celebrated and popular citizenship judge; and a champion of the successes and individual achievements of Black Canadians.

I first met Grizzle in the 1970s, when I was the editor of *Contrast*, a newspaper that represented and often spoke to, and for, the Black community in Canada. Grizzle was one of the community regulars who would drop by the newspaper's office. Often, he came with a letter or a comment on some issue of the day that he wanted published. I knew that he was one of the first Black men to run, if unsuccessfully, for political office in Ontario, but by the 1970s he practiced his politics mainly as a community activist. I also knew him to be an avid reader who attended some of the Toronto launches of my books and who, for the price of a signed book, generously supported me with his purchases, as he did for just about every Black writer gaining recognition in Canada. Grizzle liked following the careers of Black Canadians in arts, politics, media, and theatre—those who, in his youth, would have been called Proud Race Men and Women for their pioneering work in breaking into the Canadian mainstream and keeping a positive racial presence there. He collected scraps of news—and sometimes entire publications—about Black achievement, compiling an extensive collection that I happened upon when going through his numerous boxes of personal papers, now held at Archives Canada in Ottawa.

What a treasure trove he collected on the Black experience worldwide, but most notably in Canada and the United States. To my surprise, I happened upon several articles about myself as a news reporter and writer, along with entries on other prominent Black Canadians, writers such as Austin Clarke and several others who were "firsts" in their fields, or who were breaking social and racial barriers. It was obvious Grizzle collected with an eye to educating future generations about what it was like for Black people like him in North America, generally, but in Canada, specifically, in the first seven decades of the twentieth century. In his records, he presented Black Canada in relationship with what was happening in the Caribbean— or, more specifically, the British West Indies—Europe, Africa, and in all those former possessions linked around the globe by colonialism: once categorized as members of the British Empire, they were now known as the British Commonwealth. He was an original Pan-Africanist in orientation.

It was through those papers that I think I really got to know Stanley Grizzle and realize how important he remains to the story of multiculturalism in Canada. Much of what I found in the boxes I did not know, and what little I did know could now be placed in a specific social and historical context. As I researched, I kept asking myself why I knew so little about the history I was reading: why didn't I know about Stanley Grizzle's role in the Civil Rights Movement in Canada and the United States; or his role in helping the British Caribbean islands to become politically independent?

Why, I thought, did I not whip out my cell phone when I last saw him, and snap a picture as he made his way up the steps and onto that famous verandah where, as I discovered in his papers, Grizzle used to sit and entertain, sometimes sparring verbally, with US Civil Rights icon A. Philip Randolph, the pioneering head of the international Brotherhood of Sleeping Car Porters (BSCP), when he visited Toronto. Grizzle idolized Randolph, even mimicking his speech patterns, and learned from his mentor about the importance of courting the media and good public relations when promoting Civil Rights causes.

It was Randolph who was the main organizer of the March on Washington for Jobs and Freedom in 1963, and who introduced the crowd at the Lincoln Memorial to the US Civil Rights icon Dr. Martin Luther King Jr. before his famous "I Have a Dream" speech. Through Randolph, Grizzle developed a relationship with King that included an exchange of letters and conferred a standing invitation to King to visit and speak in Toronto. After King's death, Grizzle's friendship continued with King's wife, Coretta, who can be seen in those files in an iconic picture from when she came to Toronto and received an award in her husband's name from Grizzle, who was sharply decked out in his tuxedo. As Grizzle records in his papers, Randolph liked coming to his house when he was on business in Canada. He would sit and admire the neighbourhood's tall trees and comment on how different the ambiance was in Canada from what it was in the United States. Why did I not know more of these important historical relationships and their contributions to Canadian history?

In many respects, these questions go to the heart of this book. Why don't we know more about the struggle of Black men and women who fought Jim Crow-style laws and political policies so they could be recognized, not only as humans, but as full citizens of Canada? Why are their achievements in community- and nation-building often absent, or erased, from official narratives, especially from the historical ones? Why is it not understood that Canada officially became a multicultural country because—yes, it's worth repeating yet again—*because* of the pioneering work of the railway porters and the still-not-fully-fulfilled dreams of Black people like Grizzle, who, at one time, were allowed only jobs as sleeping car porters, if they were men, and in-home domestics if they were women. Why are these Black activists not celebrated or fully recognized for taking Canada off the bankrupting path of trying to be an exclusive and racist country? Why are these stories of Canadian Blackness still not told, even in this moment of multicultural awareness and racial, ethnic, and cultural reconciliation?

With this book, and in honour of Grizzle and the warriors of his generation, I hope to make a contribution toward changing some of those long-held misperceptions about Canada and, indeed, about the international struggle of Black people in Canada for social, political, and economic freedom everywhere, including the long-term impact of their efforts on particularly the social, political and cultural development of Canada.

Now, A QUICK WORD ON the thinking behind the book and my method: I want readers to hear the various protagonists' voices echo down through the ages; those who grappled with decisions about Canada's role and purpose in the world, and, specifically, Black peoples' role and social position in this country. I want this to be a *speakerly* book, where readers can truly engage the combatants, by hearing them as much as possible in their own words, and at length. By minimizing the paraphrasing of their words I will not appear to be coaching them or putting words in their mouths. So yes, I quote at length, and on purpose. It is only through their own words that readers will understand what drove the people in this book to make the decisions they did, and why we may argue that by timeless, acceptable standards—even if they genuinely believed what they were doing was morally right and good—they were wrong and even immoral in their thoughts and actions. And we will let the words of those who acted out of malice implicate them, justify our assessment of them as evil and even inhumane. This is particularly the case when looking back on the words and actions of historical figures like Prime Minister Wilfrid Laurier, whose policies aimed to make Canada into a country for white people only. It is tempting to excuse them as having less enlightened ideas, and of being representatives "of their time." But what this argument often forgets is that, even in those times, alternative views and actions were offered and the people in power ignored them. Those things and ideas we now classify as "good" weren't discovered in this present moment, or just because we arrived at the most recent date on some calendar. These powerful people of the past deliberately chose specific views and actions and rationalized their decisions afterwards. They used their power to act in their own self-interest, ignoring all other argument and entreaties. They made choices and backed them up, not with arguments for the good, but ultimately to reinforce their own political power and social status, regardless of logic and morality. What's good today was good in days gone by: white supremacy was just as evil at the beginning of the twentieth century, and many people over the years fought at great risk against this scourge. Evil is always evil, which is something that those of us living today will need to bear in mind when future generations hold us in judgment.

Originally, I intended to capture the words of porters talking about the way they lived and worked. I wanted to interview as many as I could find. But time has caught up with most of these men. The majority of those who worked during the era immediately following the Second World War have passed away. And the caregivers of the various porters who remain are often reluctant to expose them and their faltering minds and bodies to interviews. Having all but completed their human journey, the desire to protect them is understandable. The interviews that were possible were with those train porters who entered the struggle at the tail end of a special moment that changed Canada. Fortunately, they benefitted from the discussions on the trains, when senior porters would gather younger ones in empty cars, bars, and in club houses across the country to tell stories of what it was like to work on the railroad in an earlier time. In this respect, the archives now available—especially those of the Toronto division of the international Brotherhood of Sleeping Car Porters—provide much of the information in this book. But I hope readers will still get a full taste of the porters' lives from their own perspective as well as Black peoples' lives in early modern Canada.

To contextualize the quotes in the book, I provide time and place in the hope of minimizing the reader's need to consult too many notes. On a related matter, let me say a few words about the language I use in this book, some of which would otherwise be considered pejorative. Where specific words like *Negro*, *nigger*, and *Sambo* are used in the original, I reproduce them unchanged. Similarly, in solidarity with the struggles many of the sleeping car porters experienced in their time, I capitalize the first letter in "Black" and "Negro" as they did, in a nod to what they called "racial pride." The use of capitalization was a moral choice by the porters, something that, as I show in the latter part of the book, was fundamental to their desire to change the way Black people were depicted, positioned, and imagined as Canadians, and as humans. "Black" and "Negro" were sometimes capitalized in Canadian government documents, sometimes not. I use quotes to reproduce whichever form is in the original. Traditionally, no similar argument was offered for the word white, so I do not capitalize the first letter in that word.

When the sleeping car porters decided they wanted to have a hand and a loud voice in (re)making Canada into an example for the rest of the world, they found it was no easy task. So as the porters have shouted down through time, I too say "all aboard!" for we are ready to begin this very special journey into Canadian history, and the pursuit of freedom by Black railway porters.

LEAVING THE STATION
Stan Grizzle's Legacy of Social Change

FEW NOTICED WHEN THE CANADIAN Pacific Railway passenger train with a specially chartered sleeping car arrived at Ottawa's Union Station on the evening of April 26, 1954. Spring was in the air after a cold Canadian winter and the temperature in the national capital was a cool ten degrees Celsius. Winds were blowing from the north at speeds between five and ten kilometres an hour. The change of season was bringing important transformations to every part of the country; indeed, the British Empire, and the world. As they emerged from the dreadful sacrifices of the recent wars, everyone knew warmer weather and better times were on the way, not only in Ottawa but across all of Canada. Canadian newspapers were filled with advertisements for the latest summer wear, travel extravaganzas, luxury automobiles, technologically advanced stoves and fridges, as well as tips for bringing out the best in gardens, which were about to bloom.

To all appearances, Canada had long since ceased to be a bush garden made up of an endless number of isolated garrisons. Canada was, in fact, a cohesive and affluent society. Only five years earlier the country had taken a firm step toward its founding destiny: it had gathered all the white British dominions in the Atlantic under one flag with the relatively painless absorption of Newfoundland into the confederation. Canada was a now a player on the world stage. At home, everything indicated the good life could only get better. Unemployment was hovering in the range of 2 to 4.6 percent annually, about the same as in the United States, and would remain at these levels for the next two decades, as would the annual inflation rate. With a gross national product of about $8,000 per Canadian, the country easily ranked in the top ten of world economies. With a rising standard of living, Canada was an ideal place in which to live by just about any measure.

The railways—which had been counted on, from the beginning of Confederation almost one hundred years earlier, to knit provinces, regions, communities, languages, and cultures into a modern nation state—had done their work, and much of the 400,000 miles of railroad countrywide were now redundant. Mentally, however, the notion of Canadian patriotism was still a work in progress: struggles between anglophone and francophone culture still came to the fore every so often. But most people in the country considered themselves either British or Canadian. For many of the privileged groups, Canada was undoubtedly and proudly the premiere White Man's Country, and the commitment to whiteness was supposedly the primary reason for this rising prosperity.

If there was any real concern about whether this prosperity could be maintained, it lay in the realization that Canada was having difficulty attracting the immigrants who could become new citizens, new workers, and new consumers. But the truth was immigration was lagging solely because Canada wasn't attracting the type of immigrants it preferred. The world was full of people willing to make Canada their home, but these potential immigrants weren't the romanticized ideal of what many thought of as "ideal Canadians"; namely, they weren't white.

Accompanying the passengers on this train trip to Ottawa were two powerful but contradictory ideas—that Black people in Canada had been treated unjustly and that Canada could be a very different country in the future if it would just agree to change course. The delegates on the train embodied these two ideas; they lived the despair that came from the racialization they endured on a daily basis, but they also clung to the hope that Canada could become a home for people from all parts of the world, a place where the latter would live together in a peaceful fraternity. (In the same way that Canada was assumed to be racially and ethnically white, in the dominant language of the day it was also conceived as male and heterosexual.) Black Canadians wanted to live in brotherhood with diverse groups of Canadians from around the world.

Many of the sleeping car passengers arriving in Ottawa were Black sleeping car porters, or people who had once worked as porters or had come from homes and families with porters. Several were immigrants who wanted more immigrants like themselves to come to Canada in search of a better life. Since the beginning of Confederation, most train passengers had travelled almost exclusively in the care of these smartly dressed and always smiling Black porters, who manned the trains' popular sleeping cars and parlour cars. Celebrated Canadian humorist Stephen Leacock had described these porters as "smiling darkeys."[1] But these unobtrusive men on the transcontinental railway were as much iconic representatives of Canada and the Canadian experience as Mounties, moose, beavers, and iced-over hockey ponds.

As a group, and even as representatives of a racialized community, the Black train porters were politically invisible, remaining outside the social imagination of those considered "Canadians." For the most part, Black train porters were, like the old adage about children, to be seen but not heard; they were not to speak unless spoken to. On the trains—referred to as "going on the roads" or "portering"—the porters were the invisible domestic workers who prepared for the party and stayed around to clean up afterwards, and who, while circulating among celebrants, never stopped to mingle or taste the sumptuous offerings. When passengers overindulged or were sick, for whatever reason, the porters nursed them. Afterwards, the porters had to painstakingly fill out company-mandated forms, speculating on how contagious the passengers were. Often sleep-deprived on their eight-day cross-country runs, porters had to maintain enough presence of mind to ensure passengers did not miss their stops or leave luggage and any valuables behind. A missed stop was at the top of a long list of dismissible offences the porters confronted each trip. The highest reward for impeccable service wasn't a salary or liveable wage, but a gratuity based on the whims of those they had to so carefully satisfy.

In practice, train work was an opportunity to make a livelihood from tips, initially no different from the growing craze to employ hat- and coat-check women, who worked exclusively for gratuities, at trendy hotels. The porter's job was to ensure that passengers were comfortable while they were guests on the trains, and to do so as unobtrusively as possible. Like the chattel slaves in the Americas who, in many cases, were not only their elders or grandparents but also their archetypal work mentors, the porters were expected to be subservient, never questioning, always ready to issue the obligatory *yassir* and *thank you ma'am* before flashing a friendly smile, especially after receiving a tip for their good service. Though the porters were disdained in some parts of their communities as glorified chambermaids, the job itself was considered a good catch, with people often claiming that if a young Black woman wanted a secure future her best bet was to marry a porter. From time to time, white people worked as porters, but in the main, from the beginning of the twentieth century, portering was predominantly a job for Black men. And this was how Black people became defined in the national, and indeed international, imagination as servers and second-class citizens.

In a broader sense, the Canadian national narrative up to this point was clear: Canada did not have Black people in numbers of consequence and as a result it was spared the dreaded *Negro question*—the struggle, that is, between white and Black citizens over human rights and inequality then plaguing the United States. Canada was the oldest country in the Dominion, or self-ruling white colonies in the British Empire, and led the way in demonstrating to the mother country how white societies the world over could escape entanglement in the dreaded "colour line." The British could colonize the world but, in return, they'd have to pay for this achievement by having to adjudicate between catering to the wishes of white Europeans, who were supposedly a superior race of people, while keeping Black people, their inferiors, at bay. These colonies were the sites of a never-ending struggle between Europeans—who claimed, by nature, to be masters— asserting their rights and privileges, and those demanding the same treatment but who, solely because of their race, were considered better suited to be slaves or servants, and were thus not entitled to equality of treatment. In these societies there was an invisible "colour line": on one side everyone was white, European, progressive, and morally good, while on the other were people of colour, the "inferior races," who were backwards, unintelligent, and depraved. Across this line, two races of people, with unequal natural abilities, fought an incessant battle for dominance. It was believed that no society could ever hope to survive harmoniously if those on either side of this invisible colour line mixed freely. The races might be able to mingle in controlled circumstances, such as at work, but in the hierarchy of labour, the rights and entitlements that went with each race were different, and had to be rigidly respected in order to maintain social order. Inferior races had to be kept in their place; otherwise a society would be forever torn. The price to be paid for such mixing was exemplified by the bloody Civil War, from 1861 to 1865, that almost wrecked the United States—a war where American President Abraham Lincoln publicly declared that "a house divided against itself cannot stand." Generations later, America still struggles with the Civil War's legacy, while the reasons for the conflict remain largely unsettled.

Canada and the United States started out in the same position, as British colonies seeking to exploit the natural resources under the custodianship of Indigenous peoples for thousands of years, yet Canada avoided the scar and legacy of the Civil War by keeping the "inferior races" out by severely limiting the entrance of Black people into the country. Within the British Empire, and the white world in general—Australia, New Zealand, and especially South Africa, with whom Canada had always shared a "special relationship," something akin to an elder mentoring a younger sibling—Canada offered an example of how to avoid the same pitfalls as the United States. This narrative was perhaps best captured at the turn of the century, when Prime Minister Wilfrid Laurier, speaking to the Canadian Club in Ottawa on January 18, 1904, and responding to racial concerns on both sides of the border, stated "as the 19th century was that of the United States, so I think the 20th century shall be filled by Canada."[2] Laurier meant that Canada's success would depend on maintaining and enforcing the colour line that was the basis for Jim Crow-style laws in North America. Canada and the US would be the main protagonists in the battle to maintain white supremacy, but in Laurier's mind there was no guarantee that the United States, with its legacy of the Civil War and sizable Black population, would be able achieve white dominance. Instead, Canada would be the home for whiteness in the western hemisphere—a promise that seemed to be falling into place when Newfoundland joined Confederation in 1949, fulfilling a dream held by British society since the American War of Independence of bringing all the predominantly white and British dominions in the Atlantic into a single nation state.

To achieve this goal, Canadian policymakers had rejected several overtures from Britain to include the British West Indies in its possessions and allow it to enter the Canadian Confederation alongside Newfoundland. From 1776 onwards, following the secession of the United States, the idea of Canada joining with all the remaining British possessions in the Atlantic to form a single political union to rival the United States was widely discussed in British circles. Indeed, banding together in the face of anticipated US military aggression was very much part of the thinking that led to the creation of the Canadian Confederation ninety years later. By accepting Newfoundland into Confederation, Canadians thus partially attained their dream of establishing a unified British outpost in the Americas. As a white colony, Newfoundland got in; the West Indies were denied entry, however, because their residents were Black.

Institutionally, in policy and practice, Canada was officially White Man's Country and it intended to stay that way. By the first decades of the new century, many politicians and policymakers from other countries were trying to emulate what Canada had achieved. South of the border, US president Woodrow Wilson—a known sympathizer of the Ku Klux Klan and friend of Laurier—had formerly overseen the introduction of Jim Crowism when he segregated Black and white workers in the federal Railway Mail Service train cars and then banned Black workers from most of the US Post Office, the government agency being a last refuge for ex-slaves and their descendants to get federal work. The few Black workers who remained at the US Post Office in Washington did so out of the sight of the public, after being forced to work behind a screen. (This was emulated later on the Canadian railways when Black porters were required to eat behind a screen at meal times.)

Laurier's government put similar segregation strategies in place in Canada—using the government-owned railway and the civil service as policy tools. Laurier did not think Black people were his social equals and he was quick to express disdain for them. Speaking in the House of Commons on March 18, 1915, on a motion to increase passenger fares, Laurier, then the leader of the opposition, clearly spoke his mind: "The man who goes in a pullman car from here (Ottawa) to Montreal is charged only 5 cents, when this very man would give more as a tip to the nigger who attends him."[3] As Laurier explained, the government was demeaning real Canadians by requiring them to tip the porters when travelling, as if the porters were an inferior people always in need of help or the charity of others. It's also worth pointing out that Laurier's comment came around the same time some of his fellow parliamentarians, editorialists, and other public intellectuals across North America were seeking to outlaw tipping, characterizing the practice as begging and highway robbery.

By mid-century, Canada had successfully controlled the size of the country's Black population, primarily by allowing in only exceptional Black immigrants as students or to work as porters. At Confederation, Canada had a Black population of about 20,000 people—which was already down from approximately 50,000 a decade earlier—out of a total Canadian population of 3.5 million.[4] By the mid-twentieth century, almost one hundred years later, it had only 18,000 Black people, who lived mostly in Halifax, New Glasgow, Sydney, and Amherst in Nova Scotia; Saint John in New Brunswick; Montreal in Quebec; and Toronto and Windsor in Ontario— with a smattering in Winnipeg, Calgary, and Vancouver.

With a total population of about 15 million by the middle of the last century, Canada had kept its Black population to well below one percent, a small fraction of the proportional percentage of Blacks to the general population south of the border.[5] It was believed at the time that if a foreign group was larger than one percent of the total population, it might prove disruptive and not be as easily controllable.

By keeping the Black population low, Canada's leaders argued it had avoided the racial trap that the United States had created with its dependence on Black labour. It was a trap that the immigration policies of Britain, Canada, and all other white dominions, were designed to avoid. Although Canadian policymakers eyed the British West Indies as a potential pool of cheap Black labour, fear of an increasing Black presence in the country meant that Black immigration in the early twentieth century was limited annually to one hundred people—mainly men—all of whom were channelled toward a career in portering. Without the railways, the situation would have been even starker for Black people in Canada.

IN THE SPRING OF 1954, a sleeping car was chartered for porters, former porters, and their allies to visit Ottawa for a protest. The group's mission: to change the country. With the exception of a few allies, most prominently members of Canadian Jewish communities, these protestors were very much on their own. They were demanding new thoughts and actions about who could become a Canadian citizen, a status to which, in practice, only white British subjects were entitled. The porters wanted to shift the country, move it toward a future that would be very different from the one Canada had established for itself through its plans and policies.

Historically, Canada had been created as a white country exclusively for the habitation and benefit of people of European ethnicities. The porters' alternate Canadian model was one that no other European settlement in the hemisphere had attempted: a new nation state created out of all the peoples of the world, a country of equality, where specific ethnic groups would not have all the privileges and others none, and where every member of society had an unhindered opportunity to rise to the best of their own ability and imagining. The Canada the train porter protesters were proposing and envisioning would be a country based on inclusiveness and diversity; one where race would not matter. It would be a modern country in which ethnic "mongrelization," or diversity, would be natural—where the various peoples of the world mixed freely with the Indigenous people on whose lands these hemispheric colonies, dominions, and even independent republics, were constructed. It was a model for a universal brotherhood, as it was called in the day, with all of humanity sharing the same collective dignity and sense of fraternity. Except in the fertile minds of a few true believers, the dream of such a diverse and equal society had perished in a nation state that was historically and intentionally racist.

This dream of a better, more inclusive society was a common one, both at home and abroad, prior to Canada's establishment as a confederation in 1867. "In Canada, as in other recently settled countries," pioneering Black settler Mary Ann Shadd wrote in an attempt to capture this vision on the eve of Canadian Confederation:

> ...there is much to do, and comparatively few for the work. The numerous towns and villages springing up, and the great demand for timber and agricultural products, make labor of every kind plenty: all trades that are practiced in the United States, are patronized by whomsoever carried on— no man's complexion affecting his business. If a colored man understands his business, he receives the public patronage the same as a white man. He is not obligated to work a little better, and at a lower rate—there is no degraded class to identify him with, therefore every man's work stands or falls according to merit, not as his color. Builders, and other tradesmen, of different complexions, work together on the same building and in the same shop, with perfect harmony, and often the proprietor of an establishment is colored, and the majority of all the men employed are white. Businesses that in older communities have ceased to remunerate, yield a large percentage to the money invested.

Shadd encouraged Black American slaves to make their way to Canada, to this land of plenty and liberty, and, along with other ethnicities, to help build a society marked by freedom, equality, and fraternal love.

"Railroads are in the process of construction—steamboats now ply between Toronto and several towns on the lakes; and in process of time, iron and other works will be in operation, it is said, all requiring their quota, and of course keeping up the demand," wrote Shadd, with the kind of idealistic enthusiasm we associate with the founders of great nations.

> Boards from home and foreign markets, are successfully manufactured, and numerous mill-sites are fast being appropriated to saw and grist mills. In some sections, colored men are engaged in saw mills on their own account. At Dawn, a settlement on the Sydenham (river in south west Ontario) [...]

and at other points, this trade is prosecuted with profit for them. To enumerate the different occupations in which colored persons are engaged, even in detail, would but fatigue, and would not further the end in view, namely: To set forth the advantage of a residence in a country, in which chattel slavery is not tolerated, and prejudice of *color* has no existence whatever—the adaptation of that country, by climate, soil, and political character, to their physical and political necessities; and the superiority of residence there over their present position at *home*. It will suffice, that colored men prosecute all the different trades; are store keepers, farmers, clerks, and laborers; and are not only unmolested, but sustained and encouraged in any business for which their qualifications and means fit them; and as the resources of the country develop, new fields of enterprise will be opened to them, and consequently new motives to honorable effort.[6]

Canada, according to Shadd, could be a nirvana, a place fugitive slaves called Heaven, or Canaan, where the ideals of happiness, well-being, and a commonwealth could be pursued. But was this at the time the real Canada, a country that accepted Black people, with dignity, as citizens? Or was the real Canada the one that embraced Jim Crow-style laws at the beginning of twentieth century? Was the place Canada had become in the first half of the century an aberration, a digression? Had Canada made a political mistake by trying to exclusively become White Man's Country? If the answer to this last question was in the affirmative, then to correct this social monstrosity and return to the inclusivity of the past, politicians would have to adopt the porters' recommendations to make the country a place for official multiculturalism and realize Canada's true destiny.

Indeed, finding a country where Black citizens could belong, and were treated equally, was a dream that went back to the dismantling of British North America into, first, the United States of America, following the Declaration of Independence in 1776, and second, the creation of Canada, specifically the establishment of Upper Canada, which had been intended as the home of retreating loyalists from the American War of Independence. Some understand this moment—the creation of nation states in the Americas—as the beginning of Modernity itself. Both the United States, under President George Washington, and Upper Canada, under the governorship of his war rival, John Graves Simcoe, claimed to be the home of liberty and freedom. Both had to face the contradiction of

African slavery in their rival lands. Simcoe and Washington represented dueling, dialectical forces of freedom, each fighting for dominance and recognition as the spirit of the times.

"This may seem a contradiction," George Washington said, rationalizing African slavery in the United States to an English visitor to his home soon after the War of Independence, "but I think you must perceive that it is neither a crime nor an absurdity. When we profess, as our fundamental principle, that liberty is the inalienable right of every man, we do not include madmen or idiots; liberty in their hands would be a scourge. Till the mind of the slave has been educated to perceive what are the obligations of a state of freedom, and not confound a man's with a brute's, the gift would insure its abuse."[7]

This hypocritical statement would lead to a question that would bedevil race relations in the New World: *when* would Black people be fully ready for freedom and unconditional citizenship? Gradualists, who argued for amelioration and piecemeal recognition of human dignity, and their opponents, who demanded immediate recognition, would fall into separate camps. Even at the height of the Civil Rights Movement in the 1960s, this question was front and centre, and was captured best in the dialogue between Martin Luther King Jr. and a group of Christian and Jewish clergy, who recommended the Civil Rights leader take a more gradualist approach in the fight for Black dignity. In his famous *Letter from a Birmingham Prison* in 1963, King spoke to this eternal of question of *when*:

> We know through painful experience that freedom is never voluntarily given by the oppressor; it must be demanded by the oppressed. Frankly, I have yet to engage in a direct action campaign that was "well timed" in the view of those who have not suffered unduly from the disease of segregation. For years now I have heard the word "Wait!" It rings in the ear of every Negro with piercing familiarity. This "Wait" has almost always meant "Never." We must come to see, with one of our distinguished jurists, that "justice too long delayed is justice denied."[8]

By calling for immediate changes in immigration and labour policy, the sleeping car porters were similarly impressing on the government in Ottawa the urgency of *now* for the full recognition of human dignity and equality for Blacks in Canada. In doing so, they were trying to steer Canada closer to what Simcoe imagined for the country more than a century earlier.

Washington had believed Black people were not ready for liberty because they had not evolved socially from the level of brutes and were therefore incapable of benefitting from freedom. More than that, Washington argued, societies should not be thrown into chaos through abrupt change. History and tradition had to be maintained, even if at the expense of freedom for Black people. "We might as well be asked to pull down our old warehouses before trade has increased to demand enlarged new ones," Washington argued. "Both houses and slaves were bequeathed to us by Europeans, and time alone can change them; an event which, you may believe me, no man desires more heartily that I do. Not only do I pray for it on the score of human dignity, but I can clearly foresee that nothing but the rooting out of slavery can perpetuate the existence of our Union, by consolidating it in a common bond of principle."[9] For Washington, society was governed by folkways that evolved slowly over time, and that any freedom for Black people had to be deferred because society was not ready for it.

As the embodiment of the new spirit of what would become Canada, Simcoe took a different approach: liberty for Black people in Upper Canada could not wait and had to be immediate. When he established Parliament, one of the first measures Simcoe introduced as a priority, in 1793, was an act to prevent the introduction of Negro slaves. Simcoe's feelings about the subject of slavery were strong, and one of his earliest resolves was to purge the colony of this evil: "The moment that I assume the government of Upper Canada, under no modification will I assent to a law that discriminates, by dishonest policy, between the natives of Africa, America, or Europe." "The latter Act met with singular opposition," writes Duncan Campbell Scott in his biography of Simcoe. "There are no statistics available to the number of slaves in servitude in the province, but many had been obtained during the war by purchase from the Indians who had captured them in forays in American territory. Obtained from such a source, the price paid was small, and owing to the arduous conditions of labour and the scarcity of labourers in the new colony, the value of the negroes was very great." Some of the planters who retreated north with Simcoe had brought their slaves with them and kept them in bondage. However, several former slaves, who were given their freedom to fight with the British, came as free men and women. This created a problem: was Black labour to be viewed immediately as emancipated and hence to be paid for through wages and other "charges" to employers, or was it to be enslaved? As Duncan Campbell Scott explained, "The feeling even among those who admitted the necessity for the legislation was that action should be postponed for two years to allow those who had no slaves to procure them."[10] Simcoe refused to delay legislation to allow his supporters to first acquire slaves in order that, while future slave acquisitions would be banned, they would be allowed to keep the ones they'd recently procured.

Upper Canada became the second state, after Denmark, to abolish slavery on May 16, 1792, and the first British colony to outlaw slavery. The Act of George III, Chapter 27, which permitted the admission of slaves into a colony, was repealed. According to the new rules: in future, no slave could be brought into the province; the contract terms under which a current slave could be bound was nine years; and children of slaves in the province were to be declared free when they reached the age of twenty-five, until which time they were to remain with their mothers. In due time, owing to the gradual implementation of these provisions, slavery disappeared. Notices such as the following, in the August 19, 1795, issue of the (government) *Gazette*, "For sale … a negro wrench named Chloe, 23 years old, who understands washing, cooking, etc. Apply to Robert Franklin, at the Receiver-General's,"[11] became a thing of the past.

At their inceptions, then, Canada and the United States were committed to different goals, with Simcoe fighting for Canada to be a country in which the dignity of Black people was recognized as much as it was for whites. As historian Robin Winks notes, the same spirit Simcoe exhibited spread to the provinces that would become part of Canada, where at least politically, if not as fully as Simcoe envisioned it, Black people were more tolerated than in the US. Apart from Simcoe's actions, Winks writes,

> …by judicial decisions in Nova Scotia and New Brunswick between 1799 and 1801, slave-holding had been rendered difficult if neither impossible nor illegal; in Lower Canada and Prince Edward Island no action had been taken against slavery, although public opinion was clearly indifferent or hostile to it. By the 1820s a continentally directed abolitionist movement had grown, particularly in Upper Canada, which was alert to anti-slavery trends in Britain.

He notes too that, just prior to the American Civil War, "Negroes, whether fugitive from the United States or blacks from Africa or the West Indies, were on the whole treated in Canada as potentially equals, at least politically."[12]

This was the dream that, throughout history, kept the hopes of Black and African peoples alive: that they would become members of societies of their choosing and, particularly in the case of Canada, that they would become full and equal citizens. They hoped this would apply to all peoples of African ancestry, as well as other non-European peoples living in the New World.

At the heart of this was a question that had bedeviled Black nationalists and integrationists alike: Can there be a homeland for the descendants of Africans in the Americas? On the one side was the argument that former slaves and their descendants in the Americas needed their own countries to recapture and advance the human dignity robbed of them through slavery; on the other that dignity could be reclaimed through their acceptance and recognition as full citizens in their countries of residence in the Americas. But this second position raised an important question: Even if African people could find a home in a nation state in the Americas, pragmatically in European settler colonies in the New World, would they be able to live there as free individuals, enjoying the same freedom of opportunity and having the same social responsibilities as all other citizens?

Both positions were part of a wider discussion about whether modern countries had to exclusively be nations, representing a single nationalism, or whether they could be established for the benefit of many ethnic groups bound together by a simple, common desire and intention to co-exist. Could nation states be established based on values and ideas as opposed to blood and soil? Was it true that different ethnic groups, practicing their own distinctive ways of life, would always result in conflict within a common territory? Would a country hosting different ethnicities be prone to interminable cultural clashes over who should be dominant and who should willingly accept their inferiority and marginalization? Already riven by competing English and French nationalisms, would a country like Canada be able to overcome struggles between other peoples from other parts of the world? Undoubtedly, the dominant voices argued, it would be chaos if a state were too diversified and pluralistic.

Alternately, it was asked whether it was possible for diverse peoples and ethnicities, bound by a common interest and political will, to live happily together in a manufactured nation, that is a state that did not spring organically from one ethnic group. To do so would be to test an ideal associated with the American Dream, as captured by the creation of the United States of America in 1776 and the American Declaration of Independence, and then, later, by those establishing the first Black republic in the world following the Haitian Revolution. Both cases supported the argument that in a New World—effectively the beginning of Modernity—a nation state did not need to be based upon natural allegiances tied to ethnicities or nationalisms. The United States had shown that a state can be brought forth out of several European ethnicities, while revolutionary Haiti, as a Black state, by offering citizenship to people from a wider array of ethnicities, had demonstrated that a place where all people are equal in citizenship, pedigree, and standing could exist in harmony. The success of these countries, in turn, led to further questions: can patriotism and allegiance to a new country be manufactured instead of naturally determined through things like ethnicity? Can patriotism and loyalty be learned rather than inherited?

Since the abolition of slavery in the British Empire in 1838, and in the United States in 1865, many idealists had imagined that these predominantly and intentionally white societies would make room for Black people, recognizing them as equal citizens. They believed Black peoples' human dignity would be recognized and even advanced—as would that of any other ethnicity sharing this common sense of belonging, responsibility, and entitlement. In such a setting, ancestry and skin colour would no longer be meaningful social determinants of citizenship.

By the end of the First World War in the non-white world, colonized people were demanding a new social order that was not based on race. Nearer to home in Canada, Black people in the British West Indies, especially from the 1930s onwards, had been demanding the same type of responsible government that Canada had wrangled from Britain during its colonization. Some countries began dreaming of calling themselves confederations, just as Canada had, and of achieving political independence within the British Commonwealth. Independent islands in the Caribbean aspired to be homelands for Black and multi-ethnic people, but Black leaders in the region still wanted all countries to be open to Black citizenry and the creolizing of culture that results from the ethnic mixing of people from different parts of the world. Buried in these dreams was the idea, shared by some Canadians, that the islands could join Canada and the Dominion of Newfoundland in a single British confederation.

As representatives, and even symbols of this history of Canada and the Americas, the delegation of railway porters and activists arriving in Ottawa in 1954 knew they had the support of Black leaders in the Caribbean who, with their pan-African idealism, saw North American Blacks' struggle for acceptance as part of a joint international quest for freedom.

To achieve this dream—and echoing the words of Simcoe about a society that didn't discriminate between the natives of Africa, America, Europe, and Asia too—members of the porters' Ottawa delegation wanted federal government leaders to get on board with their vision of a more inclusive Canada, one that made room for Black and other people of colour in all quarters of society. By recognizing the existence of Blackness in Canada, the dominant elites would be acknowledging that, contrary to the official narrative, Canada was a Black, and not white country, since, socially and legally, one non-white dollop rendered one's identity Black. Therefore, a multiracial country was, by definition, a Black country; the culture a multiracial society produced, even when described as multicultural, was Black according to modernity's rules and practice.

Philosophically speaking, members of the train porters' delegation were inviting Canada's dominant groups to imagine living in a different world, one in which the former white elites were just one of many subjects—equal to everyone else rather than everyone else being inferior to them—and thereby shifting the focus and perspective of who really matters in society. White elites would no longer establish the norms and standards for all matters, with all other citizens deferring to their priorities, leadership, and command. As citizens, other ethnicities would matter too, regardless of how long they'd been ignored historically. Canada would become, sociologically and politically, a country of free-willed agents and subjects who determined their own futures. From their vantage point, white Canadians, as a racialized group, would have to come to terms with what it means to survive in a world where they were not automatically and exclusively in control. In this new world, emphasis would be placed on sharing and compromising rather than on exclusive ownership.

The Canada of this imagining, one where Black people were fully at home as citizens, would eventually morph into the philosophy of official multiculturalism, effectively a variant of a creolized, plural society, a noble and realizable goal, even if, as of this writing, the political and sociological will to achieve this dream still falls short of the philosophy itself. Yet there could be no change without someone daring to imagine new ways of life. This was the aim of the delegation of porters and allies visiting Ottawa: to bring about a change in how Blackness was thought of in an otherwise white social order and in the collective imagination of who naturally belongs, and has rights and privileges, in New World societies. The delegation's second aim was to ensure that the benefits won by Black people in Canada would be extended to all other racialized groups in recognition of the common human dignity of all peoples.

GETTING ON THE TRAIN IN their spring coats and sweaters, the group of Black men and women assembled at Union Station in Toronto for their six-hour trip to Ottawa, the highlight of which, they hoped, would be a meeting the next morning with Prime Minister Louis St. Laurent. They arrived as members of the Negro Citizenship Association, a loose coalition of Black activists mainly from around Toronto who banded together under the simple motto: "Dedicated to the making of a better Canadian citizen." Their aim was the establishment of a different and more inclusive type of Canadian citizenship. At the heart of this delegation were a number of Canadians who all had one thing in common besides the colour of their skin: they were men who had worked as sleeping car porters on the country's two main railways. This was a time when life in Canada's Black communities revolved around the work of these porters. In 1950s Calgary, for example, when the Canadian Association for the Advancement of Coloured People was founded by the leadership of the Brotherhood of Sleeping Car Porters, some 90 percent of Black people in that city depended on the railways for employment. In Montreal, the famed Little Burgundy community of Black people developed and thrived in the shadows of the railways' headquarters. Black communities and settlements in Halifax, Sackville, Toronto, Sudbury, Winnipeg, Edmonton, and Vancouver fanned out from the railway stations, a visual reminder that Black people were central to the railways but marginal to the wider society.

Let us now take a closer at these porters and the role they played building Canada.

THE RAILWAYS ARE ALWAYS HIRING
Working in White Man's Country

SITTING IN HIS CONDOMINIUM APARTMENT in Halifax, Harold Adams is at ease with the life he has built for himself and his family from his years working on the railroad, and with recent progress made in his country. But that was not always the case.

"I don't know how many times I came home and said I'm not going back, this work is not for me," he says as he passes out a cup of tea, perhaps with the same care he gave the strangers he serviced over thirty-five years working as a porter on Canada's passenger railways. Now he sits in his apartment among some of the memorabilia from his long years of service, reminiscing, along with fellow retired porter Thornton Williams and lifelong friend Michael Tynes, about life on the road and what has become Canada.

"When we were growing up as kids we always saw the porters when they got in from a trip," recalls Tynes with a chuckle. "They were the best-dressed guys around, they drove the cars and they had the nicest homes."

"Well, not all porters had homes," Adams chides gently, reminding him that life wasn't that kind or equal to everyone who worked as a railway porter:

> But those that did, I used to think they were members of government, members of parliament, some official, 'cause we would always see them when they were dressed up, when they were leaving to go to work. But after they got to work, and after I got on the railway, I learned that when they went to work they changed their clothes into a uniform, a white jacket with

a collar that went around the neck, and I don't like to say it but some people referred to them as monkey hats, and you had to wear that when you were on the job. In those days, you'd see very few Black people travelling in sleeping cars because it was too expensive; if they did travel, coach would be the best they could afford at that time. I am going back to the time when I first got onto the train, it was C.N.R. then... [before] they made it VIA Rail.

Williams also remembers seeing the porters around town. "There was this fellow that I didn't quite know what he did. His name was Walter. I would see Walter around town and Walter was always well-dressed and always had a little briefcase with him and I kept thinking he was a lawyer. And it wasn't until years later that I got to realize he was a porter."

Adams signed on to work for the Canadian National Railway's passenger service in 1962. When travelling away from home he wouldn't stay in hotels, but in private homes in Black neighbourhoods, as was the case in Montreal, where as many as sixteen porters might share bunk beds in the same room of a home:

When I first went there, only Blacks stayed there, but whites did not. That was the way the porters lived. Whites working on the trains were waiters, stewards, conductors, and cooks and they stayed elsewhere. [...] In Canada, segregation existed all over. Even with government jobs, there were very few Blacks until around in the '60s or late '50s, when Blacks started to get into the dockyards, but even when they did, it was [only as] porters [...] The reputations of us Blacks, in general, was that we were supposed to be good singers, good cooks, and good cleaners. And that [belief] existed in all [of] Canada.

Over a generation, these retirees have witnessed the way life has changed for Black people in Canada. There are now more job opportunities available to Black Canadians, unlike when they were teenagers. "In the days prior [...], Nova Scotia, like other places in Canada, was very prejudiced jobwise," Adams recalls. "We had men that went to high school and [...] the best job they could get was working on the train. And Blacks in general, especially men, we got spread across Canada, mostly from Nova Scotia. What they would do to recruit was to come down to Halifax, down in the valley, the small places, and anybody that wanted to work and was capable of making beds, it wasn't in those days hard work, but they took them and sent [them] right across to Vancouver. In those days, there were very few Blacks living in [places] like Calgary and Winnipeg [...] They would take them across [the country] to live [where there was work for them]."[13]

The recruiters would also visit the southern United States and, in particular, British colonies in the Caribbean, in search of porters for the railways, and seamen for Canadian ships—oftentimes recruits worked on both the rails and ships. Elombe Mottley, son of a popular politician in Barbados in the first half of the last century, recalled in an interview: "When my father was growing up, even when I was a boy going to school in the late 1940s, you could always tell who was a seaman because his children always wore a gold-plated watch, 'cause to own a watch in those days was a big thing."[14] Mottley came to Canada to study medicine at the University of Manitoba in 1958, and knew that, like so many West Indian students before him, he could supplement his income and get to see the rest of North America by working summers and winters as a sleeping car porter.

Working on the railways also provided employment for Black Canadian men and men from the British West Indies who were studying at university. They worked between classes, mainly during the peak travel periods in summer and winter. These students would return home upon graduation after studying law, medicine, and agriculture, and some would try to establish their own businesses in Black communities across the country. Eventually, Mottley decided to return to the Caribbean, joining other former porters who'd given up on Canada as a place to achieve their life aspirations. Louis Tull, a fellow Barbadian who came to Canada around the same time as Mottley, worked as a porter out of Winnipeg when he was a university student. He returned to his native island, Barbados, after his schooling to become a successful lawyer, public intellectual, politician, and minister of government. Grenadian Julius Isaacs also worked seasonally on the railways while studying law in Toronto. He was a member of the Negro Citizenship Association and, after entering private practice, rose through the judiciary to become the chief justice of the Canadian Federal Court of Appeal, the first and so far only Black person to hold the position.

From traversing the country, and talking to the passengers as they served them, train porters knew what was on the mind of the nation and the world. On the trains, the porters engaged with local and international politicians and political activists, academics and intellectuals. The trains also carried newspapers and magazines from around the world, including Black newspapers committed to racial uplift and liberation from across the continent. The Black newspapers depended on the porters for distribution into communities of interest. Porters also picked up books left behind on the trains or had reading materials recommended to them by travellers. Many of the porters were university graduates educated in the dominant social and political philosophies of the day, giving them a deep theoretical understanding of how democratic and capitalist societies like Canada operated, even if they were not allowed to reach the commanding career heights offered to their white countrymen. Many of the porters had also served in the two previous world wars and had the military discipline necessary to become leaders.

To augment their livelihood, porters often transported the latest fashions in clothes and music from one town to another and sold them at a profit. In this way, not only were they the cultural intellectuals—bringing home knowledge and new ideas—but also the arbiters of fashion and cultural trends. Halifax porters took pride in having their suits specially tailored in Montreal, as did porters living as far away as the West Coast. Montreal was considered the Harlem of Canada: anything Black people wanted—the best in Black culture—could be had there. Montreal was where the major railways of the continent converged, where the Black seamen of the world and the sleeping car porters congregated in their Blackness. It was where the Grand Trunk Railway, as a pioneering promoter of cross-Canada train travel, established its headquarters in 1852, with a Black community founded nearby that served as a home for transient Black porters who eventually brought their wives and families to settle there too.

Canada became a confederation in 1867, and its history since then can be measured in how successful men like Adams, Williams, and Tynes were in making homes for themselves and their families here. Their lives are part of the story about the struggle to change Canada and to make it a place where Black boys and girls could grow up knowing they had the dignity and freedom to become full-fledged Canadian citizens.

BROMLEY ARMSTRONG WAS A FOUNDING member of the Negro Citizenship Association and one of the delegates who travelled to Ottawa in 1954. He recalled the anti-Black discrimination that was the norm in employment at that time. Arriving in Canada from his native Jamaica in 1947 and seeking employment—which he anticipated would be a similar process to one back home—Armstrong soon realized the futility of his job search. Bromley was a welder by trade in Jamaica, part of an emerging middle class, but without

Canadian certifications and the right skin colour, he wasn't eligible to practice his trade in Canada. Armstrong knew his education and training made him capable of doing an array of management and administrative jobs. British subjects from the West Indies, and particularly the British Isles, with education and training similar to his had no such difficulty. The only difference was that they were white.

"When I was looking for work at some of Canada's flagship department stores," Armstrong recalls, "I was told repeatedly to go to the railroads since they were hiring porters. It was common practice into the early 1960s for Black men in Canada to be hired primarily as porters by the railroad companies, and many Black women were employed as domestics."[15]

Armstrong writes in his memoir, *Bromley: Tireless Champion for Just Causes,* "as a Black person living in the 1950s Canada, my soul was not well. Canadian racism and prejudice caused me to operate in an environment with narrow margins. The signs around me suggested that I could only go so far. For although Black men and women helped to fight Canada's battles during two world wars, in the early 1950s, many Canadian-born Blacks were forced to continue accepting jobs primarily on the railroads or in other service sector areas."[16]

The same was true for just about every Black immigrant and for just about every Black schoolboy or girl in Canada. One of the saddest cases in terms of missed opportunities was Toronto-born Herb Carnegie, the son of Jamaican immigrants, who by all reports and statistics at amateur and professional levels was justified in his dream of playing in the National Hockey League. But he was denied the opportunity because he was Black. More than that, he suffered the indignity of having officials acknowledge that it was only the colour of his skin that kept him out. Conn Smythe, the general manager of the Maple Leafs Hockey Club in Carnegie's hometown, Toronto, was quoted as saying that he'd "give $10,000 to anyone who can turn Herb Carnegie white," a statement that stayed with Carnegie until his death in 2012, and which he said contributed to the greatest disappointment of his life.[17]

"Although my brother and I had finished among the league's top scorers, the NHL scouts left us out standing in the cold," Carnegie wrote in his memoir, *A Fly in a Pail of Milk: The Herb Carnegie Story.* "Our disappointment was all the greater knowing that the NHL teams were losing players to the armed forces—Canada had declared war in September 1939—and many were trading in their gear for military uniforms. The rosters in hockey's premier league now had wide gaps and we knew we deserved to play in it."

"I had expected an NHL try-out and I didn't get it. Ossie and I talked about it and there was no doubt in our minds that our problem was colour. We never had an agent, we never had a lawyer, we never had a player's union, and the press was silent on the issue. There was no one to speak for us and we never made a fuss with anyone."[18] But their dream did not die quietly. The two brothers would link up with Manny McIntyre, a Black player from Fredericton, New Brunswick, to form the legendary Coloured Line that dazzled the semi-professional leagues in North America for a decade.

Near the end of his career, Carnegie was finally given a tryout with the New York Rangers. But even though he excelled in the training camp, he wasn't picked for the professional squad in what became the final degradation of spirit for him. "The scar of that experience marks my soul to this day," Carnegie wrote. "My dream would not come true, not because of a lack of talent or a willingness to work hard, but because of racism. The pain has dulled somewhat over the years, but it has never disappeared."[19] Indeed, as for so many other talented Black boys, their dreams died hard, or were sublimated when they worked, instead, on the railways.

Halifax-born Michael Tynes explains that, at school in the 1950s, it was taken for granted that working as a porter or as a seaman would be the best, indeed the only, opportunity available to Black youths. An immigrant from St. Lucia, Tynes' father worked on the ships that plied the Great Lakes and the St. Lawrence, so when his turn came to leave school, Tynes followed his father onto the water, this time into the Canadian Marines, becoming one of the first Black Canadians in the Canadian navy. Many of Tynes' school friends around Halifax ended up as porters on the railways.

Traditionally, West Indian seamen crewed on the famed "lady boats" operated by the government-owned Canadian National Steamship Company—a sister company of the Canadian National Railway—that plied the St. Lawrence and carried passengers and cargo from the Canadian East Coast to the Caribbean. These luxury liners, named after the wives or ladies of British Admirals, were the primary sea links between maritime Canada and the British West Indies well into the 1960s. The boats also provided the main communications between these islands and were a source of employment for West Indian seamen as well. Often the same people worked on the ships and on the railways, switching between the two depending on the availability of work. Some of the West Indian ship crews settled around Halifax and became important members of the local communities. When Canada closed down the service, the West Indians working as crews were offered landed immigrant status, allowing them to remain in Canada and become full Canadian citizens. By then, many had families in Halifax, and had switched to working on the railways.

To this day, stories are told among Blacks about the many notable Canadians who worked as porters, or who came from families headed by porters. One of them was Lincoln Alexander, who would become a law-yer—one of the first Black people in Canada to do so—and ultimately get elected to the House of Commons as Canada's first Black cabinet minister. He would eventually become Lieutenant Governor of Ontario—the high-est recognition for a British subject—the monarch's representative in the province. Alexander's parents were from the British West Indies; his mother was a seamstress from Jamaica and his father was a carpenter in his native St. Vincent. "Getting work was difficult, if not impossible," Alexander says of his parents' time in his memoir, *Go to School, You're a Little Black Boy: The Honourable Lincoln M. Alexander.* When he was growing up in Toronto in the 1920s, Alexander recalls, "lots of black people were reduced to doing jobs such as plucking feathers from chickens, being maids, or taking on squalid and demeaning labour. In this respect, for many people, there was not a lot of promise in life [....] Blacks at that time made up a sliver-thin portion of the city's population, and racial prejudice abounded."[20]

Of his parents, Alexander says, "Theirs was not a world filled with workplace options, so they settled on careers that were largely the default jobs of blacks at that time." His father worked for decades as a sleeping car porter for Canadian Pacific Railway, mainly on the cross-country runs from Toronto, and sometimes Montreal, to Vancouver and back. "Working the rails took him away from his wife and family for days on end, but it provided us all with the necessities of life and a modicum of dignity." Throughout his life, Alexander remained ambivalent about the family strife caused when his father was gone, friction that ultimately led to the dissolution of his parents' marriage. "When my dad returned from one of his lengthy railway journeys, he would deposit a huge pile of cash on the table, the product of tips gained from being charming and effective in his work." He continues, "Along with covering the table with his tips, he would bring us a lot of things, ranging from eggs, chickens, and turkeys to Sweet Marie chocolate bars. These were things people would give him, or he would buy along the way if he found good deals."[21]

The fathers of internationally famous jazz pianists Oscar Peterson and Joe Sealy, from Montreal and Halifax, respectively, were also porters. To this day, retired porters point with pride to the homes they built, the families they supported, and the education and better standing in society they gave their children. "For some of them," retired Halifax porter Thornton Williams says of the older men who mentored him when he went on the railway in the 1960s, "the homes they bought when on the road still exist. You have these men who did things that even guys in my time couldn't. They had a certain kind of work ethic."[22] Even though the work was never easy, for many Black men having a job on the road gave them opportunities that were not readily available otherwise, including the opportunity to travel and to have a better a quality of life, which was evident in the clothes they wore. The job also allowed them to be cultural ambassadors for their communities. Meeting and conversing with people from different classes and cultures broadened their perspectives and their views on life.

"It was an education," says Harold Adams. "You got to talk to people of all walks of life. People would talk about where they had been. You weren't there but you can almost live your life through somebody else by [listening to] their talking and their memories of what Paris is like, or England. Anything. And we carried everybody, from a gravedigger to a professor, a doctor, a lawyer. Also, our experiences in working in the bar car [were memorable], how people [were] open to you and you would walk off with somebody else's problems on your shoulders. But it was an education."[23]

James Watson, born in Windsor, Ontario, relied on railway porter work as he built a career that would make him the city's chief lawyer. Born in 1911, Watson recalled in an interview that his grandfather, James Munroe, escaped slavery in the southern United States for Windsor. "Although he had little or no education," Watson told historian Patrick Brode, "he was successful in getting a job with the railway company. I believe it was either the Grand Trunk Railway Company or its predecessor. And through diligent effort and perseverance he subsequently learned how to operate the yard engines and was eventually employed in the capacity of a yard engineer and used to operate the freight engines in the railway." Watson's grandfather would have experienced the transition when all railway jobs went from being open to Black workers to Black men being restricted to employment solely as porters. While studying at Osgoode Hall Law School in Toronto, Watson himself worked on the Canadian Pacific Railway mainly at Christmas and in the summer. "I used to take cars out, sleeping cars, when work was available, and I used to take runs to Ottawa and Montreal and Detroit and Chicago as an extra porter, and then, eventually, I was assigned as a full-time porter on the observation car of the Transcontinental train and I used to work on that car from Toronto to Vancouver. Which I enjoyed very much."

That work, available to the "spares" (on-call workers) on the porter seniority list, was to Watson's advantage even after he had graduated from law school and set up private practice in 1937 doing small-time criminal work. "It was very difficult to make a living doing that kind of work," Watson explained. "But I was able to scrape by. What really came to my rescue was the fact that I had previously obtained summer employment with the C.P.R. as a railroad porter. And when things were very slow in the office, I was able to work as a porter on weekends [...] I must say if it hadn't been for this extra work [...] things would have been almost desperate for me at this particular time."[24]

As Bromley Armstrong attested, even in the 1960s, when searching for a first job, new arrivals in Black communities in Canada were invariably pointed away from all forms of public employment and directed toward the railways. This was usually the case for Black males in their late teens to late twenties. For most Black workers, getting hired by the railways meant beating out other Black people in order to get placed on the "spares board," a list of people available for work when the railway needed them.

Dorothy W. Williams, a historian and leading activist for porters and their families, recalls in *The Road to Now: A History of Blacks in Montreal* that the railways had an entrenched method for rationing employment among Black men:

> The Red Caps, one of the first groups of resident black railroad workers in Montreal, worked only in the train stations, where they handled luggage and the boarding and disembarking of passengers. There were not as many Red Caps as there were porters. Only fifty Red Caps were employed by the C.P.R. (Canadian Pacific Railway) at any one time. Their salary scale differed greatly from that of the porters. Red Caps were hired by number.

Those numbered from 1 to 10 received wages plus tips. Numbers 11 to 50 were hired on a tip basis only.[25]

White men worked as Red Caps for the Canadian Pacific Railway, but with the colour curtain of racism descending across the country in 1912, especially on the railways, three former Black porters were shifted from working as waiters to Red Cap duties at Montreal's Windsor Station. From then on, only Black men would work as Red Caps. The white men who'd been Red Caps were given more desired positions on the trains, such as waiters or cooks.

From then on, the Red Caps were exclusively Black workers. One of the original three porters to be transferred to the position of Red Cap was Geary Parish, who started as a porter working between Montreal and Boston. By the time of his retirement in 1938, Parish was supervising forty-two men as Red Caps, with an extra twelve to fifteen on a waiting list of part-timers who could be called on to work during busy periods. Only those railway porters at the top of the seniority list had regular employment; all the other porters worked on an on-call basis. This hiring and employment rule would remain in force for most of the century. Ironically, Parish would tell a reporter for the Canadian Pacific staff bulletin that among the world-famous travellers he'd served as a Red Cap was none other than former Prime Minister Wilfrid Laurier, under whose government portering and Red Capping became work exclusively for Black men.

A similar system was also used for Red Caps and porters on the Canadian National Railway trains and stations across the country: they got paid only when they worked. Until the railway called, hours before the train left the station, the porters got by as best they could, some turning to odd jobs, some alternating between working as seamen on ships, which had the same kind of work regime as the railways. Only a very fortunate few worked their way up the railway spares boards to claim the seniority that gave them permanent work. As a result, the spare labourers would gather in halls close to railway stations and while away the time shooting pool, shooting the breeze, playing poker, craps, and other games, while waiting for the call to work. As part of this unskilled labour pool, Black women were attracted to these halls, where, having nothing else to sell, they trafficked themselves, especially to the returning porters, who had tips in their pockets. With time, these halls became centres of sorts for the Black community, and were often viewed by the wider society as places of ill-repute and possibly violence. In their halls, porters exchanged the latest news and discussed the ways of the world and the meaning of life, especially for people of African ancestry. They also schemed among themselves about how best to fight for racial uplift and social acceptance. This is how, in common imagining and by implication, the term "sleeping car porter" became synonymous with "Black." Anecdotally, it was accepted lore that every Black family had at least one member who was a sleeping car porter, although the railways, particularly Canadian National Railway, tried its best to make sure only one or two porters came from the same household.

Sleeping car porters offered what was commonly referred to as Pullman service, a kind of head-to-toe pampering of passengers by uniformed servicemen always at their beck and call. In their job, porters received the passengers on board; turned up and down their beds and seats; provided waiter service; cleaned spittoons, toilets, and ashtrays; regulated the heating and cooling to suit the travellers' comfort; polished shoes; and brushed off passengers' coats and hats when they were leaving the train. As the final point of contact with departing passengers, a brisk whisking of the coat or hat gave the porter a last chance to earn a tip. And if the tip wasn't forthcoming the first time, an outstretched palm, supposedly to help the passengers off the train, provided a second chance. With time, critics would claim that this goodbye ritual was no more than a final shaking down of passengers who, in that moment of such close contact, were forced, or even manhandled, into deciding whether to give a tip or not.

This form of porter service was pioneered by American entrepreneur George Pullman, who tried to replicate the very best in service available in the Southern great houses and parlours of antebellum America on the trains. Pullman porters were called "George's Boys" or simply "George"— terms rife with the condescension of a lordship-bondage relationship and of the paternalistic role whites assumed toward Black men, who were never recognized as anything other than boys or someone else's servant. Pullman franchised this service to railways across the continent; inadvertently lending the indistinguishable name George to all who served in these cars on either side of the border. Soon after Confederation, Pullman services were available on the government-owned railways—the Intercolonial Railway and the National Transcontinental Railway—as well as on the privately owned Grand Trunk Railway of Canada, Canadian Northern Railway, and Canadian Pacific Railway. However, when the Intercolonial Railway and National Transcontinental Railway merged with what was left of Grand Trunk Railway and Canadian Northern Railway to form the government-owned Canadian National Railway in 1923, the new entity—after initially keeping Pullman service on its runs into the United States—quickly launched its own brand of service that was Pullman in all but name.

"It is a common impression that anyone can be a Pullman porter," wrote George F. Brown in an article featured in the October 31, 1953, issue of *Courier Magazine,* which was popular among travellers.

> But when the facts are known, [and] it is very difficult to be hired for the job in the first place, then comes the test. The unobtrusive efficiency of the Pullman porter is not because the job is easy, but definitely the result of rigid training. Everyone who would like to be a Pullman porter cannot be, and that is why these men are held in such high esteem, both by the Pullman Company and the passengers who ride on the fifty-nine railroads the Pullman Company serves. Here is why: "The applicant must be an American Negro, about 25 years of age. He must have previous experience in various types of jobs and must look to Pullman services as lifetime employment. References are carefully verified and a complete medical examination must be passed. The applicant is then turned over to a porter instructor" for in-depth training.[26]

This was why, Brown wrote, that the porters were called the diplomats of the railroad. They had to be diplomatic whether dealing with fare-paying travellers and management, or communicating their happiness with their work, even if they had legitimate reasons to grouse. And, as George Pullman recognized early on, the porters dealt with the travellers and the first impression they left with them would impact future service and even determine passenger loyalty.

From the inception of his service, Pullman made it a practice to hire mainly Black workers for its services, so porters on Canadian Pacific Railway were mainly Black as well. When chattel slavery ended in the United States, Pullman targeted the resulting pool of unemployed Blacks, who had no other real options for employment. So pervasive was the Pullman porter in Black communities in North America that Carter G. Woodson, an authoritative Black writer at the turn of the century, took note of the Great Migration of Black people fleeing Jim Crow conditions in the US South to the Northern states starting in the second decade of twentieth century. "A large number of educated Negroes, therefore, have on account of these conditions been compelled to leave the South. Finding in the North, however, practically nothing in their line to do, because of the proscription by race prejudice and trade unions, many of them lead the life of menials, serving as waiters, porters, butlers and chauffeurs," Woodson wrote. "While in Chicago, not long ago, the writer was in the office of a graduate of a colored southern college, who was showing his former teacher the picture of his class. In accounting for his classmates in the various walks of life, he reported that more than one third of them were settled to the occupation of Pullman porters."[27]

Wages were low for porters so they had to rely on tips from passengers to make a living, a situation Pullman encouraged so porters would maintain the highest quality service in the hopes of a small monetary token of appreciation. Later on, tipping and hustling, or the bootlegging of merchandise on trains and in their communities, would outpace wages as porters' main income source. In 1909, on the Intercolonial Railway, Pullman's sleeping car and parlour services in the US were exclusively Black, while in Canada, the railway corporation and its union signed an agreement formally limiting Black employment on the railways to porter services only. This policy was indirectly confirmed in the House of Commons on January 18, 1912, through a question to the new Conservative Minister of Railways and Canals, Francis Cochrane.

"Is it the policy of the Department of Railways to promote Pullman car porters to the positions of Pullman car conductors?" asked Liberal parliamentarian Alexander Maclean.

"No," said the Minister.

Maclean followed up: "Did the Prime Minister of Canada, in the year 1908, or in any other year, at Halifax or elsewhere, declare it as the policy of the Conservative Party to promote Pullman car porters to the rank of Pullman car conductors?"

"The department is not aware," Cochrane responded.[28] By then, Conservative Party leader Robert Borden had replaced Liberal Wilfrid Laurier as prime minister, but even though the governing party had changed, the policy of segregating porters and conductors based on colour remained fully established as government policy.

By June 26, 1924, the Canadian National Railway's employment policies were well in place when the corporation's president, Sir Henry Thornton, and the powerful federal deputy minister of railways, Major Bell, made their annual appearance before the Standing Committee on Railways and Shipping in the House of Commons. The pair was asked by the committee to explain the railway's policy "with regard to having coloured help in the dining services and in the porter and parlour car services." While the president claimed he could not provide an answer, the deputy minister did. "Practically all the coloured help on our own cars are citizens of the country," Bell stated. "On the Grand Trunk we run Pullman service, and that is entirely manned by coloured help, except for some of the conductors."

Asked if the same answer applied to more upscale and exclusive parlour cars, which offered a higher level of service than the sleeping cars more readily available to the public, Bell responded, "In the parlour service in our own railway, I think you will find white men, generally speaking."

"I appreciate that this is rather a ticklish question," Conservative Joseph Harris pressed on, "but will you express an opinion as to what your policy is going to be with regard to keeping coloured help in your dining car service throughout the whole system?" He was referring to the proposed absorption of the Grand Trunk Railway, which hired Black workers for all services, into the Canadian National Railway, which limited Black workers to being porters.

"We have very few in the dining car service," Bell admitted. "I think they are practically all white men. It is only the porters who are coloured, and as a rule it is very hard to get anyone but coloured help for that."[29]

Two years later, the segregation of the railways was supported by regulation, in a formal agreement between Canadian National Railway and the Canadian Brotherhood of Railway Employees. The formalization came in a December 1926 report by a board of conciliation under the Industrial Disputes Investigation Act. The report followed an inquiry into a claim of racial discrimination when Canadian National Rail, on taking over Grand Trunk Railway, replaced all Black workers in the dining car service with white ones. The Black workers claimed these actions were "creating [...] in the minds of our coloured employees engaged in similar service, an uneasiness as to the security of position, an uneasiness which might, in the minds of these employees, be attributed to colour prejudice."[30] The conciliation was indeed necessary as the company, the union, and the government tried to tamp down Black porters' concerns about a successful attempt by Canadian Pacific to break up attempts at forming a union for porters in 1918. In 1920, the railway dismissed seven porters who'd been involved in the formation of a Black porters' union, the Order of Sleeping Car Porters, the previous year, sacking workers with between three and twelve years of service. When the government refused to recognize the Order of Sleeping Car Porters, Black workers ended up having to rely on the Canadian

Brotherhood of Railway Employees, with its all-white executive, for representation. After six years of foot dragging, the board was ready to respond and, apparently, to put the Black workers in their place.

The report noted, "that the removal of these coloured employees and replacing them by white help was due to no other reason than of the difficulty it [railway] experienced in securing competent help. It strongly resented any allusion as to it being prejudiced toward its employees on account of colour." The conciliation report sided with the railway and noted that the members of the board had assured the Black workers there was no prejudice against them, offering as proof the company's claim that the railway had put some of the replaced workers in other positions. They were made porters and, without any seniority in this new position, were placed on the spares board with the possibility of working only when the need for extra employees came up. These Black porters had lost their right to secure work. "In a measure this was satisfactory," the report said. "It did not, however, settle or dispose of the matter of seniority rights, or the uncertainty of positions presently held by coloured employees."[31] To this end, the board invited the union and the railway to come up with an agreement between themselves.

"Should the Railway, at a future date, deem it necessary to replace such coloured crews with white help," said the memorandum of agreement signed on December 17, 1926, "the committee representing the employees affected will be called into conference with officers of the department and an amicable arrangement made to take care of the employees displaced." This statement probably didn't provide any comfort to the Black workers, since it implied that the practice of replacing Black with white workers would continue—the question was how the replacements were to be handled. "It is also agreed that coloured kitchen help will be continued on trains where coloured help is at present employed in kitchens, and in the event of any change, the employees' committee will be called into conference and amicable arrangements made in the same manner as herein provided." With this, the agreement established that service of this type was exclusively for Black workers. All other types of work on the railway would be open only to white people. The memo stated:

> Coloured employees who have been removed from positions on dining cars but who have been continued in the service of the Company in other positions, or who have been granted leave of absence for sickness or otherwise, will retain and continue to accumulate seniority for the purpose of filling

vacancies or new positions on dining cars operated with coloured crews. Coloured dining car employees, who are assigned as parlor car porters, will exercise their seniority in retaining or bidding on such positions and will also retain and accumulate seniority to secure and retain positions on dining cars operated with coloured crews.

All employees referred to in this memorandum of agreement who have been, or may be displaced as a result of the change from coloured to white waiters and have no regularly assigned runs, will be continued on the payrolls of the Company at a rate not less than ($90.00) dollars per month until such time as they are placed on regularly assigned runs.[32]

As a condition of employment, all porters had to sign a statement that effectively indicated they had no right to a job with Canadian Pacific Railway: "I hereby agree to work as such for the company on any of its different runs as my service may be required," the statement said, "it being understood that my engagement may be terminated by the company without notice and without assigning any reason therefore, at any time except during the course of any particular run and moreover that it is subject to the terms herein stated."[33] As Stanley Grizzle noted in his papers, no other class of employee at the railway was required to sign such a statement.

This approach by government and railway established legal racial discrimination in Canada and would remain in force on the trains up to the 1960s, when Black porters were finally able to undermine the system of having two categories exclusively for white and Black workers.

Serendipitously, the head porter on the car taking the delegation to Ottawa was a man from Toronto, George Garraway, who would become one of the first to benefit from the activism of the people in his charge. A few years later, he would break through the North American colour barrier by becoming one of the first Pullman porters on the continent to be promoted to conductor.

Portering on the "roads" became a Black ghetto with no promotional exit or expectation for improvement. White employees who insisted on working as porters always had the option of seeking a transfer elsewhere or finding another type of job. This was not the case for Black workers. For example, on Canadian National Railway, a Black man who began his railway career as a porter would retire a generation later as a porter. He might possibly be promoted to porter-in-charge, where he did the same supervisory chores as a conductor, but he would never be made a conductor.

Indeed, the very constitution of the conductors' union indicated that membership had to be white. The most significant change in a Black porter's career over a lifetime of service would be a shift from temporary to permanent status, and, in time, moving up the seniority list, possibly as high as supervisor-in-chief. All other railway workers—conductors, engineers, brakesmen—were entitled to apply for promotion within their group or to a more prestigious work classification.

To reinforce this colour line, the railway and the corporation segregated railway employees into two self-contained groups—Group One for porters only and Group Two for all other employees. Group One was all Black; Group Two was non-Black. This was the way the railroad operated for almost six decades. Porters on Canadian National Rail in particular would have to continue fighting their own union, the Canadian Brotherhood of Railway Employees, for equality of treatment and for recognition as full union members for decades. They eventually ended up openly fighting their union leadership and going over the latter's heads to appeal to the Canadian Labour Congress and the federal government to end workplace segregation. This was years after the delegation of porters arrived in Ottawa in 1954 to try to get the government to introduce anti-discrimination fair-employment-practices legislation, and to enforce it.

"DID YOU RING, SIR?"
Modern Luxury and Black Labour

IN 1891, A REPORTER FROM the *New York Sun* shadowed porters on the Canadian Pacific Railway transcontinental run to give readers a firsthand account of the working conditions of the men on the luxury service. Pullman train travel was in its glory days and many people found the romance associated with the company endearing. Those fortunate enough to travel by train were eager for specific details before embarking on their journey. Travellers were crossing the North American continent with ease, with easterners in Canada and the United States travelling to the west coast in mere days and in the lap of luxury. The excitement was palpable across the entire continent, as travel was becoming more accessible and less expensive and time consuming.

Four years after the end of the bloody Civil War and the elimination of chattel slavery in North America, 3,000 miles of track spanned the US from coast to coast, allowing transcontinental rail service for the first time. This important milestone was intended to help heal the wounds of separation, hatred, and distrust, and to remake the United States of America as an indivisible nation state. In a race to achieve the same unity for Canada, Donald Alexander Smith, the chief financier for the nascent Canadian Pacific Railway, had driven the final spike into the ground, joining two sections of railway track at Craigllachie in British Columbia and making the dream of cross-country railway travel in this country a reality. This was also the final spike in the mythological creation of a Canadian nation linked by ribbons of steel from sea to sea, bringing isolated regions and provinces and their unique geographies and beauty into a united entity now reachable to every citizen.

"A nebulous dream was a reality: as an iron ribbon crossed Canada from sea to sea," says a plaque placed later at the spot. "Often following the footsteps of the early explorers, nearly 3,000 miles of steel and rail pushed across vast prairies, cleft mighty mountain passes, twisted through canyons. Here on November 7, 1885, a plain iron spike welded East to West." As Pierre Berton wrote in his book *The Last Spike*, the picture of the actual bonding of the country through the last spike became one of the most iconic in Canadian history. "Banks feature it on calendars; insurance companies reproduce it in advertisements; television documentaries copy it; school pageants reenact it."[34]

With the transcontinental tracks in place, travellers were anxious to get moving, whether to search for new markets or to enjoy the geographic and diverse wonders of Canada. The addition of sleeping quarters on the trains meant passengers did not have to interrupt their travels to stay overnight at hotels or boarding homes. In this new age of travel, passengers would board at one station and stay onboard until they arrived at their final destination. On-board passengers could mingle with their peers, conduct business, rest in their berths, and partake of exquisite food and drink. Uniformed helpers would babysit small children and the elderly would have a friendly helpful assistant who was almost a travelling companion. Every action by and between passengers and porters would be carefully choreographed in keeping with the exacting standards that were the hallmark of this form of train travel. Like other railways across North America, Canadian Pacific wanted to provide the best passenger experience. To achieve this it needed the Pullman Corporation, fast becoming renowned for its luxury and nurturing Black helpers. The Pullman Corporation offered their services on Canadian railways, including the Intercolonial Railway, which operated mainly in the east, and the Grand Trunk, which operated primarily in central and western Canada.

The porters' strict uniform code was enforced throughout decades of service. Over time, the code stipulated that porters on tourist and coach cars had to wear "grey, single-breasted, straight buttoned sack coats, trousers of the same material; regulation cap with badge lettered 'Sleeping Car Porter.' White shirt and black four-in-hand tie to be worn at all times. Black shoes, nicely polished." The exception to this rule was in the warm months between May and October, when a "white jacket may be worn throughout the day." Under this code a uniform coat could not be worn over a white coat, and porters always had to wear a uniform cap when receiving and discharging passengers.

When working in the buffet and observational cars, porters wore a bow tie and white coats at all times. They also had to wear a white apron when performing duties. The porters were allowed to unbutton their coats when selling or collecting tickets, but in such cases they had to be wearing a vest when the coat was unbuttoned. "Employees must see that their uniforms are regularly pressed and cleaned, so that they will at all times present a neat and tidy appearance. Caps must not be worn on the back or side of head, and they are to be changed when they become crushed."

Not only did porters have to report for duty in uniform, their personal habits also had to be exacting. "Smoking, drinking intoxicating liquor, chewing tobacco or gum, or the use of toothpicks, playing cards or gambling on trains or on Company's premises is strictly prohibited," Canadian Pacific stipulated in its rulebook for porters.[35]

With cross-country travel growing in demand, the Canadian Pacific Railway was advertising its continental runs complete with sleeping car porters as the truly modern mode of travel. The Canadian National Railway and the Grand Trunk Railroad in their advertisements and posters also promised the finest in travel at great speed. The railways were making international travel available to a growing middle class. Passengers arriving on ocean liners from Europe, Asia, and elsewhere now had access to sightseeing trips across the continent via rail. The creature comforts available in sleeping and parlour cars ensured that travellers received the same kind of attention expected for guests in antebellum great houses.

The Pullman service was based on the concept of porters as good housekeepers, receiving visitors into their homes and entertaining them in a manner befitting the highest standards in society. Attentive to details of service and the wishes of their guests, porters could not afford to be careless. Carelessness was a scourge against which the railway was always warning its porters. John Harewood, now of Ottawa, recalled in a conversation how, as late as 1959, he would pay the price for any inattentiveness. A year earlier, Harewood had arrived to study at the University of Toronto and received the plum job of sleeping car porter on the Canadian Pacific Railway. Just out of training, Harewood, on a Toronto to Ottawa trip, was asked by a male passenger who had been drinking heavily to bring him a cup of coffee. The passenger was unsteady, his hands shaking, and in the handoff of the cup some of the coffee spilled on the passenger. When Harewood returned to Toronto he was called in by management and told the passenger had complained. Harewood was dismissed. "I was told the passenger is always right," he recalled.[36]

Porters had to be on their toes from the moment they arrived to prepare the car hours before receiving passengers until the last passenger had disembarked and the car was cleaned. Each porter was responsible for servicing the passengers in their car and placed his name at the car entrance as if it was the nameplate on his home. Not only was a porter expected to run his car impeccably, he was supposed to help any other porter in need of assistance. The porters were part of a team and each had to show that he was capable of remaining qualified for membership in this exclusive corps of workers. They had to be mindful of their attitude to passengers because the passengers were their superiors. In addition to addressing passengers with a broad smile and calling them Sir and Madam, the porters also had to ensure they did not display what the railway called *undue familiarity*. "This is one of the most numerous causes of complaints against employees," the railway warned in a circular. To prevent misunderstandings it was recommended that porters "avoid intimate conversation with their passengers and under no circumstances should they sit down in the presence of passengers, but should conduct any conversation while standing."[37]

Over the decades, well into the middle of the twentieth century, it was common for the Canadian Pacific Railway and Canadian National Railway to boast of their exquisite service. Passengers were catered to from head to toe, down to the nightly polishing or blackening of their shoes and the pressing of their clothes. The finest meals and drinks were offered in dining cars equipped with their own menus and chefs, and there were smoking rooms and cars equipped for playing cards or listening to music from a piano or, eventually, from the radio services then coming into vogue. At night porters turned down the beds for passengers and in the morning roused them awake. In between there was always the cord hanging by the berth attached to a bell. One pull and a porter would come running. Along the way the porters would faithfully point out scenic sights, fetch drinks from the club car, clean toilets and spittoons, and, most important of all, remember to alert passengers ahead of their destination. When passengers disembarked the porter would brush off their clothes, collect their luggage, and see them off with a smile and an open palm for any gratuity.

The *New York Sun* reporter offered readers a glimpse behind the curtain at the men who provided these services, capturing the roles and conditions of sleeping car porters, which would remain roughly unchanged over the next seventy-five years. It was only when unions were able to wrestle concessions from the railways and when technology, such as faster trains, came into effect in the 1950s—slicing as much as a full day of travel from a transcontinental trip—that routines began to change. The article also showed how Black men had to resort to deception—such as pretending they were happy when they were not or appearing to be wide awake and bright eyed instead of chronically sleep deprived—to survive. The smiles on the faces of the porters masked much of the pain and frustration they felt about their jobs and limited opportunities; the same smiles and impeccable service also contributed to the romantic image of train travel and the happy porters who made it possible.

The myth of the happy Black crews on the railways was partly based on the deceptions of advertising posters, such as those which showed Pullman porters, with their smiling Black faces, pulling back the blinds in a sleeping berth and asking, "Did you ring, sir?" These advertisements boasted: "Service? Courteous Pullman employees are proud of their art in extending travel hospitality. They help make your Pullman trip a memorable event."

But the smiles and service were not so much voluntary as demanded by the railway rules, which supervised almost every action of the porters. A pocket card issued by Canadian Pacific Railway offered the following helpful hints:

Co-operate in maintaining our high-class service. We're proud of it. You're on the team now—play the game.

Cultivate patience and good disposition.

Be Courteous. Yes, Madam! Good Morning, Sir! Thank you, Sir! Are easy words to use and pay-off generously in terms of goodwill.

Be Tactful. "A Soft Answer Turneth Away Wrath."

Be Safety Conscious. You owe it to yourself and the other fellow, too.

Take Advice Gracefully. Your Supervisors know the score and are anxious to help in a friendly way. Remember Teamwork is the keynote in making a perfect score.

Take Pride in your Work; it is an important part of the game. There is no better tonic for self-esteem than knowing your job thoroughly, and then putting up an outstanding performance.

Be Conscious of your opportunity for making friends for the Canadian Pacific. Much depends on you.

Be Mindful of the comfort of those about you. You'll get a lift out of the expressions of gratitude that will come your way.

Respect the other fellow's right to privacy. He'll appreciate your thoughtfulness.

Keep your car clean and orderly. There is a place for everything. "Good Housekeeping" takes on added significance in the confines of a sleeping car.

Be Tidy. A smart and snappy appearance, especially in uniform, is a tremendous Morale Booster.

Remind passengers about collecting all their personal belongings before they detrain. They'll appreciate your interest. It's an important point of service, too.

Check the linen and equipment when you take a car over, and take good care of the car property. These are essential moves in playing a Good Game.[38]

Indeed, the importance of checking the linen deserved a circular of its own titled "Instructions to Sleeping Car Conductors and Porters relative to handling Linen and other Car Equipment." In modern cars, it instructed, linen must be packed "with folded edges outward." The clean linen should be stacked on three shelves: the top containing 130 sheets; the center holding the remaining sheets and "the complete suit of slips [pillowcases]"; the lower containing 250 towels "when packed in rows, one bundle above the other."

"When stripping berths," the circular said, "fold top sheet from foot to head. Remove and fold blankets. Remove slips from pillows, leaving pillows on mattress at head; pull the three sheets toward middle of bed, fold together from sides toward center, enclose slips, and roll tightly from head to foot into bundle. Roll linen from each berth in separate bundle and, before removing berth curtains, take roll to soiled linen locker and pack orderly and closely toward back of locker."

Soiled linen could be removed from the car only after all passengers had disembarked, but in cases where there had to be a quick exchange of linen at passing stations, "porters must, within a reasonable time before arrival at such stations, sack and have ready to turn in the quantity of linen required to be exchanged."[39] Conductors were required to send telegrams ahead requesting new linen while it was the porter's responsibility to carefully count the pieces needed. If a porter could not account for all his linen at the end of a trip he risked having it deducted from his wages; and if it happened too often it was grounds for dismissal.

The reporter for the *New York Daily Sun*, wanting to find out the story behind the smiling Black porters, boarded the train in Montreal and watched the porters on a trip to Vancouver and back. For most travellers, all that really mattered was the ride itself and the conditions of service. No one cared to think too much about the working conditions of the porters since the uniformity and excellence of service were taken for granted.

A Long Run, a version of which was reprinted on September 12, 1891, in the *Manitoba Daily Free Press* revealed that the

> only employees of the Canadian Pacific who are with the express trains all the time between Montreal and Vancouver are the sleeping car porters. They travel nearly three thousand miles without a break and are on the road for nearly six days. It is a pretty hard life, but at both ends of the routes the porters have an opportunity to rest, though even then they hardly got sufficient recuperation. For two or three nights the porter is not likely to get over three or four hours sleep a night, and he is lucky if he gets that. He is his own conductor, and collecting the sleeping car tickets and accounting for them add considerably to their work.[40]

The reporter was touching on a condition of work that had concerned workers and travelers alike in the era of long-distance travel: when should a train's employees be allowed to sleep and for how long? The public was concerned that train travel could be unsafe when the train's speed was coupled with exhaustion and uncertain sleep. A number of accidents had resulted in a loss of life. On May 8, 1917, representatives of railway unions in Canada appeared before the House of Commons Special Committee on Railways to discuss intended changes to the country's railway laws. The union representatives were concerned that even with the proposed changes the regulations governing the operations of trains didn't go far enough. The unionists felt that the government was not doing enough to limit the number of hours employees could be forced to work without a mandatory break. Earlier that year the railway union representatives had sent a memo to Prime Minister Robert Borden and had lobbied government ministers to impose limits on the number of consecutive hours the railway employees worked.

William L. Best, Canadian legislative representative for the Brotherhood of Locomotive Firemen and Engineers, told the parliamentarians that he was "hopeful that the trainmen's organization and the conductors will see the matter in the same light as we do, that it is a case of necessity, [...] a matter of national importance, to conserve the human element involved in the railway industry. [...] When a man has spent, say, ten or twelve hours, or perhaps up to that time, if his physical condition is normal, he can render very nearly one-hundred percent efficiency. As he gets up to twelve, sixteen, twenty-four, thirty-six, or forty-eight hours, as I have often had to do without rest at all, many times eating meals at intervals of twelve hours—a man cannot give one-hundred percent [...] Many of our accidents occur when men have been long hours on service."[41]

Joining Best were representatives from the Order of Railway Conductors, the Brotherhood of Locomotive Firemen and Engineers, the Brotherhood of Locomotive Engineers, and the Brotherhood of Railroad Trainmen. Conspicuously absent was any representation for the porters. It was proposed that the Board of Railway Commissioners, as regulatory agents, should be mandated to make orders and regulations "limiting or regulating the hours of any employees, or class of employees, with a view to safety." But even for these union representatives the measure was too far-reaching because it governed all classes of railway workers, and in their minds those classes were not all equal. When asked by the parliamentarians if they supported the proposed change, the union representatives demurred, indicating that while they agreed with the sentiment behind the amendments they were concerned about the wording. Finally they conceded that their concern was with the wording itself and that they would prefer to adopt the same legal language that was being used in the US.

"In the United States," explained Charles Lawrence of the Brotherhood of Locomotive Engineers, "they have a law where if a man, *in connection with the operation of a train*, is on duty sixteen hours continuously, he must not go on duty again until he has had at least ten hours' rest. If he is on duty sixteen hours in the twenty-four, that is a few hours on and off, he must not go out until he has had eight hours rest."[42] This was the language adopted for the new legislation. But since the porters were working *on* the trains and not *operating* them, their consecutive hours of service would not be regulated in the same manner as conductors, brakesmen, engineers, and other employees who worked in operating capacities. Also notable in the international railway unions' bylaws: they prohibited Black workers from membership.

The newspaper report meticulously captured the transcontinental travel experience of the porters as well as it could.

Leaving Montreal at 8:40p.m., [the porter] is certain to have a busy time at Oshawa shortly after midnight, and then he has his boots to black, and he is lucky if he gets a wink of sleep before two or three a.m. He takes a pillow and lies down in the smoking room when no passengers are there, and catches catnaps if he can. He is likely at any moment to be roused by a bell summonsing him to one of the berths, and the bed is sure to be kept busy after daybreak.

This is followed by the long stretch into Winnipeg, the geographic centre of Canada east-west and a thriving passenger market of Canadians and Americans who arrive in Winnipeg either to head further west or to travel to eastern parts of the country. Still no real sleep for him.

After leaving Winnipeg he has a comparatively easy time across the plains, though he is compelled to be up after midnight both at Regina and at Calgary. At all important stations he has to go to the telegraph office with a statement of the accommodations unoccupied in his car, so that the station agents ahead may dispose of berths. He has a busy time through the mountains. As a rule he loses nearly his entire carload at Winnipeg, and it fills up there at once with passengers from the south. He loses his passengers again at Banff, and their places are supplied by tourists who are going on from that pleasure resort: then many of his passengers get off at Glacier and others come on, so that nearly all the time he has much to do in the way of keeping his accounts besides his duties as porter.

The porters would not only be telegraphing about the availability of berths but the condition of the cars. They developed a code so that any mice found onboard would be referred to in the report as diamonds, rats would be sapphires, bedbugs pearls, roaches rubies, lice opals, and dogs emeralds. Well into the second half of the next century, the porters' rules of conduct demanded that when "there is any indication of vermin on cars a written report should be submitted at home terminals or turnaround stations and if it is necessary to wire, the above mentioned code words should be used."

Continuing to describe the odyssey of the average porter on duty, the article continues: "At Vancouver he lays over for two days, and as a rule he sleeps in the car, occupying it all the time for the round trip. When he returns to Montreal he has been away fourteen days. Then he has a longer rest. He is off duty for five days, except that he has to take his turn reporting at the depot at night to assist the outgoing porter in taking care of luggage. His five days' rest puts him in pretty good condition for another two week siege."

Finally, the article turned to the conditions of service.

The porters say the trip is rather trying, but that there is nothing like getting used to a thing. The company pays them forty dollars a month, and they expect to make at least as much more in fees. All of them are colored men from the States, and have served on some of our branch lines. They say they like the service of the Canadian Pacific, for the company treats them well. Once in a while a man is switched off his regular run, which does not please him very well. For instance, he may reach Winnipeg, going east, with an empty car, and he is likely to be sidetracked for further orders. He has plenty of leisure then, but the fees which form so large a part of his income are not forthcoming, and he prefers more profitable activity.[43]

Particularly offensive to the porters were the circumstances around "dead-heading," when a train switched off a run and the porter was in charge of a rail car with no passengers. In this situation the porter was deemed not to be working and was not paid a salary for the travel on top of having no passengers to hustle for tips. A porter might be taken off the original run and switched to another headed in a different direction, which would unexpectedly extend the length of time the porter would be away from home while also compromising his earnings. The porters found their work unsatisfactory if they returned home without their pockets full of the loose change and bills they would have received from passengers. Very quickly into their careers porters learned to master the art of successfully soliciting tips, and to augment these payments many of them turned to bootlegging wares on the trains or shipping needed goods from town to town for resale. It was with great difficulty that the porters were able to make a living, and later, in retirement, most lived in poverty.

Working conditions for Black railway porters were precarious from the beginning. In 1898, the federal government found itself dealing with a controversy when six Black porters were fired in the fall by the government-owned Intercolonial Railway. When asked to explain the situation in the House of Commons, Andrew George Blair, the Liberal minister of railways and canals said that, after checking into the matter, the "coloured porters" had not been fired but had been shifted to other duties. "When it became necessary to reduce the staff in connection with the sleeping car service," he explained, "and to supply one person instead of two when the slack time came, instead of the coloured porters being dismissed, they were retained in the employ, and were given practically as good salaries as they had ever received."

With this explanation the minister indicated the conditions under which Black porters were hired on the Intercolonial were a good guide to the conditions on Canadian railways in general. "A coloured man who is taken into the service, if he has had no experience, starts at twenty dollars a month; if he has had some experience before, he starts at twenty-five dollars; and thirty-five dollars is the maximum salary allowed. Where their services as porters were not necessary in connection with the sleeping cars they were offered, and most of them accepted, employment as waiters or otherwise, as well as salaries of twenty dollars a month and their board; so they were doing very well."

The minister said the porters would be re-employed in the busier summer season when the railway had two porters on a car instead of one, as in winter. "The real trouble with coloured porters is that they are in the habit of getting tips while on the sleeping car services," the minister explained, "and their tips amount to more than their salary, so that they are better paid than any of the other employees on the train. When they drop out of that, they lose the tips, and their salary does not count."

But even at that time opposition parliamentarians accused the government of condoning racism by defending the treatment of Black porters. "The honourable Minister has not explained the statement he made the other day, that there were more coloured men employed on the Intercolonial now than at any former period," Conservative Member of Parliament for the Ontario riding of Bothwell James Clancy said. "Here is something that appears rather strange. Six of those porters were employed, and in the fall, they were either dismissed or given positions equivalent to dismissal, by that freezing out system to which my honourable friend referred. It is a well known fact that the salary of twenty dollars per month, where they are at their own homes a great part of the time (and unable to get tips), is a very small salary, and that the men in those positions depend largely on their tips. In other words, their salaries are paid by the travelling public rather than by the railway company."

Having made the point about the porters' poor wages, Clancy questioned why the men were treated this way in the first place. "It is rather strange," he said, "that five out of the six—men against whom there was no complaint— were dismissed from the car service and found themselves without employment or had to take a kind of employment at such reduced rates that they were unable to live. It is unfair to say that they were offered positions, unless the positions offered were as good as the one they lost. I am afraid the honourable gentleman will have to give a better explanation than he has given so far from what appears to have been a case of drawing the coloured line."

This was not the first or last time that the government led by Prime Minister Wilfrid Laurier was accused of racism and of importing Jim Crow style discrimination from the US by segregating workers on the railways.

"Men of that kind," Clancy added, "when dismissed find it very difficult to get employment again, because of the strong feeling against them on account of their colour. They have not the same chances in the race that other men have, and, therefore, the government should be more careful not to act unjustly towards them."[44] Neither the minister, nor any other member of the cabinet, including Prime Minister Laurier, responded to Clancy's charges.

Eventually the conditions of service forced the porters to link up with other porters across North America to form unions. Cottrell Lawrence (C.L.) Dellums, a leader of one of the most successful unions, helped the legendary A. Philip Randolph organize the porters into a fighting force in the Chicago-based Brotherhood of Sleeping Car Porters. The porters first won a union contract against the Pullman Company in 1935, and ten years later they signed a similar contract with Canadian Pacific Railway. Dellums would become the president for the international union after spending his working life as a porter and seaman for Canadian Pacific. Dellums' personal story demonstrates how pervasive the colour line of segregation was across North America, including the exclusion of Black people from all but the most menial jobs.

After deciding he could no longer make a living working on ships, Dellums joined a line of men outside a hotel in Oakland, California, who were applying for Pullman porter jobs. "I was in desperate straits for a job," he recalled. "I had been around here long enough to realize that there wasn't very much work Negroes could get. It was a common saying around the billiard parlors here in West Oakland that the ways a Negro could make a living in the Bay District then were very limited. One was to go down to the sea in ships and the second was to work on the railroads or for the railroads down in the yards and thirdly, illegally [....] You could find no Negro hotel waiters or bellhops. It was rough."[45]

Working conditions had changed in some respects since the inception of Pullman services, but even though porters were technically making a higher monthly wage, the working hours were deplorable. Under the first contract porters signed with Canadian Pacific in 1945 their pay increased from about eighty-eight to 132 dollars monthly. A working month was limited to 240 hours and subsequently reduced to 208 hours by 1954, with a week of paid vacation annually.

"When I went to work for the Pullman Company in January 1924," Dellums said,

they paid sixty dollars a month, by the calendar month. If you worked all the calendar month, you *might* get sixty dollars; but the odds were ten to one that you'd never get sixty dollars while you were a young porter. Now once you were there long enough to have enough seniority to hold a regular run, as long as you didn't miss a trip during that calendar month, you'd get your sixty dollars. But the runs were not regulated. The company set up their runs the way *they wanted* to set them up. Let's say one porter might have a regular run from Oakland to Seattle. You'd total up the number of hours that he was actually on duty in an ordinary thirty-day month, and he might work three hundred hours. Then there might be another porter working right out of the same place, let's say running Chicago, and he might work 350 hours. Both of them would get the sixty dollars. [....] We had an actual record of one run where the porter worked 485 hours a month! And he got the same sixty dollars. Then others worked as little, I believe, as 335 hours—that was the minimum any regular assigned porter worked. They all got sixty dollars.

Now the extra porters, which were the young men who went to work, would have to work what they called "the extra board"; they didn't get paid until they went out. There was no way for them to make sixty dollars, because the Pullman Company had all kinds of schemes to prevent paying. The most noted rule was that they didn't pay PM time. Now that meant that if they ordered the porter to do work at 12:01 PM his pay wouldn't start until midnight. They never started a porter's pay on PM time. Of course it was common for porters to go to work at three or four o'clock in the afternoon and the pay wouldn't start until midnight. Later on, when the company was forced to make some changes, they set up 'a mileage month,' which was eleven thousand miles. If a porter worked beyond that distance, he got thirty cents for each hundred extra miles that he worked. Now when they did that, they didn't start his pay until the train moved. The porter could go to work here in the yards in West Oakland at five o'clock in the afternoon and start receiving passengers at 7:30 or eight o'clock. But the trains might not leave until 11:30, midnight, or maybe one o'clock in the morning. His pay didn't start until the train moved because then the time-book showed only the departure of the train and arrival of the train.

The problem for the porter without seniority was that he had to start pre-paring the trains hours before the passengers arrived and the train pulled out of the station. It was a trick common to all Pullman franchises to keep wages low. "Most of the trains in those days left the original terminal at midnight," Dellums explained,

> and a porter would have to be in the yards at least two hours, sometimes three hours before the departure. He had to go two or three hours before the reception of the passengers so that he could get the car ready and the beds made down so that the people could lie down when they come on, if they wanted to. The train may not leave for hours. You know there were any number of trains that didn't leave until after midnight, but in all those cases the passengers were allowed to get on the train and go to bed at nine o'clock. The porter would have to have that car ready and start receiving possibly at nine o'clock. He would have to stand around out there in the rain, snow, sleet or whatnot, all that time, waiting for people to arrive and board the train if they wanted to. He was supposed to be out on the ground, on the platform, waiting. But his pay would start when the train departed.
>
> When the train arrived at its destination, his pay stopped. But he had to put the passengers off, get their baggage off, and get them all discharged and then go back in the car and make sure that all the beds were properly put away. If the trains arrived early in the morning, sometimes over half the beds might still be down. So then he would have to kind of tidy up the car, pick up all the soiled linen and count it and put it in sacks, make up a linen slip to show how much clean linen he was putting into how many sacks, and then pile it all up. So he could be as long as two hours getting off the train if it arrived early enough in the morning. No matter what time of the day it arrived, he couldn't get off in thirty minutes. Yet his pay stopped when the train arrived. So you see there was no way for him to make sixty dollars. I never did so.[46]

The situation was not much changed when Harry Gairey signed on to work as a Pullman porter on the Canadian Pacific Railway in 1938, his second stint on the railways. "My first job was dishwashing, and in the kitchen, for the Grand Trunk [...] My first night, they were coming from Montreal, going on to London. They took me down to Coboug (Ontario) because the train was late. I had to wait in the station until about two in the morning. I went right through to London that night, and the next day we went to Windsor."

Gairey continued:

Toronto was our headquarters. We started out here at nine in the morning to Montreal and we arrived between five and five-thirty. Then we would come back the next morning and go right through Toronto to London. Get to London, Ontario, at approximately ten p.m. Clean up the kitchen and then we went to the quarters—Grand Trunk provided us with quarters in London. The next day we serve lunch and go to Windsor, stay there till four p.m. and back on to Toronto. Go home, Grange Avenue. And then the next morning we repeat it over again, over and over again, same story. Every morning we had to go somewhere, every day. Thirty dollars a month. If the train was late you didn't get any overtime. You would work actually around the clock. There was no union. No day off. It was just a continuing thing. If you stay there all night and all day, you get thirty dollars a month. Thirty-one days, you get thirty dollars a month. But it was good pay at the time. There's nothing you could do; if you protested against this—I wouldn't have anyway—then you had no job. You are in a strange land, you have to keep going. […] The second cook was getting forty-five dollars a month, and the chef cook, like Joe Bailey on the café car, he would be getting seventy-five dollars a month. And in the dining car they would be getting around eighty, eighty-five dollars a month because they fed more people. […] And then I went into the dining room, waiting on tables, and I liked that very much. Because you see, the waiter was getting thirty dollars a month, same as a dishwasher, but they made tips, they made between fifteen, twenty dollars a day at that time in tips. So that was very good.

One of the biggest challenges for porters was staying awake when they were so sleep deprived. "The most difficult job I had was keeping awake," Gairey wrote. "We only got three hours sleep a night, four nights on the road. That's twelve hours sleep for four days. So my biggest job when I finished my work in the day was to keep my eyes open and not get caught sleeping. That was an offence, but somehow I managed to make it." But even when porters did get a few winks, the quality of the sleep was unpredictable.

"Just sitting up after you've finished your work," Gairey reminisced.

You have nothing to do, you're just sitting there; your passengers don't want anything, you have a little stool you sit on. If there is a vacant sleeping car section you could sit in that and I guess you could fall off asleep, you can't miss any stops, stopping at all these stations across the country. So it was a sort of an uncomfortable sleep but it was a big help if you could get a little nod in. I was really vulnerable as far as sleep was concerned. That was my specialty. I loved to sleep. But I hardly got time to sleep, with three hours sleep a night. We worked twenty-one hours and had to be on the train eighty-four hours to go to Vancouver. You'd go to bed from twelve to three; three o'clock the man in the next car wakes you up (there is a hook up between the cars in case any passenger rings the bell in either car you can hear it). He goes to bed and you have to watch both cars [....] so even though you had three hours you couldn't say you will sleep for the rest of the night because if something happened to you in your car and you can't answer for it, you gone. What you do when passengers are sleeping, you shine shoes.[47]

IN MIDST OF THE FIRST World War, Canadian Minister for the Militia and Defence Sir. A. E. Kemp noticed a familiar face missing when he took the Canadian Pacific Railway train between Ottawa and Toronto. So he took time out of his busy duties, which included those of minister of overseas military forces—the combined duties of overseeing the Canadian war effort at home and in Europe—to write a personal letter of enquiry to his friend Lieutenant-Colonel Frederic Lum Wanklyn. A well-known businessman around Montreal and director of several companies across Canada, Col. Wanklyn was general executive assistant to the powerful president of Canadian Pacific, Thomas Shaughnessy, and, ultimately, employer of all the porters. "I daresay," Kemp wrote in a letter dated May 10, 1917, "you have heard of Steve Shanks, the porter who has been running on the C.P.R. between Toronto and Ottawa from the time the road first opened. He was a great favorite with the travelling public and popularized the Railway because of his genial ways and fine temperament."[48]

C.P.R. had taken over operations of the Toronto-Ottawa passenger service in 1881 when it purchased the St. Lawrence and Ottawa Railway and the Canada Central Railway and merged their operations into one service. They also started to offer the very popular overnight sleeper train service that was heavily in demand by politicians and businessmen. It was not until the 1920s that the Canadian National Railway began a competing service, and between them the two services were so popular that often parliamentarians would rise on points of privilege to complain about the way they were treated on the trains, especially when their sleeping privileges were not up to the standards they expected.[49]

As they travelled, passengers conducted business with other businessmen and politicians, treating the service as a travelling office and as a place where they could eventually retire for trouble-free sleep, arriving at their destination in time to start a new day of work. Over time porters created a bond with regular passengers and got to know their tastes, preferences, idiosyncrasies and even the secrets of some of Canada's top elites who in return relied on the porters for special favours during the trip, which could be eight hours or longer depending on the weather. Politicians and businessmen knew they had to be generous with their tips to ensure consistently excellent service. In exchange the porters sought out particular politicians, business people or regular travellers for advice and to lobby them on matters of concern to their church, community or family. The bond which developed over time between passenger and porter was real. Over the many years of his porter service, Steve Shanks had developed connections with many passengers, including the man now inquiring about his whereabouts.

"I understand he is no longer going to be able to take up his duties again," wrote Canadian minister for the militia and defence A.E. Kemp. "In fact, I had my daughter visit his house in Toronto a few days ago to find out what the trouble is, and it appears that he has Bright's disease." Shanks' sickness was a disease of the kidney, which is associated with high blood pressure and diabetes, conditions prevalent among Black people. With his kidneys failing and little prospects for recovery because of the state of medicine at that time, Shanks could no longer work. He and his family were destitute.

"I don't think he has managed to save very much money," Kemp continued, "and as he was such an exceptional character I am sure that the hundreds of people who came in contact with him would like to help. My object in writing you is to ascertain whether or not the C.P.R. know anything about his present difficulty; whether there is any money coming in to him by way of pension, what it is, and whether it is payable together with any other particulars with which you might be able to furnish me; as I feel, as I am sure many others do, that I would like to "chip in" and give the family a lift in the way of raising a mortgage on their property, which is worrying them."[50]

Colonel Wanklyn replied the next day that that Shanks' case was already before the railway's Pension Committee and would be considered at the next regular meeting the following Monday, which was in two days time. This was the in-house union the railways had established to stave off efforts by the porters to form a union. Eventually it would establish an employee mutual assistance committee in the 1930s that acted as a benevolent society, providing such assistance as a small pension and death benefits. "Shanks is only sixty-two years of age, but has a long and favorable record, and I have no doubt that his case will meet with satisfactory consideration."[51] He promised to write again as soon as he learned of the committee's decision.

The following month, the minister wrote again, reminding Wanklyn of his commitment to keep him informed of the decision by the pension committee. "Can you tell me whether or not this man is in destitute circumstances as I should be glad to contribute some thing to the comfort of his family," he wrote on June 29, 1917. "He was a most popular Officer for a great many years in the employ of the C.P.R."[52] Sir Kemp might have also been concerned that, at 62 years of age, Shank was at least three years short of qualifying for a pension. The next day Colonel Wanklyn responded, "I am pleased to inform you that the Pension Committee have allowed him $20.00 per month, retiring allowance, as from the 1 March, 1917."[53]

This was one of the happier endings for a porter. Many others in similar circumstances did not have anyone to champion their cause, let alone a renowned government minister respected throughout the entire British Empire and with the clout to get things done, and who might have followed through to *chip in* his own personal funds to supplement the meagre pension.

It was uncertainties such as these that eventually drove the porters to form unions, and even after they were unionized, the conditions of workers did not totally change from what they were at the inception of the era of greater train travel in North America. Unionizing did not come easy.

GETTING BACK INTO MONTREAL AFTER working all night, fifty-six-year-old porter Charles Ernest Russell could hardly keep his eyes open and occasionally might have nodded off. This lack of sleep was so chronic that porters joked among themselves that instead of *sleeping* car porters they were, indeed, *sleepy* car porters. The on-duty conductor wrote him up for sleeping and as he was leaving his car, thinking undoubtedly of how quickly he could get home and to bed, Barbados-born Russell was called to the Superintendent's office for a hearing on the charge of sleeping on duty. As a result, he had to miss breakfast. But it would take some time before the meeting got going, during which time Russell had to wait while trying not to sleep. He was not allowed to leave the office and head home until noon that day, dog tired and after denying the charge.

Russell was fed up with this kind of treatment. He had been working as a porter for the Canadian Pacific Railway since 1918 and was a senior employee. He was also the chairman of the company-sponsored Welfare Committee, an in-house union for porters that administered company funds and provided pensions to a maximum of two hundred dollars per month to retirees. Despite his efforts, Russell was unable to improve working conditions for his members. He had handled many grievances for the porters, most of them stemming from what Russell felt were false accusations that, if left unchallenged, often resulted in the accumulation of demerit points and, ultimately, dismissal. As Russell would recall, among the accusations porters faced were minor personality clashes with white conductors or write-ups by conductors stating that porters had become too familiar with women passengers, most likely to be white. Not only did the porters claim many of these accusations were trumped up, but that they revealed a pattern: the false charges tended to accumulate the closer the porter got to the age of retirement, an obvious attempt by the company to avoid paying pensions. Sleep deprivation remained at the top of the list of grievances.

Russell decided the situation was untenable. On May 4, 1939, he wrote a letter to A. Philip Randolph, marked personal and confidential, that began, "Dear Sir: I am a porter of the Canadian Pacific Railway, domiciled in the City of Montreal and I am General Chairman of the Welfare committee. I have been thinking a long time to approach you as to weather [sic] you would consider our application, to become members of your organization, as there are a great many of us who feel that the present time is most appropriate for us to become organized."[54]

The letter must have brought back memories for Randolph, who fourteen years earlier had been approached by a fashionably dressed man on the streets of Harlem. The man took off his Panama hat, introduced himself as the president of the Employees Representation Plan for Pullman porters in New York, and asked if he could have a word with Randolph.

The porter was Ashley Totten, a West Indian born in the Virgin Islands who was the head of a nascent Brotherhood of Sleeping Car Porters union. Totten was noted for militancy but he also knew that, as a Pullman employee, he would be a marked man if he led another open attempt to form a union. The Pullman Company had crushed the porters' efforts to establish a union four times in twenty-five years—in 1900, 1910, 1913, and 1918. Each time the issue of sleep deprivation topped the organizers' list of concerns. Each time most of the leadership was fired. To assuage the demands for a union, Pullman set up the Employees Representation Plan after they crushed the 1918 drive.

Randolph was the firebrand speaker and publisher of the *Messenger*, which advocated unionism as a means of building Black solidarity and called for the establishment of a Pullman porters' union. Totten invited Randolph to speak to the Porters Athletic Association at the Elks Lodge in Harlem on August 25, 1925. With five hundred porters in attendance that night, the brotherhood was officially launched at the meeting, with Randolph serving as the union's public face and Totten the unofficial representative. Totten soon became a full-time organizer after being fired for disobeying a company command to return to New York from Chicago, where he'd been scheduled to attend a meeting alongside Randolph to organize that city's porters. Totten not only disobeyed the company but took to the floor in a barn-burning speech imploring the porters to join their colleagues in New York in the Brotherhood of Sleeping Car Porters. Thereafter Totten would join Randolph in a crusading drive across the United States. By the time Russell wrote Randolph, Totten had taken on a more administrative role, mainly as the result of a physical beating he took in Kansas City, where he was stationed as a union organizer. Two years prior, Russell and all porters across North America had taken note when the Brotherhood of Sleeping Car Porters signed its first contract with the Pullman Company, an achievement since heralded as a high point in Black and African American history, and a key development in the struggle for civil rights.

Six days after Russell wrote the 1939 letter, Randolph replied:

> May I say that I think it is unquestionably sound, proper and advisable that all the sleeping car porters, parlor car porters, buffet car porters and those porters performing service of this kind, should be in an organization, whether they work for railroads of the United States of America or in the Dominion of Canada.
>
> The organization of this class of workers into one union is certain to give these workers strength to protect their interest and improve their lot. The carriers are bound to give you more consideration when they realize that you are members of an international union.
>
> Therefore, may I assure you that the Brotherhood will be glad to accept the porters of the Canadian Pacific Railroad as members.[55]

So began the international union's drive to organize porters in Canada, a long struggle that ended with success. The union would remain the main bargaining agent for porters at Canadian Pacific Railway until its passenger service went out of business in 1978. Randolph ended his letter by saying he was coming to Canada the following month and was willing to "get in touch with you so that you may arrange to get some of the porters in the Canadian Pacific System into a meeting for us to address along these lines."

Russell responded on June 1, 1939, with caution. While his committee saw the necessity of such a meeting and would try to contact other porters, they would have to be careful. "I must point out that members of the committee cannot openly take active part," he wrote, "for the reason we would be made the scapegoat, hence we are prepared to give you the names and addresses of those we think are desireous (sic) of being unionized."[56]

Russell and his colleagues had good reason to be cautious. Several earlier attempts at forming a union for Black workers in Canada had failed, most spectacularly in 1920 when Canadian Pacific Railway broke the first Black union in North America, the Winnipeg-based Order of Sleeping Car Porters. The company also fired the union leaders, sending a clear message to anyone thinking of unionizing. Its rival Canadian National Railway had already refused to recognize all attempts at unionizing. But instead of extinguishing the porters' desire to organize, the railways' efforts drove the union movement underground where it smoldered, awaiting an opportunity to burst out into the open.

Randolph responded on June 7, 1939, saying, "I do not wish you to do anything which may cause you to be penalized in any way by the Companies."[57] He said he would be happy to receive Russell's list of names so he could contact the porters when he was in Montreal in early July.

"I hope your visit to Montreal will prove a success," Russell responded on June 22, 1939. "Again I must thank you for the kind thoughts of the danger to myself and my co-workers, but, we have begun the fight and it must be carried to its logical conclusion." He sent Randolph a complete list of full and part-time employees, but ended his letter with the warning: "Again, I must remind you that myself and co-workers, will not be present at any of the meetings you may hold, but I shall arrange to meet you somewhere strictly private, when we shall be able to discuss any plans you may have in mind."[58]

As promised, Randolph and his assistant Bennie Smith held recruiting meetings in Toronto and Montreal. Reporting on the drive, the Brotherhood said in its newspaper, The Black Worker, that about one thousand people turned up in Toronto to hear Randolph speak on "The Fight of People of Colour for Economic Justice." In 1942, a local in Winnipeg was set up with A.R. Blanchette as its secretary treasurer. Shortly afterward, Randolph set up the Canadian Association (sometimes referred to as League) for the Advancement of Coloured People—patterned on the National Association for the Advancement of Colored People in the United States—to fight for a civil rights bill and for fair employment practices legislation at the federal and provincial levels. Membership of the Association/League was open to "Negroes, Hindus, Chinese, Japanese Canadians and any liberal white people who are dedicated to the struggle for the liberation of the darker races."[59] With the head office in Calgary, the CAACP had offices in Montreal, Toronto, Winnipeg, and Vancouver.

But organizing the porters was not easy. As Russell had predicted, Canadian Pacific Railway fought the unionizing drive, beginning with the dismissal of as many of the Canadian ringleaders as possible. Charles Henry Baldwin, born in Woodstock, Ontario, helped to organize the Toronto area local and was bold enough to take the application for certification to the company. Not only was the proposal flatly turned down, but with the help of what he called "stool pigeons" who snitched on him to management, Baldwin was ultimately fired, forcing him to find other employment to support his wife and eight children. Baldwin went back to school at age forty-seven and became a civil engineer. Canadian Pacific Railway pressured the federal Ministry of Labour to call a vote by porters to decide between the Brotherhood and the company union. The Brotherhood won the vote 470 to seven. Bargaining began some time later and a first contract was signed on May 18, 1945.

But Stanley Grizzle remembered something else of note that happened at that time. "The C.P.R. Company, which had traditionally reserved sleeping car porter jobs for Black men only, did on May 17, 1945, the day before signing the collective agreement, hire the first white man as a sleeping car porter in Toronto," Grizzle wrote in his papers. "The union was certified as a bargaining agent on 25 March, 1945. The collective agreement became effective June 1, 1945. Other white men were hired that year in Montreal, Winnipeg and Vancouver. Thus, with the mere stroke of a pen, the porters' ranks became integrated. That is power."[60]

Not all porters welcomed this change. Some felt that they would lose job security if white people were now considered for these jobs. But with this small step, instigated by the porters, Canada's segregated society started to change, with different ethnic groups mixing as co-workers for the first time in many years. Even so, a great deal of work still needed to be done. Fortunately the porters were up to the task. They still had many more battles to fight against entrenched racism and discrimination.

THE COLOURED COMMONWEALTH
Reckoning with a Racist Past

THE ARRIVAL OF THE DELEGATION of porters and their supporters in Ottawa in 1954 showed that Black Canadians were finally finding a unified voice. Canada was developing into a full-fledged nation state and the porters knew the eyes of the world were watching how the country treated its non-white populations.

The timing of the delegation's visit wasn't coincidental; the porters and other delegation members were conscious that Canada was searching for a new role in global affairs, one that was evolving rapidly. By July 7, 1956, an editorial in the *Globe and Mail* argued that the predominantly white British Commonwealth was becoming the "Colored Commonwealth," and that there would be a new role for Canada, as a direct result, in international relations: "Canadians, in their rapidly changing Commonwealth, will have to go beyond mere tolerance, mere fairness: they must win and deserve to win, the friendship of the colored dominions springing up beside them."[61]

Across the country, but notably in the capital, there was the sense that something truly transformative was happening in Canada. Indeed, that the idea of Canada itself was evolving, with competing ideals of what the country could and should become jostling for dominance. Old ways of thinking appeared to be giving way to new ideas about nation-state building and Canadian identity and culture. If Canada were a railway, you'd say it was at an important juncture, the forces of history and even racial determination having brought the country—with all the passengers on board or waiting to climb on—to a special moment. The delegation wanted to further this along by joining the nationwide discussion.

Internationally, Canada was moving into a more central position on the world stage as a moral force for good. Internally, political elites were debating what the country's policies should be at home and abroad to make a difference in a changing world. As the train was pulling into the station that Monday evening, news was already breaking across the Atlantic Ocean in Geneva about the steps to negotiate the end of the Korean War, only the latest scar on humanity that had resulted from a half century of international conflicts and genocides caused by European imperialism. Canada found itself positioned as a bridge between warring parties. When the thorny question of seating arrangements for the fifteen delegations to the 1954 Geneva Conference was settled, Canada was placed between the main combatants. On one side of Canada would be the United States and its allies; on the other would be China and North Korea. Canada was positioned as an honest broker in international affairs—a perception that would continue to develop in the coming decades with Canada's role in United Nations peacekeeping.

After a half-century of tentative moves toward formal independence, an emboldened Canada was actively asserting its sovereignty in all areas. Canada epitomized the voguish buzzword of "self-determination," having moved, under its own direction, from being a colony, or a European settlement, to a modern nation state with a pristine image as a middle power in the Cold War between the Soviet Union and the United States. As historian Robin Winks argued, this tapped into the "vital lie" that Canada was fated, by geography and temperament, to be humanity's bridge or middle ground. "One preoccupation of Canadian statesmen from the late nineteenth century to the present time has been to seek out a special role for Canada to play in international, and, earlier, in Imperial affairs," Wink said in his 1968 pamphlet "Canadian-West Indian Union: A Forty-Year Minuet." "Restricted to a relatively narrow area of international activity by the hard realities of distance from Europe and proximity to the United States, Canadians have tended to build for themselves an image of the honest broker, the fair-minded middle power which could interpret French culture to English and English to French, Britain to the United States and America to Britain, the 'white dominions' to the 'coloured Commonwealth'."[62] At the time, Canada was seen internationally as a lynchpin, coupling-pin, and golden hinge.

Domestically and worldwide, there was also an uglier, competing image of Canada: as a country willing to spend social and political capital to preserve itself as a white British colony with a racialized hierarchy. Ideologically, privileged white Europeans, acting as superiors, were at the top of this chain, while at the bottom were the groups deemed naturally inferior and incapable of becoming genuine members of the modern nation state. The latter groups included, most notably, Indigenous peoples, who were perceived as naturally unsuited for membership in the higher social arrangements of western countries. Indeed, not only were Indigenous and other people of colour considered ill-suited for western society, it was presumed, out of a mistaken belief that they were neither physically nor socially evolved enough, that they might even be physically and mentally harmed in an incomprehensible environment. It was thought that exposing such people to the expectations of social justice or making them recipients of equal treatment would be a waste of time and resources; they were incapable of appreciating a standard of living higher than what nature intended for them; it would thus be unkind to include them in the wider Canadian society.

For a long time, this purported benevolence was the main weapon used to control Black migration into Canada. Such language was common not only in Canada but in Britain and other white dominions in their quest to control non-white immigration and citizenship. Ironically, in implementing this ideology, Canadian policymakers cited, as supporting evidence, a long list of Black intellectuals and nationalists, several of whom had argued along the same lines about the suitability of Black people for North American society since the end of slavery in the United States.[63] Rather than seeking integration into a common citizenship, these Black nationalists argued that former slaves should give up on the expectation that they could fit into or expect civil rights in societies not initially intended for them. By fighting for better treatment, Black citizens were destined to be constantly at odds with their society, creating dissent and unhappiness for everyone. The Canadian establishment relied on this entrenched belief that whites were different from all other races and should be kept apart for the good of all; in their view, separation was what Nature, or God, intended.

Noted British scientist Robert Knox (1791–1862), a lecturer of anatomy, zoology, and member of the French National Academy of Medicine, was widely respected for his scientific explanation of why races should not mix; and, most of all, why they should not mix in lands outside of Europe where Europeans were the colonists. Following a popular series of lectures in London, he expanded his ideas into a book titled *Races of Men: A Fragment* (1850), which became a major treatise on European settlements in the Americas. For Knox, only one thing would be certain: "the strong will always grasp at the property and lands of the weak. I have been assured that the conduct is not at all incompatible with the highest moral and even Christian feeling"—a statement eschewing the notion that morality determines such practices. Colonial states were not likely to be based on fraternity, brotherhood, or "love of thy neighbour," as so many Christian theologians had argued was the foundation for Canada. As Knox noted,

> I had fancied that it was but I have been assured of the contrary. The doctrine which teaches us to love our neighbor as ourselves is admirable no doubt; but a difficulty lies somehow or other in the way. What is this difficulty, which all seem to know and feel, yet do not like to avow? It is the difference of race. Ask the Dutch Boor [sic] whence comes his contempt and inward dislike for the Hottentot, the Negro, the Caffre; ask him for his warrant to reduce these unhappy races to bondage and to slavery; to rob them of their lands, and to enslave their children; to deny them the inalienable right of man to a portion of the earth on which he was born? If he be an honest and straightforward man, he will point to the firearms suspended over the mantelpiece—'There is my right.' The statesmen of modern Europe manage such matters differently; they arrive, it is true, at the same result—robbery, plunder, seizure of the lands of others—but they do it by treaties, protocols, alliances, and first principles.[64]

Knox argued that settlements are governed by what he called "physiological laws" that ideally match different races of human beings to specific landscapes. He contended, too, that it was unnatural for those who are natural inhabitants of one part of the world to expect to survive as transplants in another part. He cited the example of the Saxons of Western Europe, for him the fittest of human species and races: "Under the influence of climate, the Saxon decays in northern America and in Australia, and he rears his offspring with difficulty," Knox said. "He has changed his continental locality; a physiological law [...] is against his naturalization there. Were the supplies from Europe not incessant, he could not stand his ground in these new continents. A *real native* permanent American, or Australian race of pure Saxon blood, is a dream which can never be realized."[65]

These so-called laws, propounded by Knox, would be the basis for Canadian immigration policy: first, there would be a constant demand for Saxons, or white people, from western Europe as immigrants, with a preference for British citizens; second, Knoxian laws would be the basis for Canadian government claims that Blacks and other people of colour could not reasonably be expected to survive, far less thrive, in a climate to which they were not naturally suited. "Each race has its own form of civilization, as it has its own language and arts," Knox explained,

> I would almost venture to say, science; for although exact science, as is being based on eternal and indisputable truths, must ever be the same under all circumstances and under all climes, it does not follow that its truths should ever be formulated after the same fashion. Civilization, or the social condition of man, is the result and test of the qualities of every race; but it would be unfair to judge the European Saxon by this standard, seeing that the entire race, insular and continental, is crushed down by dynasties antagonistic of their race.[66]

Europeans had to be careful not to get crushed by non-white cultures.

Another implication of these "laws of nature" was that there should be no mixing of peoples from different races either as families or in states—for the union would be beset by conflict between the stronger and weaker traits or elements associated with specific people. This would be the case if a stronger, more advanced group like the Saxons of Europe mingled with elements of the so-called lower races. If the lower races were in the majority, it would just be a matter of time before the stronger succumbed to the weaker, and society reverted to the latter's lower, naturally uncivilized manners. Mixing the races would produce "social mules" who were unnatural in any setting or geography as well as incapable of reproducing and perpetuating themselves and their societies: "Nature produces no mules; no hybrids, neither in man nor animals," Knox warned.

"If we look to the period of Rome's conquest, we shall find no amalgamation of races ever happened," Knox wrote.

> In Greece it was the same. It would seem, indeed, that happen what will, no race, however victorious they may be, has ever succeeded in utterly destroying a native population and occupying their place. Two laws seem to me the cause of this. Should the conquering party be numerous there is still the climate against them; and if few, the native race, antagonistic of the conquerors, again predominates; so that after most conquests the country remains in the hands of the original race.[67]

The implications of these laws were clear for countries like Canada and the United States, which were intended for settlement by European Saxons for the good of their race. White people living in the Americas would have to face two pivotal questions: "Can a mixed race be produced and supported by the intermingling of two races? Can any race occupy, colonize and people a region of the earth to which they are *not* indigenous?"[68] The answers to those questions came in the form of legislation and policies, which led to the creation of White Man's countries in sites of European colonialism in North America and Australia, and apartheid in South Africa.

"On various occasions in the past I have called attention to the fact that the government does not encourage the immigration of coloured people," W. D. Scott, superintendent of immigration, wrote on Canadian government letterhead in 1914. In his letter to shipping agents, Scott explained the prohibition policies that would remain in place for decades.

> There are certain countries from which immigration is encouraged and certain races of people considered as suited to this and its conditions, but Africans, no matter where they come from are not among the races sought, and, hence, Africans no matter from what country they come, are in common with the other uninvited races, not admitted to Canada unless they comply fully with all the provisions of the Immigration Act.[69]

The approach to establishing settler communities like Canada and the United States was to create a racial profile and rules for immigration based on social understandings and natural limits. This is why the development of Canada was at times described as akin to the creation of garrisons in the wilderness, where communities attempted to thrive behind forts and barriers that kept undesirables and bad elements out, and provided a haven for those within the gates.

Alternately, the development of Canada has been analogized, by thinkers such as Northrop Frye, as a bush garden, where wild land was cleared of natural inhabitants in the form of undesirable brush, trees, plants, and weeds. In the garden, nature's frontier, the preferred social plants would take root and thrive. Fragile and unsuited to the Canadian land and climate, the plants were always in danger of dying out unless given special care, attention, and protection from natural threats in the garden. In this analogy, whites of European Saxon ancestry were the plants trying to thrive in the garden, whose settlement was enclosed by a garrison; the other, undesirable plants were the Indigenous people of the area, as well those indigenous to Asia and Africa, who needed to be kept out of the garrison and/or the garden—often, as Knox suggested, at the point of a gun. Once established, this garden had to be physically preserved by keeping out the undesirables who would so easily overrun the cultivated space if given a chance. It was for this reason that policymakers believed a whites-only immigration policy so vital.

By the beginning of twentieth century, North America was awash in the kind of thinking promulgated by the American propagandist Madison Grant in his popular book, *The Passing of the Great Race: or, The Racial Basis of European History* (1916). Not only did nature dictate that Europeans were a superior race to all others, Grant argued, it also punished the races biologically for mixing. The child born of two unequal races would always show the traits of the lower race. "Whether we like to admit it or not," Grant wrote, "the result of the mixture of two races, in the long run, gives us a race reverting to the more ancient, generalized and lower type. The cross between a white man and an Indian is an Indian; the cross between a white man and a Negro is a Negro; the cross between a white man and a Hindu is a Hindu; and the cross between any of the three European races and a Jew is a Jew."[70] This way of thinking still governs our classification of children, who have invariably been called such things as "half-breed," "mulatto," or, in today's descriptor of choice, "mixed-race." No matter how they are described, the child is usually classified as a member of the group on the lower scale of a racialized ethnic hierarchy.

Eventually, such behaviours and attitudes toward social order became codified as mores, and even as laws intended for the betterment of society. Once discerned and incorporated into daily living, it was understood that these rules and regulations should not be tampered with, or dispensed with, because, by undermining the structures and ideologies that keep the machine of state running smoothly, it would lead to the unravelling of the society. As a result, especially in the first part of the twentieth century, supporters of the Canadian system were reluctant to introduce social changes that went against historic practices. They also resented any government that wanted to introduce changes that might undermine prevailing norms and practices. If the government tried to make changes, it would be imposing stateways at the expenses of folkways, as the conservative social activist and proto-sociologist William Graham Sumner argued in his pioneering 1906 work *Folkways: A Study of the Sociological Importance of Usages, Manners, Customs, Mores and Morals*.

Out of this framework grew the difference between those of the in-group and all those excluded in the out-groups; it also would lead to such social passions as patriotism and ethnocentricism—a belief that one specific ethnic group is always right and superior. These beliefs would be the basis for continued agitations between those who were favoured and those who were excluded, and who wanted change so they could be included. "The insiders in a we-group are in a relation of peace, law, order, government, and industry, to each other. Their relation to all outsiders, or others-groups, is one of war and plunder, except so far as agreements have modified it. [...] Other foreigners who might be found in it are adopted persons, guest friends, and slaves."[71]

The ideas in these books were widely referenced, directly and indirectly, in immigration debates that backed arguments for gradual change on the grounds that, for change to be meaningful, it must first enter society's consciousness as folkways and then be adopted through education. Orders from government imposing change would not only be socially disruptive but could lead to unintended consequences, making society worse off for everyone, including those the government intended to help. Moving too quickly and precipitously to introduce change that undermined folkways, historically developed for the survival of the society, would lead to chaos.

Canadian government officials and leading elites, along with their counterparts in the southern United States, were undoubtedly students of Sumner. They never equivocated in their argument that any demands for social justice had to conform with the dominant folkways and had to allow enough time for folkways to change before any meaningful differences could take place.

At that time in the Canadian experience, "native" and "Aboriginal" referred to First Nations peoples as well as Chinese, East Asians, Africans, and their descendants. They were the Red, Yellow, Brown, and Black peoples of the world—all lumped together, in common parlance, as shades of Black—naturally positioned and imagined as inferior to whites.

Though the delegation arriving in Ottawa was most concerned with the fate of Black people, what they put forward would be in the name of all disadvantaged groups. Canada's train had arrived; determining on which track it would depart—thereby mapping out the future of Canada—would be the focus of discussions between the train porters, their supporters in the delegation, and Canada's political officials.

Even though, with increasing affluence, air travel was coming into vogue, it was not coincidental that the Negro Citizenship Association delegation travelled to Ottawa by train for their important meeting. This 1954 delegation reached Ottawa, literally, because of the sleeping car porters. One of them,

Harry Gairey, had used his employee discount as a supervisor on the Canadian Pacific Railway to secure reduced-price tickets for the entire delegation. Gairey was a founding member of the Negro Citizenship Association and its first treasurer, so, apart from working as a porter, he was known among Black people in Canada and the Caribbean as one of two people to approach on immigration matters. The other person was Donald Moore, a former porter and the president of the Negro Citizenship Association, who, as a result of leading this delegation and his continued fight for policy changes, would come to be affectionately known as the grandfather of Canada's new immigration policy.

Another Canadian Pacific Railway porter, the dynamic unionist Stanley Grizzle, was a leading member of the delegation and was listed as one of the people who would be speaking to the government. Grizzle represented the Brotherhood of Sleeping Car Porters on the Canadian Pacific Railway and had long been an advocate for anti-discrimination employment practices.

Grizzle was one of the main organizers and researchers behind the delegation to Ottawa. The other was Blanche Eastman of New Brunswick who was commissioned by the Negro Citizenship Association to study presence of Black people in Canada over time. According to Grizzle's files in the National Archives, not only did he do most of the research and lobbying of politicians, human rights groups, and trade unions, he also paid the passages for the trip out of his union's local funds. He did this after his appeal for funding support from the union's international headquarters in Chicago and from the Canadian organizer was turned down, leaving the Toronto local to make the contribution on its own. "Our local will be very happy to assist the Negro Citizenship Association in its protestation to the Canadian government," Grizzle wrote to Moore on April 2, 1954. "Our assistance will be in the form of a financial donation."[72] Grizzle was also in the forefront of lobbying provinces to introduce legislation outlawing discrimination in work and accommodation. He helped lead a charge by the international union of sleeping car porters for this kind of anti-discrimination legislation across North America, starting with a petition by the union leader A. Philip Randolph that forced US president Franklin D. Roosevelt to set up a fair employment practice committee in 1941. He had previously led a delegation in a meeting with the Ontario Premier Leslie Frost, which resulted in the province becoming the first jurisdiction to introduce fair employment legislation in 1951.

While helping to organize the lobbying of governments and negotiating for his members with the Canadian National Railway, Grizzle was also at work helping with the founding, in 1956, of the Canadian Congress of

Labour, a national umbrella for trade unions. At the founding convention in Toronto, he introduced four resolutions condemning discrimination, specifically in the way Canada restricted Black immigration and the human rights of all non-white peoples. Grizzle would ultimately be one of the first Black people to run, albeit unsuccessfully, for elected office under the banner of the socialist Co-operative Commonwealth Federation (CCF) party. Eventually, he would become the first Black person to become a Canadian citizenship judge.

The Ottawa delegation was headed by Moore, a businessman, whose first employment in Canada was as a sleeping car porter, a job that led him to fully appreciate what he called the vast discrimination Black people faced in the country. Moore was born in Barbados, in 1891, and came to Canada at the urging of boyhood friend Stephen Springer, a sleeping car porter in Montreal. Springer had visited Moore in New York, where, after arriving in May 1912, he was struggling to make a living. Springer persuaded Moore that he would have better job prospects in Canada, so in February 1913, Moore arrived in Montreal and—as was usual for Black men seeking work—applied for a job as a sleeping car porter.

In *Don Moore: An Autobiography*, Moore recalls that his first trip as a porter on Canadian Pacific Railway was to Winnipeg, and then to Toronto. Arriving on a Sunday, Moore went for a short stroll around the Toronto train stations and fell in love with city. "Here, I thought, is the place for me. Toronto must be a great place in which to live [...] On my return to Montreal, my home base, I asked to be transferred to Toronto."[73]

Moore resigned from Canadian Pacific Railway in 1916 and, two years later, enrolled in the dentistry school at Dalhousie University in Halifax. Like many professional students, especially those from the Caribbean studying in Canada, Moore also worked one summer as a porter on Canadian National Railway before coming down with tuberculosis. Moore would become a successful businessman and a respected community leader, often affectionately referred to as Uncle Don. Any Black person having an immigration or citizenship problem came knocking on his door. Finding that there was essentially no one formally representing Black people in Canada, especially immigrants, particularly those who'd been rounded up and kept in prison pending deportation, Moore stepped in and built up a reputation, not only in Canada but also in the Caribbean, as an intermediary between Black immigrants and the federal government. It was in this capacity that he was chosen to explain the Negro Citizenship Association's brief to the government.

The delegation understood the importance of its meeting in Ottawa. The organizers had made no secret of their intended audience with the Prime Minister in their community discussions. As Bromley Armstrong, one of the delegates, recalled: "news of the Ottawa meeting caused a flurry of activities in Toronto's African-Canadian community. Nearly two hundred copies of a brief outlining the NCA's position were prepared for distribution, and they accompanied invitations to organization and churches across Canada asking them to be part of the April 27 delegation." Black elites in Halifax, Montreal, Vancouver, and other cities were consulted on the message that would be delivered to the federal government. Discussions were held in the mainstream churches as the Black churches in Canada were notably silent on the issue. Moore later lamented, when reflecting on the delegation's alliance-building, "Support was regretfully lacking from one area of the black community where such support should have been automatic—the black churches. No word was received from any Negro church up to the time the delegation left for Ottawa."[74]

Though Black churches had played a key leadership role in the United States' Civil Rights movement, which had also formally begun in 1954, these churches did not automatically play the same role in Canada. This does nothing to discount the significant roles played by the Cornwallis Street Baptist Church in Halifax, founded by Black refugees in 1832, the Union United Church in Montreal, and the Pilgrim Baptist Church in Winnipeg, which were all historically involved in the organization of the porters into a political force. But, overall, the Black population in Canada did not exactly mirror the one in the United States: in Canada, Black social activists were primarily led by unions instead of churches, due to the influence of sleeping car unions and their allies on other trade unions.

In place of the Black churches, the Roman Catholic, Anglican, Salvation Army, and United churches gave support, as did several Jewish religious and community leaders. This was another difference between Black people in Canada and in the United States—a sizeable proportion of Black Canadians were West Indians or were their descendants. West Indians traditionally worshipped in mainstream churches, so in Canada many gravitated to those churches, even if they were not always fully accepted. The leader of the delegation, Don Moore, had been a member of the Methodist church in Barbados, but on arriving in North America, first in the United States and then Canada, he found that he was not welcomed as a congregant to the same extent as he was back home.

It was well known in Black communities across North America that one of the best ways of spreading news, or ensuring an upcoming event would be well publicized, was to tell it to the sleeping car porters. When the delegation of Black representatives arrived in Ottawa, not only were the eyes of Canadian Black communities on them, but the eyes of Blacks across all of North America, the Caribbean, Latin American, and Europe were as well—all the result of the sleeping car porters and their counterparts, the Black international seafarers, spreading the word.

DELEGATES TO THE MEETING CARRIED a brief for the government that they had painstakingly prepared over the previous months. The brief's main draft was written by Donna Hill, a white political activist, who, along with her Black American husband, Dan Hill, had come to Canada from the United States. Dan Hill would later become the first director of the Ontario Human Rights Commission. The Hills were among the early activists fighting for the human rights of Blacks and other ethnic minority groups in Canada. Donna Hill had been at the forefront of the struggle for equality in employment and for anti-discriminatory practices in housing, public accommodations, and restaurants, often joining teams of Black and white people to test how restaurants and places of accommodation serviced visible minorities.[75] Research from the Brotherhood of Sleeping Car Porters— the union representing CP Rail porters—provided the background for much of Hill's brief, as well as the ideology fuelling the activism behind the delegation. Last-minute updating of Moore's opening statement, and incorporating additional thoughts and supporting evidence, was completed on the train from Toronto.

"In our appearance before you today," the brief stated, "it is our desire to call to your attention certain phrases of the Immigration Act and the Immigration Regulations which seem diametrically opposed to the high principles of Canadians and Canadian ideals." It noted that the Immigration Act of 1923 that was then in force seemed to have been written and revised over the years with the express intent "to deny equal immigration status to those areas of the Commonwealth where coloured people constitute a large part of the population."[76]

The draft's first task was to attack Canada's definition of who was a British subject and who was permitted to immigrate to Canada from the established white dominions. "Our delegation claims this definition of British subject is discriminatory and dangerous," the brief said. "It is discriminatory because it creates two classes of Her Majesty's subjects—on the one hand you have subjects predominantly white, on the other, subjects predominantly coloured. The first class are deemed 'British subjects' for the purpose of the Immigration Act, the other class, by implication, are not British subjects."

"It is dangerous," the draft continued,

because it instills a feeling in these divided groups, as well as in Canadians, that there are superior and inferior races, and it has the tendency to raise animosity between people born in different geographical areas. Social and biological sciences have established definitively that there are no superior races. "All human beings are born free and equal in dignity and rights." And Her Majesty Queen Elizabeth, as recent as December 25, 1953, pronounced herself as dedicated to the concept of an equal partnership of all Commonwealth nations and races—and urged acceptance of this concept upon all countries of the Commonwealth.

This was a reference to the queen's traditional Christmas Day speech, perhaps the one time every year when all subjects in the colonies and dominions to whom it was addressed were united in a single endeavour.

The draft said the legislation was dangerous for another reason as well. As a democratic nation, it stated, Canada was committed to promoting world peace:

and the false feeling of a superior race has already shattered the peace of the world as experienced in the Second World War. We believe Canada will not countenance, in any way, anything which may lead to sowing the seed of race hatred; neither will she act contrary to the 'Canadian understanding of the equality of all people.' She must take drastic measures not only to remove race hatred, but to destroy it completely forever. This classification of British subject is dangerous to the peace of the world.

In making the argument for immigration from the West Indies, the brief said Negroes had shown that they could survive in all climates and that, when given the chance, they were easily "assimilated" into the Canadian society:

In most communities it must be noticed that Negroes have become an integral part of existing political, social and religious groups; they may be found in the ranks of skilled and unskilled labour, farming, business, trades, and in the most technical professions. They work side by side harmoniously with like workers of other races; they may be found in any level of society. In various municipalities and provinces, regulations have been, and are being, adopted to remove any residues of discriminatory practices. Examples of these regulations are to be found in the Ontario Racial Discrimination Act, and Manitoba's Fair Employment Practices Act; even our own Government has seen fit to pass the Canada Fair Employment Practices Act. This could not have been done had it been felt that Negroes could not become an integral part of Canadian society.[77]

Though the draft did not state so, it was widely known that Black activists, especially in unions representing porters, had been in the vanguard of the attempt to change these discriminatory employment practices. With the porters, the two issues of employment and immigration merged. Indeed, as the *Daily Mercury* newspaper in Guelph, Ontario, had stated on October 19, 1953, "discrimination against colored railway parlor car attendants may be the first large-scale complaint heard under the new Fair Employment Practices Act" that had come into effect a few months earlier.[78]

Emphasizing the point of good citizenship by Negroes, the brief said, "the customs, habits, modes of life, or methods of holding property in the West Indies are essentially the same as in Canada, and no change is necessary when these people become part of the Canadian way of life."[79] To this end, the brief recommended: broadening the definition of British subject to include all British subjects of all ethnicities and colours, and citizens of the United Kingdom and Commonwealth; allowing for the migration of British West Indians, without regard to racial origin, as long as they had sufficient means to maintain themselves until they found employment; allowing nephews and nieces under twenty-one years of age to join family already in Canada; recognizing persons of exceptional merit, including skilled workers such as nurses, draughtsmen, stenographers, and graduates of Canadian educational institutions; and setting up a Canadian Immigration office in the British West Indies to handle prospective immigrants. By the time they presented the brief, the leaders of the delegation had made a small breach in the fortress that kept Black people from immigrating to Canada. With the brief itself, they executed a full-scale attack on the fortress itself and its ideological underpinnings.

FIVE MONTHS EARLIER, IN DECEMBER 1953, primarily through Moore's efforts, the Negro Citizenship Association had won what would turn out to be a symbolic victory when they persuaded the Canadian government to allow a registered nurse from Jamaica, Beatrice Massop, to immigrate to Canada. When her initial application was turned down in 1952, Massop turned to Moore for help. With Canada facing a shortage of nurses and nursing assistants, the delegates were hoping Canada would allow in qualified women from the British West Indies to help fill these jobs. They would later extend this category of "persons with exceptional merit" to include women formally trained in the homeland as domestic servants. This might have been the most explosive recommendation in terms of its potential to change Canada. By exploiting the exceptional merit category, the Black activists would end up opening doors to welcome the first major influx of British West Indians in Canada, especially in the 1960s and 1970s, when Blackness had a moment of ascendency in the country.

The 1954 Ottawa delegation's recommendations in their brief, if and when implemented, would shape ideas of what Canada was, and who could become Canadian. We're still living the legacy of those recommendations as Canada continues its evolution away from the White Man's Country it had long been into a Canada that, in subsequent generations, has been described as "multicultural" and the "first post-modern country;" a country where ethnic nationalism has given way to people of all races and ethnicities living together in common humanity and citizenship. At the time, the delegation aspired to create a Canada that would be a just society, where individuals would receive all to which they were entitled simply by virtue of their membership; enjoying, that is, all the rights, obligations, and entitlements that come from being a citizen. Equally, all citizens would be recipients of social justice: they would not only claim an entitlement or right to share in all that the society produced—whether good or bad—they would also receive their due. There would be the political will to make social justice not only an ideal, but a daily practice. In this vision of Canada, individuals would know with absolute certainty that they were citizens by the way they were seen, treated, and assumed to be naturally Canadian—the way they were automatically included in all thoughts and actions related to being Canadian. Citizens would enjoy the instinctive recognition that their humanity was valued and they were fully functioning and engaged Canadians. With such unrestricted opportunities, Black citizens would be as equal as any other member of a free and democratic society. As Canadians, they would be as free as any other Canadian.

The end of the Second World War nine years before, and the changing world order and Canada's increased role within it, had opened up opportunities the delegation intended to exploit. Europe, and many other parts of the world, was in tatters socially, politically, and economically, and Canada was in a position to both help and benefit. Canada had plenty of "empty" land, which leaders understood it could use to generously resettle people displaced by the war and to ramp up production of wheat and other cereals to reduce world hunger. New arrivals in Canada would also find plentiful work in the mines or harvesting natural resources like timber, gold, iron, and the limitless waters waiting to be harnessed. There was also a need for nurses, bookkeepers, electricians, messengers, and household domestics. All these new immigrants would join with the now old-stock Canadians of British and French extraction to construct an almost new society—one of affluence—where everyone would enjoy the fruits of Canada's struggles for freedom and democracy in the last war. Canada had ended the war rich in land, money, and reputation, but poor in the number of Canadian hands needed to make the country into the industrial manufacturing giant it clearly had the potential to become. An energized Canada, conscious of its strengths, resources, and potential for good works internationally, thus had much to offer in these emerging new world affairs.

The United Nations Declaration of Human Rights, which had been drafted by Canadian law professor John Humphrey, would be the focus of that new international body. This declaration, affirming the dignity of all human beings, contains many of the ideas and ideals that the porters and their allies were struggling to bring to full acceptance in Canada. But penning and supporting such a declaration laid bare a historic conflict within Canada itself: on one side was the very obvious hypocrisy of the Canada of old, which began with the dispossession of Indigenous lands for the construction of a racist state; and on the other was the new Canada suggesting to the world that the issues of race, ethnicity, and nationalism that had caused past wars should have no social or political significance in and among countries in the United Nations.

In seeking to find a common voice, the union members of the Negro Citizenship Association had been working behind the scenes with representatives of other despised minority groups, most notably the Jews, to point out the flaws in Canada's commitment to the high ideals of human rights. "As a member nation of the United Nations and a signatory to the Declaration of Human Rights, Canada has the duty of maintaining and expanding democracy within her own borders," a delegation of trade unionists—called the National Committee on Racial Tolerance of the Canadian Congress of

Labour—had said in a brief to the Canadian minister of labour, Milton Green, at an Ottawa meeting two years prior, on May 27, 1952.[80] The brief called for the Canadian government to adopt a fair employment practices act and policies to outlaw racial discrimination in employment, thereby joining a movement gathering steam across North America to ban racial discrimination in the workplace. The call for fair employment practices first came from the international union, the Brotherhood of Sleeping Car Porters, a decade earlier, and had already led to the removal of barriers that prevented Black people from entering military service in the United States and Canada. In return for a 1941 promise by US president Franklin D. Roosevelt to set up a fair employment commission, A. Philip Randolph, as leader of the international Brotherhood of Sleeping Car Porters' union, had backed away from his threat to organize a march on Washington to protest discrimination against Black people. Randolph and the union would instead use the Fair Employment Commission as an opportunity to push for fair employment practices in all North American jurisdictions. Black military men, who had fought for freedom around the world, had returned home to find a lack of opportunities in both countries and in the Caribbean.

The Canadian unionists wanted governments across the continent to go further. "Notwithstanding the healthy degree of political democracy which exists in Canada, there is serious ground for complaint regarding the treatment accorded to Canadians who belong to racial or religious minorities or who are foreign born," the Canadian brief said. Ironically, the committee was calling for legislation to eliminate practices still common among many of its members, particularly those unions that restricted membership to white men only, thereby preventing Black people from gaining employment in industries and services where union membership was a requirement for the job. Such was the case, for example, with the unions representing railway conductors and locomotive engineers.

"The Congress asserts that the denial of a job to any Canadian, for no other reason than that his race, creed, his colour or his ancestry is not that of the majority, is a violation of one of the most fundamental tenets of democracy: equality of opportunity," the brief argued.

Such discrimination has no scientific basis; it is based wholly on prejudice. It is contrary to the religious and moral values on which this country was founded. It saps the morale, and destroys the faith in Canadian democracy, of hundreds of thousands of our people, who see themselves treated as second-class citizens. It builds barriers of hatred and distrust within the community, making genuine national unity impossible. It deprives Canada of the best efforts of countless thousands of her people and leaves her poorer for it.[81]

The wording of the brief was similar to what the Toronto division of the Brotherhood of Sleeping Car Porters was writing in its own briefs and resolutions. Division president Stanley Grizzle had been bombarding every convention and high-profile meeting of trade unionists in Canada with resolutions and letters to make the fight against discrimination in immigration, work, and accommodation a political priority. Grizzle had become the go-to man in the labour movement for getting figures on the effects of discrimination in Canada and for arguments to undercut the reasoning used to support discriminatory practices. In talking about how discrimination limited the citizenship rights of Canadians, the committee, even without mentioning them directly, was highlighting the denial of citizenship rights being faced by the so-called "Canadian Negro." Now a delegation from the Negro Citizenship Association, with Grizzle and train porters among them, as well as some of the top Black Canadian activists and intellectuals, was arriving in Ottawa to plead the case themselves. They believed in the power of ideas as a starting point to shape the way people live and get along with each other. They also believed that all human beings were reasonable and could be persuaded to confront the inhumanity caused by their ideology and practices.

As the delegation prepared for its meeting, there was the sense of an awakening in Canada, but the country was still uncertain about how much of the past to retain and how much of an idealized future—one that would be radically different from the past—could, or even should, be feasible. Canada was on the cusp of shedding its image as a backwater colony of the British Empire to become a shining example to the world of a fair and honest leading power in the seemingly rudderless British Commonwealth then replacing the British Empire. Internally, however, Canada had some housekeeping to complete before it could truly become that shining light to the rest of the world. Uppermost among its challenges was the very basic question of national identity: who should have the right to become a Canadian and to use that status to help determine Canada's future and its position in the world? Indeed, Canadian citizenship would be the touchstone issue of all of the delegates' discussions in Ottawa.

It was taken for granted that immigration would be the means through which the country could fulfill its potential by effectively choosing its citizens. The big question was whether Canada should continue to give citizenship preference only to white British subjects. In debates across the land, and those in *Hansard's* official records of Parliament, there was no doubt about this preference.

So who was a British subject? In practice, Canadian policy was firm that this title, for immigration purposes, meant only white people; that is, Europeans living in the British Isles, Australia, New Zealand, South Africa, the US, and the Irish Free State. Europeans who had resided in Black British colonies were also included. The order-in-council regulations under the Immigration Act, which had been updated only four years before the delegation's meeting in Ottawa, prohibited the landing of certain immigrants in Canada. It was also clear in its definition of who *was* permitted to enter:

> A British subject or a citizen of Ireland entering Canada, directly or indirectly, from the United Kingdom of Great Britain and Northern Ireland, Ireland, Australia, New Zealand, the Union of South Africa or the United States of America who has sufficient means to maintain himself until he has secured employment: Provided that for the purposes of this Regulation the term "British subject" shall mean a person born or naturalized in the United Kingdom of Great Britain and Northern Ireland, Australia, New Zealand or the Union of South Africa, or a citizen of Ireland who has become a citizen of the United Kingdom by registration under the British Nationality Act, 1948.[82]

To this end, entry was limited to British subjects from the dominions, citizens of the United States of America, and French citizens born in France or in Saint-Pierre and Miquelon. In addition, the Immigration Act made clear that because of their cultural practices certain applicants were prohibited because of "the peculiar customs, habits, modes of life or method of holding property in his country of birth or citizenship or in the country or place where he resided prior to coming to Canada." Entry into Canada by people from Asia was limited "to the following classes of person or persons: the wife, the husband or the unmarried children under twenty-one years of age of any Canadian citizen resident in Canada who is in a position to receive and care for his dependent."[83] Even when limited in this way, immigration was further restricted by quotas: India was limited to 150 people annually, Pakistan 100, and the then-named Ceylon 50. Anyone seeking to immigrate to Canada from these countries also had to be a spouse or a child under the age of twenty-one, and everyone must have a direct family member already in Canada to avoid the blanket prohibition.

In Ottawa, the Negro Citizenship Association was petitioning on behalf of those who would not qualify to immigrate to Canada. Immigration from the British West Indies would be the test, as the delegation sought to exploit the hypocrisy and contradictions of colonialism and imperialism. Those of European descent were allowed in; those whose race or ethnicity was African, Asian, or American Aboriginal—those who had, in other words, practically made the West Indies the first multicultural society—were rejected. The contradictions of colonialism and imperialism were on full display in this policy: Canada would either be a good and faithful member of the British Empire and—by living up to British ideals of equality and international norms for respecting human dignity—the emerging Commonwealth, or it would be an outcast on course for the kind of pariah status the Dominion of South Africa would eventually experience. The delegation planned to argue that Canada could not be both at the same time—it had to shift its focus—and that, from this point forward, Canada must reject its racist history if it wanted to achieve a genuinely pluralistic future.

THE MORNING OF THE MEETING, the delegates set out from the YMCA, and YWCA, where they had spent the night. Fog would rule most of what was a gloomy day of wind, snow, ice pellets, cold rain, along with rising and falling temperatures. The weather very much suited the meeting with its highs, lows, and government obfuscations. It would start with two surprises—one for each side.

Prime Minister Laurent was travelling and asked his minister of immigration, Walter Harris, to meet the delegation on his behalf. Indeed, this was not that big a surprise, as Grizzle had heard through his government contacts that the meeting would be with the minister. As soon as he'd found out that the prime minister would not be in attendance, Grizzle dashed off a letter to him, dated April 26, 1954, before leaving Toronto. The letter said:

> The Toronto C.P.R. Division of the Brotherhood of Sleeping Car Porters' membership wishes at this time to protest the Canadian Government's Immigration policy as it affects Negroes. It is quite obvious to us that the citizens of the West Indies, British Guiana, India, Ceylon and other British dominions and colonies are not classified as "British." We further are of the

opinion that this distinction was made to keep people of colour from becoming Canadian citizens. We sincerely hope that the present government will very soon remove from Canada's Immigration policy this vicious "colour line."[84]

The letter ensured the prime minister received their delegation's message unfiltered.

And this was when the second surprise occurred. Harris and his staff, who were used to receiving delegations and deputations, were amazed at the number of people descending on their office. Thirty-five members strong, the delegation was unlike anything they had seen before from Black Canadians, causing a mad scramble by staff to round up enough chairs to seat everyone. The so-called Negro community, and the sleeping car porters in particular, had learned an important lesson in political activism: coalition-building and large numbers were powerful. Still, the delegation was smaller than the fifty Moore had originally intended. It wasn't the first time they'd used numbers to overwhelm. Four years earlier, as a delegation of the Brotherhood of Sleeping Car Porters, they had used the same strategy on Leslie Frost, the premier of Ontario, when they met with him to advocate for anti-discrimination legislation in the workplace and lobbied for the Fair Employment Practices Act.

Grizzle—who also had a hand in drafting the brief to the premier with his Jewish allies—recalled a startled Frost saying, "This is the largest group of coloured people I've seen in one place, all my public life."[85] That delegation was more than one hundred members strong. Grizzle had learned something from his main mentor, A. Philip Randolph, who, as the head of the Brotherhood of Sleeping Car Porters, had always used the threat of overwhelming numbers of protestors to get different American presidents to bend to his demands for civil rights. Randolph had initially done it by threatening a march on Washington in which thousands of Black people would protest against segregation in the US Armed Forces. The threat resulted in a 1941 executive order by President Franklin D. Roosevelt to set up a commission looking into fair employment practices in government services, thereby starting the official dismantling of Jim Crowism. Randolph used the same strategy seven years later, to force President Harry Truman to integrate Black people into the military. Randolph later made good on his threat when he organized the famous March on Washington for Jobs and Freedom, where Martin Luther King Jr. would give his famous "I Have a Dream" speech.[86]

That morning in Ottawa, when the federal immigration minister Harris started to apologize for the size of room, Harry Gairey was prepared and quickly stepped in. "I wouldn't worry about that," he said, referring to the seating, "because we just want to present this brief to you, and the injustices, and introduce the president."[87] With that, Donald Moore, the president of the Negro Citizenship Association and main spokesman for the delegation, took over.

Moore began by citing the long list of groups, unions, churches, and community organizations across the country that were supporting the delegation. The Negro Citizenship Association, he explained, "was born in response to the continued appeal of our brothers and sisters who were experiencing untold indignities and hardships occasioned by the wholesale rejection of their attempts to be legally admitted to Canada. At that time, not even close relatives were admissible."[88] Moore was reminding Harris of a prolonged, ongoing battle in the Canadian House of Commons, in which allies of the porters and the Negro Citizen Association had been calling on the minister to change Canada's racist immigration regulations. The country was being asked by a neglected and marginalized group of Canadians to account for its past behaviour and to imagine a future radically different from its past.

Minister Harris would give the delegation what would later be described as a polite hearing, but little else.[89] Very little of what they brought to his attention in their brief would have been new to him: he would have heard much of what they had to say earlier and repeatedly both in parliament and in the telegrams of protest sent by the association and its allies since the issue first came to his attention. Apart from denying there was discrimination against Black West Indians, he defended the Canadian immigration policy as it was then constituted; but mostly he just sat and listened. The temperature in room felt as chilly as those outside the building.

After the meeting ended, Moore remembered that either in his haste or because of his nervousness he'd managed to misplace his hat. "After the session was finished I couldn't find my hat," Moore recalled. "It was a sight to see the minister looking under chairs in an effort to find a hat for a delegate who didn't have the sense enough to keep his hat on his head."[90] Still, even if the meeting did not result in the immediate responses the delegation was hoping for, the fact that it happened at all was a major victory. It had been a long time coming and a long journey for both the delegates and Black people in general, and it was no small thing to be able to command the attention of a senior minister of government, even if only for a short while.

"I KNOW NOTHING ABOUT THAT"
Legislating the Colour Line

WHEN THE NEGRO CITIZENSHIP ASSOCIATION, dominated by the sleeping car porters, decided to take their protest to Ottawa in 1954, the delegation well knew the system they were up against. Still they were taken aback that they were not receiving a warmer reception by the government. As the porters crisscrossed North America on the trains, they had witnessed for at least half a century the worst aspects of Canada's social system, specifically in the way it excluded much of humanity from participating in the building of the country and in determining the nation's future. Having been denied full participation in society because of their skin colour and ancestry, the porters were themselves emblematic of this exclusion.

Since 1909, the sleeping car porters had been segregated on the government-owned railways, and then again on the privately owned railways, where they could work *only* as porters, with no possibility of promotion or changing jobs. The railways offered a wide array of the country's best jobs—from rail-yard workers, to firemen and engineers, to presidents and chairmen, who lived in huge mansions and roamed the country in the private cars that were the perks of the job—yet the porters were entitled to only one type of work: as lowly-paid passenger helpers with no job security. The porters experienced this abrasive social inequality on a daily basis, and they wanted different lives for themselves in Canada. The porters knew they were likely to face further marginalization by fighting back, and that they might even harm the Black community they represented. They'd noticed how the historic, albeit mythological image of Canada—as a country of acceptance and inclusion that welcomed Black people fleeing persecution, slavery, and other forms of hardship—had essentially reversed itself.

So how were these inherently unequal structures put in place? What tools did policymakers use in the six decades leading up to the arrival of the delegation in Ottawa? How did Canada make segregation, first used with railway workers, an instrument of a wider policy for nation-building and citizenship? One of the simplest methods was to keep the Canadian Black population as small as possible by controlling who could enter and stay in the country. A second method was to severely restrict the opportunities Black people in Canada had to enjoy what might be called the good life: all the goods and services the country produced. The most effective way of achieving this goal was to deny certain groups of people the right to choose their jobs, which, in a high-grade consumer society, limited their ability to accumulate and share in the nation's wealth. The railway porters knew the racial policies that informed the running of the country and the railway system that built it were inseparable. By limiting their job opportunities, the Black porters were unable to participate fully, both socially and economically, in Canadian society.

Immigration and settlement in a specific state are usually governed by countervailing push-and-pull mechanisms. The economic conditions in the Black world—which included Africa, and, closer to home, the southern United States and the Caribbean—were then terrible enough to push people to immigrate north for a better life. On the other side of the equation, the conditions in the receiving country should be attractive enough—or comparatively better than those at home—as to pull immigrants away from their homeland to settle in the new country in the hopes of a better life. The "push" in this situation was thus the poor economic situation in mainly Black countries, and the "pull" was the need for labour and Canada's affluence. Traditionally, any economic advantage a receiving country offered might be a sufficient reason to attract people from poorer countries or states, especially those looking for work, even if the social conditions they encountered once there were not ideal. Immigrants and their children would eventually, of course, demand fuller citizenship benefits and recognition, including social, political, and welfare rights. Some feared that when it came to people of colour, this may eventually result in social unrest, which was a key reason Canadian policymakers had argued for minimizing Black immigration.

Canadian immigration officials made it clear to potential Black immigrants that it would be better for them, both physically and psychologically, not to live in Canada. Applying the racial theories of Robert Knox,

Canadian policymakers told potential Black immigrants that Canada might look good and inviting from afar, but once they arrived they would find it even more difficult to survive than they had in the lands they were fleeing. They further argued that Black immigrants would not be naturally suited to the country—either to the geography and physical conditions or to the social mores and general society. At ports of entry, medical examiners were instructed to bar Black applicants from entering and to place them in the classes of prohibited individuals outlined in the Immigration Act. This meant that the easiest way for a Black person to get into Canada was to be recruited by the railways from the southern United States and the West Indies, or to arrive as a Caribbean university student with the expectation of returning home upon graduation.

The Canadian government equally ensured that those Black immigrants who got into the country and stayed did not prosper: there was no work for them, and when they were employed it was hardly at a liveable wage. They were ostracized, and segregation and social prejudice dominated their lives. This was achieved in numerous ways, including the growing number of segregated schools for Black people and the policies which ensured that porter work was the most prestigious employment available. Those who applied for other types of work, especially in government services, were quickly told they were like birds flying past their nests: they didn't know their place. A few Black immigrants operated businesses or professional services, but their clientele came mainly from the small, isolated Black communities scattered across the country. In these communities, families headed by train porters—or by tip-dependent Red Caps, lavatory attendants, hotel doormen, and elevator operators—were the main financial supporters of the Black businesses and professions.

For all practical purposes, Black people, even when born in Canada, were viewed as having a different nationality and treated as if they belonged elsewhere. They were simply Negroes, a term of aboriginality that was applied to all Black people from around the world and which refused to differentiate them by nationality. Theoretically, they were all part of a Negro nation that had no geographic boundaries. It was this experience that compelled the Negro Citizenship Association to convey the discriminatory way Black people were being treated with respect to Canadian citizenship and employment, two issues that had preoccupied Canada over the previous decade.

These immigration and employment policies were put into practice in government services and agencies across the land. The delegation members knew they had to tackle both pillars of the social system: who got in and who got what work in Canada. They knew it was necessary to dismantle not only these pillars but much of what was considered to be Canada itself. From the highest levels in the land, the message had long been that Black people were not Canada's natural citizens. And one of the main proponents of this message, the person who led the way in cementing this message, was Prime Minister Wilfrid Laurier.

THE FIRST TIME THE LIBERAL government's policy of restricting the employment of Black people in the civil service was raised in the Canadian House of Commons, in the opening days of March 1911, Prime Minister Laurier responded abruptly. "I know nothing about that," he said.[91] Opposition members returned to the question frequently thereafter, without getting a straight answer from Laurier or his ministers. But the questions continued. It seemed to critics that Canada was imposing a colour line, an idea that, despite their open indifference to the question, increasingly came to haunt the Laurier government. Government ministers would avoid directly answering questions on the issue in Parliament in a variety of ways. One was by disputing who had the right to respond to questions. A minister might also dodge a question by saying the necessary information was unavailable to him. As heads of their government, prime ministers are supposed to be aware of any fundamental policy changes emanating from the various parts of their administrations. Prime Minister Laurier's claim that he did not know about the colour line thus seemed disingenuous.

The question of the so-called colour line—where societies, primarily in the Americas, faced the choice of existing separately and distinctively as white or Black communities within the same country; or, alternately, being integrated in what would eventually be called multicultural states with a common citizenship—was on everybody's mind during Laurier's leadership and beyond. Celebrated African American scholar W.E.B. Du Bois suggested that the choice to enforce colour lines was central to the development of future societies. "The problem of the twentieth century," he emphasized in his 1903 book *The Souls of Black Folk*, "is the problem of the color-line, the relation of the darker to the lighter races of men in Asia and Africa, in America and the islands of the sea."[92] Du Bois would spend much of his intellectual life fighting on the Black side of the colour line, especially as head of the US-based National Association for the Advancement of Colored People (NAACP), on which the Canadian Association for the

Advancement of Coloured People and the National Black Coalition of Canada (NBCC) were patterned—two national groups that tried, with limited success from the 1950s onwards, to unify Black Canadians in a single human-rights coalition.

Concerned about the well-being of Black people around the world and not only in the United States, Du Bois had taken note of the enforcement of a colour line in Canada. As editor of the NAACP's journal, *The Crisis*, Du Bois questioned why Canada was restricting Black immigration. The secretary of the Department of the Interior, L.M. Fortier, responded to Du Bois on behalf of the Canadian immigration department, saying "[t]here is nothing in the Canadian Immigration Law which bars any person on the grounds of colour, but since coloured people are not considered as a class likely to do well in this country, all other regulations respecting health, money, etc., are strictly enforced and it is quite possible that a number of your fellow countrymen may be rejected on such grounds."[93] This response was published in *The Crisis* on April 11, 1911, merely a month after the issue was first raised in the Canadian parliament, and two years after Laurier imposed segregation on the government-owned national railway by permitting differential hiring practices. At best, this statement confirmed that Black immigrants were evaluated differently; but it also provided evidence of the government's belief that Black people weren't physically or socially suited to Canada.

Increasingly, members of Parliament and other politicians were forcing Prime Minister Laurier and his government to answer questions about the kind of country they wanted, and about whether Black people could be Canadians on the same footing as the European immigrants they preferred. When opportunities to make a clear decision presented themselves, Prime Minister Laurier and his government didn't hesitate to come down on the side of the colour line that made Canada white. Unlike the United States, which was trapped by its existing Black population, the Canada that Laurier wanted to establish for the twentieth century and beyond was to be the sole white country in the Americas. This would be quite an achievement given that, due to less discriminatory settlement patterns, it was believed that the rest of the Americas would fall prey to such social evils as miscegenation— the mixing of races—and ethnic and national mongrelization, where none of its people would have the socially desirable pure (white) bloodline.

With such a small Black population, Canada could argue that the latter would not be a problem, certainly not in the same way that caused Du Bois, ruminating on the plight of Black citizens in the United States, to ask, "How [as a Negro] does it feel to be a problem?"[94] As a founding father of American sociology, Du Bois knew that citizenship was a matter of social equality, whereby all citizens are recognized and treated as equals. When it is clear that inequalities exist, when groups are treated less well than the norm, a social problem exists. Social inequalities are therefore citizenship matters. If the Black people in a state are not treated fully as equals, by definition a social problem exists. Canadian elites had created a system that allowed them to say they did not have these problems, yet social inequalities clearly existed.

"Even though they persistently buttressed a color line during the Jim Crow era," Sarah-Jane Mathieu writes in *North of the Color Line: Migration and Black Resistance in Canada, 1870–1955,*

> most white Canadians were unwilling to concede to racism's salience in their society. Fear of blackness, "negrophobia" Canadians called it, gripped white Canadians just as white southerners panicked over their insurgent black population. It is imperative that historians remember that by the middle nineteenth century, Canada and the Southern United States had a lot in common: both regions were largely agrarian economies eager for transition to industrial ones; both had a history of removing their Indian populations in order to make those agrarian economies possible; both struggled with harsh farming terrain—too hot or cold for too much of the year; and both were caught up in major railway-building projects also meant to unify and solidify the regions' identities.[95]

At the beginning of the twentieth century, Canada's image in relation to Blackness contrasted with the mythology surrounding the Underground Railroad, which positioned Canada as a free monarchial country that openly welcomed Black people, particularly slaves, fleeing oppression in the United States. This was the story that came to prominence prior to the American Civil War, when slaves were encouraged to flee southern plantations and follow the North Star until they arrived in a "Place Called Heaven": Canada, the land of freedom for all human beings regardless of the colour of their skin.

Canada West, and specifically Toronto and southern Ontario, had been sites for abolitionist opposition to American slavery. George Brown, recognized as both a father of Canadian Confederation and the founder of the

Globe newspaper, the forerunner to the *Globe and Mail*, championed the anti-slavery cause and called on all Canadians of conscience to fight against slavery. Well-known US abolitionist Frederick Douglass visited Toronto several times and spoke forcefully at meetings in condemnation of slavery in his homeland. The reach of the controversial Fugitive Slave Act—under which escaped slaves found anywhere in the American Union had, legally, to be returned to the bondage from which they'd escaped—ended at the Canadian border. On the escape route out of the south, a network of abolitionists would provide safe havens for the escapees, with each sanctuary serving as a station on this imaginary railroad whose terminus was in Canada. The novel *Uncle Tom's Cabin* captured the story of these escapes to freedom and stoked the myth that Canada was both anti-slavery and supportive of Black people. The celebrated ex-slave and activist Sojourner Truth, known as Moses to the enslaved seeking freedom, used southern Ontario as a base from which to make forays into Egypt—the code name for the United States—to assist slaves in their escape to Canadian freedom.

Much of this contemporary mythology concerned the transformation that occurred in slaves the instant they arrived in Canada. A conductor identified only as Captain Chapman described the rejuvenation of the human spirit that he'd witnessed while delivering runaways to Canada by boat. Throughout the trip, the "cargo," as they were called by code, were pensive, seemingly lethargic, and even morose, no doubt concerned that they might be intercepted. Indeed, Chapman said,

> while they were on my vessel I felt little interest in them, and had no idea that the love of liberty as a part of man's nature was in the least possible degree felt or understood by them. Before entering Buffalo harbor, I ran in near the Canadian shore, manned a boat, and landed them on the beach [...] They said, "Is this Canada?" I said, "yes, there are no slaves in this country"; then I witnessed a scene I shall never forget. They seemed to be transformed; a new light shone in their eyes, their tongues were loosed, they laughed and cried, prayed and sang praises, fell upon the ground and kissed it, hugged and kissed each other, crying, "Bless de Lord! Oh! I'se free before I die."[96]

The Underground Railroad was frequently invoked by Canadians to emphasize the fundamental moral distinction that made Canada a better country than its southern neighbour. But even then there was opposition to the Underground Railroad in some Canadian quarters, including among those who would eventually favour the slave-owning southern states during the American Civil War. This was an opposition largely repressed by the government, but never eradicated. With time, opposition to Blackness would assert itself as the dominant view among Canadian elites, especially those in government. This opposition came to a head in the government of Prime Minister Laurier.

On March 9, 1911, when the issue of restricting government employment of Negroes was raised again in Parliament, the Liberal minister of naval affairs, Louis-Philippe Brodeur, claimed he had never heard of the issue even after it was drawn to his attention that the matter had been discussed in the daily newspapers. At this point John Reid, a conservative parliamentarian from Grenville, Ontario, asked a question directly of Laurier by zeroing in on a specific case.

> I draw the attention of the Prime Minister to another case where a coloured gentleman, who was at the head of the examination list for the Census Department, instead of being put in that position was given an inferior position by the Minister of Agriculture, looking after the black Minorca hens on the (government) farm. I trust the Prime Minister will not allow this kind of thing to spread throughout the departments (of government).[97]

Once again, the prime minister professed that he had never heard of the matter. Believed to have originated in Africa, Minorca hens are black birds with black beaks and feet and a red comb. Applying the theories of Robert Knox and his followers, Minorca hens were perceived, like Black people, to be ill-suited to Canada's habitat—because of its large comb, the hen was allegedly susceptible to frostbite and death. As a social creature, it was thought to prefer foraging on its own in rough terrain instead of living in groups in domesticated pens and henhouses; it was also not good at brooding and taking care of its chicks. By nature, and in social thinking, Minorca hens were perceived as stereotypically Black. A Black person employed tending Minorca hens in Canada was therefore conceived as the height of absurdity and futility. For a Black person, it was an insult. The message it sent was that the person and the hen were ideally suited for one another because they were alike: both were naturally black and not suited to live and thrive in Canada.

Such bad-faith treatment of Black people in the Americas had long been a part of the story of Black inequality going back to the end of slavery in the United States, when it was understood that white people would never allow the sons and daughters of former slaves to succeed. No matter how hard Black people tried and how well-intentioned they were, the dominant white groups often conspired to deny jobs and opportunities for social mobility to Black people. Potential bosses would make naïve Black applicants feel like they were seriously being considered for a job all while intending to deny it to them. Likewise, the applicants often carried around letters that they believed bore positive recommendations to help them get a job, when instead the letters proved to be a cruel joke that did the very opposite. This is perhaps most clearly depicted in Ralph Ellison's novel *Invisible Man,* where a young man carries seven letters of recommendation to various employers, all personal friends of the letter-writer, only to later find out the truth of what he was carrying. "I beg of you, sir, to help him continue in the direction of that promise which, like the horizon, recedes ever brightly and distantly beyond the hopeful traveler," recommended the fictional letter in Ellison's novel.[98] This Black man, who takes an examination in hopes of becoming a naval officer, finds himself enduring obstacle after obstacle placed between him and the horizon.

"Mr. Speaker," Parliamentarian O.J. Wilcox began in his questioning of March 23, 1911,

for the reason that on three different occasions during this session the question of the colour line being drawn in a department of government has been brought up in this House, I desire to ask my hon. friend, the Minister of the Interior, a question or two. [...] I have received a communication from one of my coloured constituents asking what all this talk is about, and if it is true that my hon. friend is drawing the colour line in his department. [...] My hon. friend from St. John (Mr. Daniel) brought before the House the fact that one George Simpson, of Toronto, who had passed a very difficult examination for a position in the Naval Department, whose character was most creditable, of whom the president of the Young Men's Christian Association, according to the Ottawa 'Free Press,' had spoken of as a most admirable young man, was not given the position to which his examination had entitled him, but was transferred to the Department of Agriculture. I have also been informed [....] that some time ago a young coloured man applied for a position in the Census Department. He was also transferred to the Department of Agriculture. I know of my own certain knowledge that last session the Rev. Mr. Hackett, [...] a bishop of the Episcopal Methodist Church for the province of Ontario, who has sixteen different churches under his charge, was ruthlessly and indiscriminately ejected from the corridors of this House. That would lead me to the conclusion that the colour line was being drawn.[99]

Wilcox went on to lament the difficulty of telling the history of coloured people in Canada. "Facts and dates are the language in which any race of people write their history, and for the reasons that the facts and dates relating to the coloured people have not been preserved, I regret to say, as well as they should have been, we have not before us their complete history." He suggested that the history of coloured people in the United States could be used as a guide for understanding Black people in Canada, "for the past 47 years since they were emancipated, and it is no exaggeration to say that no race in the world has made greater moral and intellectual progress since then." He spoke too of the US government's acknowledgement of the value of coloured people in the army during the Spanish-American War, noting that "Medals of honour and certificates of merit were granted to coloured soldiers for distinguished services in the Cuban campaign." This same argument—that Black people were loyal and willing to fight and die for Canada, one of the highest markers of citizenship—would be utilized by the Black delegation when they met with the federal government in 1954.

Wilcox next quoted from the *Winnipeg Tribune* from the previous day, March 22, 1911:

With regard to Canada, popular sentiment which has compelled the dominion government to place the virtual probative tax of $500 a head upon every Chinese entering the country, and which has shown itself so hostile to Indian and Japanese labour in the western provinces, now is manifesting a pronounced disposition to exact from the government at Ottawa stringent legislation barring the American negro from the Dominion.

"I desire to ask the minister," Wilcox finished,

if there is any sentiment in this country that he knows of in favour of placing a head tax of $500 on coloured people coming to this country, the same as he does with regard to the Chinese.[100]

Once again the government stonewalled. When Laurier's powerful minister for the interior, Frank Oliver, responded, he pretended not to understand the question. Oliver, who was responsible for immigration and settlement in Canada, would be the point man for determining admission of Black immigrants to the country. When Wilcox repeated his questions, Oliver deferred responding, claiming the matters were not under his jurisdiction.

CONSERVATIVE MEMBER OF PARLIAMENT WILLIAM Thoburn rose in the House of Commons on April 3, 1911, to broach the issue of the colour line that was then consuming Canadians.

"I would like to ask the government," Thoburn asked, "if they think it in the interests of Canada that we should have negro colonization in our Canadian Northwest? Would it not be preferable to preserve for the sons of Canada the lands they propose to give to niggers?" Thoburn was one of the most strident critics against Black immigration, with his speeches reported widely across the country. With the matter of what kind of immigrants Canada should be accepting formally brought to the table, two main features of Laurier's anti-Black policies were brought together for a national discussion.

"I draw the attention of the minister of the Interior to an article bearing on this question, which appears in one of our newspapers," Thoburn continued:

The article is headed, "Many Negroes Coming Over," and is as follows: "Winnipeg March 28—The arrival of a party of two hundred negroes from Oklahoma last week bound for free homestead land in Athabasca landing district northwest of Edmonton, is raising a good deal of protest throughout the west and the opinion is freely offered that steps should be taken by the Dominion government to put a stop to a class of immigration that the experience of the Southern States would indicate is hardly to be classed as desirable. The party, which came into Canada by way of Emerson last week, was subjected to the most rigorous examination by the immigration officials, who found themselves unable to stop a single member of the party. All had plenty of money, were in perfect health and apparently of good moral standing. They talked freely and stated that they feared neither cold nor privation, and that all they were seeking was free land and a chance to make homes for their families.

The final action of the Canadian government in admitting to that country negro families from Oklahoma whose members possess $5 each is having the effect of furthering the colonization movement among Oklahoma's negroes, especially in Okfusgee, Muskogee, and Creek counties, where there is a large negro population. The first immigration to Canada during the past week was of ninety families, 500 negroes in all, from the vicinity of Clearview, in Okfusgee county. They sold all their property in this state, intended to take up homesteads in Canada. Many other negroes are making preparations to start and indications are there will be a general exodus."[101]

Feeling persecuted in Oklahoma, former slaves had started to eye western Canada in general, and Alberta in particular, as a place where they could settle and thrive. This was to be their Promised Land. Canada wanted homesteaders, and these American Black immigrants were ready to help develop the land. In addition, it was clear that the white people of Oklahoma did not want them and were encouraging the state's Black residents to move out. "In 1910 a Clearview, Oklahoma, newspaper owned by a Black, printed an article titled, 'Alberta, the Home of the Colored Race.' During that year numerous Black people 'scouted' the area, returning to Oklahoma and bringing their families and friends back in the following year. A 1911 report from Enid, Oklahoma, reprinted in the *Edmonton Capital*, stated in part: 'Within the next few months it is estimated that at least one thousand negroes will leave from the northern and central part of this state for Alberta where they will form colonies in the vicinity of Edmonton."[102]

Immigration minister Oliver responded to Thoburn that,

The government can only do as parliament authorizes it to do. Parliament has passed a certain law in regard to immigration, and the government is administering that law. There is no provision in the law to prevent negroes from coming into Canada, and until parliament makes such a provision, it will not be possible for the government to take action on its own responsibility. As to the facts of the case as stated by my hon. friend there is practically no question. There are already in the prairie provinces several settlements of negroes from Oklahoma. When these people came to Canada they got the same rights as anybody else. Any person coming from another country into Canada and having the necessary qualifications is entitled to a homestead, and negroes get free homesteads the same as any other people. So far they have been treated exactly the same as other people have been, both in their admission to the country and in regard to taking up land in the country. They will have to be continued in that treatment until parliament authorizes some other action on the part of the government.[103]

Oliver gave, in effect, the same answer that his underling L.M. Fortier had, but he fell short of mentioning the all-important regulations that would be used to control admissions. The big difference was that Fortier's message was intended for foreign notice and was part of a public-relations campaign where government officials sought out immigration agents and publications available to Black people in their homelands to bluntly tell them that they were not welcome in Canada and the grounds for barring them.

The alarm over Black immigration was spreading in Canada. A petition dated April 25, 1911, which circulated in Edmonton and elsewhere, warned the prime minister of "the serious menace to the future welfare of a large portion of Western Canada by reason of the alarming influx of negro settlers [....] We submit that the advent of such negroes as are now here was most unfortunate for the country, and that further arrivals in large numbers would be disastrous. We cannot admit as any factors the argument that these people may be good farmers, or good citizens." The petitioners indicated they were certain that Black and white people were not meant to live together and that any such society would degenerate into lawlessness caused by the Black members. "It is a matter of common knowledge," the petition claimed, "that it has been proved in the United States that negroes and whites cannot live in proximity without the occurrence of revolting lawlessness and the development of bitter race hatred, and the most serious question facing the United States today is the negro problem." The best way to prevent these developments in Canada, the petitioners argued, was to prevent Black people from coming to the country in the first place.

> We are anxious that such a problem should not be introduced into this lawlessness as has developed in all sections in the United States where there is any considerable negro element. There is no reason to believe that we have here a higher order of civilization, or that the introduction of a negro problem here would have different results. We therefore respectfully urge that such steps immediately be taken by the Government of Canada as will prevent any further immigration of negroes into Western Canada.[104]

But there was also opposition to the emerging government policy and public panic then spreading over Black immigration. The Liberal parliamentarian Archibald Blake McCoig, representing the Ontario riding of West Kent, which, along with the riding held by Wilcox, was home to many Black residents, argued that: "In my section of the country, there are a good many coloured farmers who are amongst the most industrious and successful citizens of the Dominion." His consituents were concerned, McCoig argued, that the government was going to place a tax upon coloured people coming into the country from the United States. "The Minister of the Interior," he said,

> gave me a letter assuring me that so long as these coloured people were enti-
> tled to enter under the law, they would be admitted as freely as any other
> people who came to our country. I am glad to know that the government has
> taken that stand, because I would regret deeply if this government of which I
> am so proud and which I am so glad to support should in any way discrimi-
> nate against coloured people, especially when we have among us men of the
> race who do their share to build up this Dominion. I hope the government
> will continue along the lines they have set out on, and allow the coloured
> people to come in so long as they are prepared to perform the duties of citi-
> zenship which are expected from every man in Canada.

"In regard to whether there is any sentiment in Canada in favour of placing a $500 head tax upon negroes coming into the country," Oliver responded, "so far as my information goes there is a very strong sentiment on the part of a great many people in this country against the admission of negroes; but as to the intention of the government,"[105] Oliver referred McCoig to what he'd said pre-viously: the government could only do what Parliament authorizes them to do.

The exclusion of immigrants, Oliver had argued earlier elsewhere, was based on "whether the proposed immigrant is ordinarily considered desirable or ordi-narily considered undesirable. The immigrant ordinarily considered desirable is the man who wishes to go on the land, and if he does not want to go on the land the presumption toward him is not so favourable."[106]

Conservative parliamentarian John Daniel for the City of St. John in New Brunswick then called the minister's attention to a story of 165 negroes from Oklahoma who had been

> stopped at the boundary [and who had] intended to go on the land and
> settle as a farming community; so that, according to the minister's own
> statement, they belong to the desirable class. Under these circumstances it
> would seem plain to the ordinary observer that they were excluded because
> they were not of the right colour.

Oliver responded that he did not know where the information on the excluded negroes came from as his own was that "they were not stopped at the boundary, and that they were not excluded." He was then reminded that the information came from a news dispatch that had been read to the house the previous night. "If it was in the dispatch," he said, "so far as my information goes, it was not correct, because I have no information that the people were stopped at the boundary, or that they were excluded. My information is that some members of the party were excluded, but the larger number of them, having complied with the conditions laid down in the Immigration Law and the regulations, were admitted."[107]

Indeed, the Black immigrants from Oklahoma had been stopped and turned back at the border. They wanted to homestead in western Canada—one of the main criteria for Canadian immigration—but were instead told they were unsuited for the country. By then, moral panic had spread across the land at the prospect of Black people overrunning the country and endangering whites. Even if there were no laws to prohibit Black immigration, as Oliver had stated, some of his department's regulations had the same effect.

Government regulations aimed at keeping Black people out of Canada would control Black immigration well into the 1950s. One major change in the regulations occurred in 1920, when the definition of a British subject was altered to exclude Black subjects living elsewhere in the British Empire. Black subjects, specifically those in British possessions in the Caribbean, were denied the automatic right to enter and settle in Canada as British subjects, thereby shutting off the country's biggest vein of Black immigration. And having brought Black immigration firmly under control, the Canadian government was now turning its attention to what it saw as the next threat to Canada: Asian immigration, which it believed, in some cases, might prove to be even worse than Black immigration.

"It is perhaps ironical," writes historian Robert Huttenback in reviewing immigration practices in the British Empire, "that the Canadian Liberals did, after all, lose the election of September 1911, although the issue that defeated them was the recently signed reciprocity agreement with the United States, not Asian immigration. Be that as it may, Sir Wilfrid Laurier and his government, despite a marked lack of enthusiasm, had forged, for political reasons, the legislative basis for a "White Canada.'"[108] Borden and subsequent governments would build on the structures put in place in 1909 by Laurier, who even in opposition continued to show his disdain for Black people, and particularly for porters. Laurier's policies were most apparent on the Canadian railways: the way work was segregated, so that only Black people were porters; the way Black were denied promotions or consideration for any other positions on the railway; the way porters were recruited in international regions for cheap Black labour, while all other Black immigrants were denied entry; and the way Black immigration was limited only to those who would work on the railways. These policies set in place the employment and social practices that would govern Black Canadians' way of life well into the second half of the twentieth century.

BY THE TIME THE BLACK delegation launched its protest in Ottawa discrimination was a stark reality for Black people, Jews, indigenous peoples, and South East Asians in Canada. None of these groups were considered truly Canadian and were thus not entitled to the benefits and full protection of the state. Alistair Stewart, rising in the House of Commons on April 9, 1946, would contribute to the combatitive tone that would emerge in the porters' protest seven years later. Stewart, the Co-operative Commonwealth Federation representative for Winnipeg North, was engaging the issue of a new Canadian citizenship law, and wanted to put on record what this new law would mean for coloured Canadians. This would prove to be a defining moment in Canada's development as an independent country.

Other parliamentarians had ignored how the issue of racial bias in Canada was a sign of disunity, but Stewart tackled the matter and its deleterious effects on those communities most affected by it. First, he criticized Canadian society for marginalizing people whose first language wasn't French or English, recalling that he had earlier suggested the need for a resolution in Parliament calling for a "bill of rights protecting minority rights, civil and religious liberties, freedom of speech and freedom of assembly; establishing equal treatment before the law for citizens irrespective of race, nationality or religion or political belief; and providing the necessary democratic powers to eliminate racial discrimination in all its forms." Though many groups in Canada were affected by racism, including Germans, Ukrainians, and Polish people, Stewart argued, the two groups hit hardest were Jews and Black people. "Anti-Semitism, racialism of a type," Stewart argued,

> is one of the most deadly enemies of any democratic community. It not only hurts those against whom it is directed but warps and twists the minds of those who practise it; yet we find it again in the government service, in the department of immigration; we find it in the allegedly cultured places in the country, in universities such as McGill and Toronto [....] We must

never rest until we have wiped it out [....] and given to the Jewish people the same rights and the same privileges that every other Canadian has.[109]

Here Stewart was probably anticipating the growing partnership between Jews and Negroes, who would become allies lobbying for the recognition of human rights in Canada. In North America, these two groups often advanced in lockstep, something that members of the international Brotherhood of Sleeping Car Porters were pushing for under a wider rubric of the brotherhood of all humanity. Throughout the 1940s and thereafter, activists from the two groups would host events in major urban centres on both sides of the border to discuss issues around human dignity.

In their mutual fight for anti-discrimination legislation in employment and housing, Black and Jewish groups were supported by the Brotherhood of Sleeping Car Porters under the national leadership of A. R. Blanchette, and the local leadership of Toronto president Stanley Grizzle. Working actively with them were members of Jewish groups from the leadership of the Canadian Labour Council (C.L.C.) and from the council's political arm, the Co-operative Commonwealth Federation. But first, and perhaps ironically, both groups were working hard behind the scenes to remove the C.L.C. from the grip of its founding president, Aaron Mosher, who was also the leader of the powerful Canadian Brotherhood of Railway, Transportation and General Workers Unions (CRTGWU). Mosher, a Jew, would become a member of Canada's white elite. As perhaps the most powerful railway unionist of his day, he openly conspired with governments from Laurier onwards to segregate Canadian railways and to limit Blacks to working only as porters. His leadership was eventually challenged by more enlightened unionists, including Jewish groups in the syndicate, who disavowed his social policies. Once under new leadership, one of the C.L.C.'s achievements was to coordinate a campaign leading to a vote to amalgamate the Black and white units of the CRTGWU, effectively bringing segregation in railway work to an end. But that would not happen until the 1960s, and this development would only follow once the Black porters and their allies had taken their case to Ottawa.

Alistair Stewart was one of the porter's oldest and most steadfast allies. In 1946, Stewart demonstrated Canadian society's worst inequalities by pointing to the experiences of Black people. Stewart gave the example of a "girl" in Winnipeg who answered an advertisement for a course in practical nursing approved by the federal Department of Public Health and Welfare. The advertisement required candidates to be eighteen years old, have a grade-eight education, and be of good health and moral character. Following a telephone interview, the applicant received a letter saying she had been rejected because "accepting an applicant of your nationality would be a new thing in the history of our practical nursing school."

Stewart continued:

> What nationality was that girl? She was Canadian, but her skin was dark; and because her skin was darker than ours she was refused one of the fundamental rights of a citizen of this country. That is not the only case; I could go on citing example after example, but there is one more about which I must tell the house. This is the story of a young man who came to Canada from the West Indies. He went to university and obtained a degree in science. He became a licensed pharmacist. He went to Dublin and there took two years of pre-medical training and three years of medical training; then, because his money ran out, he returned to Canada. He was coloured [...] but because he was coloured he was condemned in perpetuity, apparently, to do nothing but work as a porter on the railway.[110]

Two months later, Stewart again highlighted in the House of Commons the systemic limits that prevented Black people from getting jobs in the federal civil service. All applicants for federal positions were required to specify their skin colour, which made it easy to weed out Black and other non-white people from the application pool.

"I should like to ask a question of the Secretary of State," Stewart said on June 19, 1947. "In view of the equal rights of all Canadians as citizens, regardless of creed or colour, why is the word "colour" used as question 17 in the civil service application form?"

"The hon. Member spoke to me about this question," Liberal Minister of State Colin Gibson said, "and I have made inquiries through the chairman of the civil service commission. There is of course no doubt whatever as to the eligibility of all Canadian citizens, regardless of colour, race or creed, for appointment to the civil service. I understand from the chairman of the commission that the question on the application form as to colour is to enable the commissioners, when an application is received from a member of the negro race, to place the applicant in a position which will be congenial."[111]

A collective sigh must have gone out across the country, for here was a minister of government confirming the limits placed on Black people in society. News reports across the country quoted the minister as saying that evaluations were necessary to determine Black peoples' proper place. Following a national uproar, the minister was back on his feet at the resumption of Parliament the next day. "Mr. Speaker," Minister Gibson said,

> As a matter of privilege I should like to refer to an article which appeared in the press last night and this morning concerning a question asked yesterday [...] The article states: *State Secretary Gibson said today in the Commons that applicants for civil service positions were asked to state their colour so that the civil service commission could place them in the "proper position."* The words "proper position" are in quotation marks. Those were not the words I used. As will be found in *Hansard,* what I said was: ... the question on the application form as to colour is to enable the commissioners, when an application is received from a member of the negro race, to place the applicant in a position which will be congenial.[112]

An obvious question then, was whether a *congenial* position was the same as a *proper* one, or one to which the applicant is societally best-suited? Had Gibson merely confirmed the policy—in place since the days of the Laurier administration—that deemed Black Canadians to be most suitably employed not as inside civil servants but as outside workers looking after black Minorca hens? This was more than mere semantics, as very few Black people got civil service jobs at all, and when they did, the positions were mainly menial ones. Perhaps mindful of this history and the ongoing discussion of Black people and their positions in a segregated workforce, Stewart returned to the issue on June 25, 1947, when he asked the minister "What positions are considered 'congenial' for 'a member of the negro race' by the civil service commission?"

"As already stated," minister Gibson replied, "negro applicants for positions in the public service of Canada are entitled to and receive the same rights as members of any other race. No special positions are reserved for them, but an endeavor is made by the civil service commission to appoint them to the positions the conditions of which will be satisfactory both to employee and to employer."[113] Which was just another way of saying to Black people that the railways were always hiring. Segregation's mechanisms held firm and were perpetuated, at an inestimable cost to Black Canadians.

THE END OF EMPIRE
Reimagining Immigration

THE BLACK DELEGATION'S TRIP TO Ottawa was the culmination of decades of lobbying and alliance-building by groups like the sleeping car porters, who lay the groundwork for change by placing political pressure on the government over the joint issues of immigration and employment and how they impacted Black Canadians. When they arrived in the Canadian capital, the delegation knew they had the support of a small cross-section of Canadian elites, who had begun to speak up in the media and in Parliament. Apart from the allies they were assembling at home, the porters and others committed to their cause were also building international support, especially in the United States—through the efforts of the porters' international union and as part of the nascent Civil Rights Movement— and in the Caribbean. The arrival on the political scene of a new type of West Indian leader—one who saw his mission as part of a Pan-Africanist liberation movement that affected an entire diaspora of Black people all over the world—was making a difference. Within Canada, however, the meticulous task of building public support was still slow.

"Speaking of racial discrimination, as so many of us do these days," an October 3, 1945, *Winnipeg Free Press* editorial argued, "when is some Member of Parliament going to take up the case of porters on our Canadian railways? These men have been subjected to many years of the most unfair type of discrimination because they happen to be negroes."[114] With the conclusion of the Second World War, only a month earlier, the newspaper, whose motto was "Freedom of Trade, Liberty of Religion, and Equality of Rights," was being true to its ideals as it advocated for greater freedoms for individuals and minority groups throughout the world but also, most importantly, at home.

Winnipeg itself was known as a city of progressives and activists, and these included a strong group of unionized porters who'd long been fighting against racial discrimination, not only on the railways but also inside their own Canadian Brotherhood of Railway Employees (CB-RE), a union that, from the turn of the century, was supposed to represent them, but had failed to do so under the leadership of Aaron Mosher. Considered the leading nationalist voice among Canadian unionists, Mosher had tremendous clout with government and business alike. The CB-RE's hold was primarily over the government-owned Canadian National Railway, and its approach to racial issues was the opposite of the Canadian Brotherhood of Sleeping Car Porters, the dominant union on the main private railway, Canadian Pacific. The railway porters, who were fighting discrimination and prejudice both within their own institution as well as in the wider society, had first to build a wider community alliance to get around the fact that they belonged to unions with opposing ideologies. This was one of the reasons the porters helped set up the Negro Citizenship Association. The NCA provided a unified voice for the porters through which they could lobby nationally and internationally for change, and even against their own union when necessary.

In the wake of the Second World War, with life presumably returning to peacetime normalcy, important questions were emerging in Canada about citizenship. Who was a Canadian? What should Canada stand for? What were the rights of Canadian citizens? For nearly a generation, there had been political lobbying for clarification about whether British subjects in Canada, racialized as whites, had different rights in the country than British subjects native to other colonies in the Empire. There was a desire in many quarters in Canada for human rights bills and codes, at the federal and provincial levels, to help clarify and reinforce citizenship issues. In Canada, there was a renewed urgency to the discussion about the rights of all residents, and questions were being asked about whether some members of the population—who called themselves citizens and claimed exclusive rights and entitlements to the good life in Canada—had more privileges than others.

For Black political activists in communities across Canada, the first challenge was to get the major political parties to acknowledge Black people as among the country's constituents and as citizens worthy of recognition for the work they did for the country. Since Black people in Canada were so dependent on the railways for their livelihood, this recognition would initially come through an acknowledgement of how vital the railways were to the country. And the role of the railways during the Second World War provided Black activists the opportunity to drive this point home.

Since the first call to join the war effort in 1939, the major railways transformed themselves in order to transport soldiers from across the country to the ships that took them to war in Europe, Africa, Asia, and the Caribbean. Canadian railways transported the men and equipment needed in the national effort, while moving even more resources and manufactured goods to markets at home and abroad. Praise for the railways, primarily for their owners, but also for the workers, was universal. In Parliament, traditionally opposed political parties were united in acknowledging the railways' role in helping to preserve and even promote a way of life based on a culture of free men and women living in liberty in a free country.

On May 16, 1944, parliamentarian Major James Coldwell, the leader of the opposition Co-operative Commonwealth Federation, spoke in the House of Commons about the War Appropriation Act as it applied to transportation.

> Today we can ask ourselves the question, where would we have been during this war had we not had these transcontinental (railway) systems. I think [we] will do well at this time to express the gratitude we all feel to the railway systems, and particularly to the men who have done this remarkable job. I have met railway men during this war who have travelled thousands of miles every month and who from time to time thought they were going to get a good night's rest but who have been called to take out another train of supplies that were needed for the war effort.[115]

With Canadians debating the merits of the country joining the fledgling United Nations and endorsing its Declaration of Human Rights, parliamentarians and other opinion leaders were busy discussing citizenship rights, especially for refugees and people displaced by the war in Europe. The porters and their allies recognized a political opportunity to work closely with the dominant political parties, especially the Co-operative Commonwealth Federation. The CCF had strong ties with organized labour in Canada and

Stanley Grizzle, increasingly recognized as a union leader, cultivated close relationships with other unions that became their political mouthpieces in Parliament. In an unpublished manuscript in his papers, Grizzle writes about his contact with Coldwell, who had been a union leader before entering politics, and how he'd influenced him:

> I remember travelling with M. J. Coldwell. He was the leader of the C.C.F. party in Canada and we had some great discussions about the labour movement and struggle for equality and he had great respect for Randolph [international president of the Brotherhood]. It certainly convinced me that the democratic socialist party, which Coldwell was the leader of, was genuinely interested in economic equality of all people.[116]

In the years prior to the delegation's arrival in Ottawa, the issue of Canadian citizenship and its requirements was frequently debated in the government. Parliamentarians and public intellectuals across the country were specifically concerned about how to determine who was a citizen and whether race should be a determinant factor. It was a question that began with the very notion of who should be allowed to immigrate to Canada, since this was the first stage in the selection process. Questions were raised about Black people both already living in Canada as well as those born in other areas of the British Empire: did they have a constitutional right, as British subjects, to enter and live in Canada and, ultimately, to be recognized as Canadian citizens? And if they *were* viewed as Canadian, did they have the same rights as white Canadians?

Sleeping car porters challenged the prevailing norms of citizenship and the expectations of rights in Canada that had emerged out of the Second World War. Because of their Blackness, the porters were tethered, generation after generation, to a caste-like system that denied them job opportunities in the wider society, and they challenged Canada's assertion that it was a liberal democracy predicated on respecting the individual rights of all citizens. As the *Winnipeg Free Press* reported, at a time of growing affluence and much discussion about democratic freedom, the governing classes in Canada were conveniently ignoring the loud social message of those Black citizens, who were limited to working on trains in dead-end, low-paying jobs. What kind of capitalist system was Canada practicing, the paper wondered aloud, when it disallowed entire groups of people from selling their labour as they wished

and prevented them from moving from place to place, even across borders, in search of work?

"These men are Canadian citizens," the newspaper said,

> and it would only seem logical that they graduate from porters to conduc-
> tors. During the war the railways scoured the country for men to train as
> sleeping car conductors. Yet even during this emergency they refused to
> raise the color bar against their negro employees. All this may come as a
> shock to decent Canadians who want no part of Hilter's vile racial theories
> in Canada. Nevertheless, we do have racial discrimination on our railways.
> What does the parliament of Canada propose to do about that?[117]

Under the rubric of citizenship, the rights to employment and mobility—
to move in search of employment as British subjects within Canada—were
intrinsically bound together.

ON APRIL 24, 1953—ALMOST A year before the Black delegation arrived in
Ottawa—an ally rose in the House of Commons to question immigration
minister Walter Harris about his administration's Canadian immigration
policies. Immigrant policy had always been a major plank in the government's platform for helping Canadians secure the good life, especially in
terms of how immigration helped the country meet its employment needs.

"I wish to discuss for a few minutes the question of immigration from
the British West Indies," began J.W. Noseworthy, the CCF parliamentarian
for Toronto's York South. Harris was a rising star in the ruling Liberal Party,
a lawyer and a war hero who, a decade earlier, stepped away from his parliamentary duties to fight in France for four years during the Second World
War. A few months after this confrontation, he would become a popular
minister of finance at a time when the Canadian economy was expanding
rapidly and developing a stream of high-quality jobs for native-born and
immigrant Canadians alike.

"In my opinion," Noseworthy scolded, "the policy which is followed
by the government in regard to immigration from the British West
Indies is immigration by discrimination on the basis of colour. I know
that the minister objects and says that such is not the case, but [from
what] I can gather it is about the only conclusion one can reach regarding the government's present policy."[118] Since the policy was based on
colour, he argued, it was effectively creating distinct categories of British

subjects, and those with Black skin were receiving unequal treatment to that of white British subjects.

For the sleeping car porters and members of the Negro Citizenship Association, this was one of the opening salvos in the battle that, a year later, would bring them to Ottawa. In using the phrase "immigration by discrimination," Noseworthy was borrowing the language of the sleeping car porters, who had first used the phrase in the union newspaper to describe Canada's immigration policy. A few months earlier, through the efforts of Stanley Grizzle, the Negro Citizenship Association had succeeded in getting the national umbrella organization representing trade unions in Canada to publicly attack that policy. Noseworthy was not alone in adopting the porters' language.

"The general position of the Congress on immigration as was stated is that we should bring in as many immigrants as the country can absorb," the Canadian Congress of Labour said in a year-end brief to the government prior to Noseworthy's speech, "and that we should not discriminate on the grounds of race, creed or colour." The union membership also passed on another resolution to the government that condemned the policy of "discrimination against coloured persons, particularly from Commonwealth countries, and (which) threatens civil liberties through arbitrary deportations for a variety of grounds, including acceptance of public relief."[119]

On their own, and mainly through Grizzle's activism, the Negro Citizenship Association had bombarded various government officers in Ottawa and the media with letters requesting statistical information on Black immigration to Canada, how well Black people fared in the country, and how well they were enjoying citizenship privileges. The confrontation, when finally brought to the House of Commons, would force Canadians to determine who they were as a nation: had Canada been established for the benefit of anyone who was British, or was Britishness simply a disguise for racialized whiteness? Immigration and employment policies would test how committed Canadians were to international protocols such as the UN's Universal Declaration of Human Rights, which prohibited discrimination based on race. Article 2 of the Declaration states:

Everyone is entitled to all the rights and freedoms set forth in this Declaration, without distinction of any kind, such as race, colour, sex, language, religion, political or other opinion, national or social origin, property, birth or other status. Furthermore, no distinction shall be made on the basis of the political, jurisdictional or international status of the country or territory to which a person belongs, whether it be independent, trust, non-self-governing or under any other limitation of sovereignty.[120]

This article was of particular significance for people living under colonial regimes, such as those in the British West Indies, and who wanted to immigrate to Canada. Emerging political leaders in the British West Indies argued that their people should be the beneficiaries of such equality, starting in places like Canada and elsewhere in the British Empire.

The UN Declaration was an important weapon. And a year after the delegation visited Ottawa, Grizzle and his union intensified their lobbying at the local and international levels to embarrass Canada for not living up to it. At the international convention for the Brotherhood of Sleeping Car Porters on June 27, 1955, in Montreal, the union had appealed "to liberal and labour forces in Canada to join with their Negro fellow citizens to bring about a liberalization of Canadian policy on immigration."[121] The appeal was picked up in labour publications and disseminated nationally and internationally. The Vancouver branch of the United Nations Association heeded this call. Following an alert from Grizzle, A. Philip Randolph, as president of the International Brotherhood of Sleeping Car Porters, sent a letter to his Montreal-based field organizer for Canada, A. R. Blanchette, encouraging him to co-operate with efforts to highlight Canada's failure to live up to their United Nations obligations.

"You will note that the Vancouver Branch of the United Nations Association of Canada wish [sic] to get information concerning the color exclusion policy of the Canadian Department of Citizenship and Immigration in order that it may be able to frame the resolution for presentation to the United Nations Association National Office in Ottawa which may result in some change in the above mentioned policy," Randolph wrote on December 28, 1955. In the letter, he encouraged Blanchette, as the union's top official in Canada, to contact local divisions of the Brotherhood and to ask them to gather information on how many Negroes had been barred from entering Canada in the previous three years. This was research Grizzle had already started, and he had passed the information on to the field officer. But any further action had to be approved by Randolph. So, with help from a branch of the United Nations Association, Randolph was made to believe the plan had originated with him.

In granting his approval, Randolph wrote to Blanchette, "I consider this a highly important matter and hope that you will give it your careful attention. I may [sic] the means by which we may be able to break down this reprehinsible [sic] practice of color caste and exclusion policy of the Canadian Department of Citizenship and Immigration."[122] Working through the union bureaucracy, Blanchette wrote Grizzle on January 9, 1956, forwarding the correspondence from Randolph and the United Nations Association branch in Vancouver. Blanchette also asked for a copy of the brief to Ottawa from the Negro Citizenship Association to use in his lobbying. Before their arrival in Ottawa, the delegation organizers had started to prep the public by circulating a draft of their proposals to the government, pressure they would maintain by continuing to circulate the proposals even after the meeting.

The ensuing confrontation with the government about its immigration policy would result in an evaluation of what Canada's future role would be in the British Empire and the world in general. Would the government continue to side with members of the whites-only Old Dominion Club, of which it was a founding member and leading champion? Or would it come in line with the emerging desire for a multiracial British Commonwealth, with Canada as a leader? One notable quirk in the debate was that, technically speaking, British subjects from the West Indies could migrate to Canada as freely as could British subjects anywhere else in the world. Grizzle had been told as much when he contacted Minister Harris in 1952 to ask whether "British West Indian Negroes" were eligible for admission into Canada, information he then shared with Blanchette. "While there is no clause specifically applicable to residents of the British West Indies (in the prevailing Order-in-Council on immigration)," Harris wrote on May 20, "such persons are dealt with under paragraph 4 of the Order-in-Council" defining who was a British subject. "Each application for admission receives careful consideration and is dealt with on its individual merit."[123]

On February 13, 1955, in a follow-up to the Ottawa meeting, Donald Moore of the Negro Citizenship Association wrote the new minister of citizenship and immigration asking that the legal definition of British subject be broadened. "It is not proposed at the present time to broaden the categories of persons admissible as immigrants from the British West Indies," Minister J. W. Pickersgill responded on March 3, "but to continue to consider applications for the admission of close relatives and meritorious cases as in the case of many other countries. [...] we are always prepared to consider any individual cases of applicants who appear to have outstanding qualifications."[124] For members of the Ottawa delegation, Canada's limited definition of "British subject" was out of step with opinions held through-out the British Empire and the emerging Commonwealth of Nations.

"During the centuries of Imperial growth and power," explains Ian R. G. Spencer in his book *British Immigration Policy Since 1939*, "Britain had never introduced or accepted a distinction either between the citizenship and nationality of the monarch's subjects resident in different parts of the Empire or between the monarch's citizens and the monarch's subject."[125] In the absence of this distinction, dominions like Canada had instead tried to define who was a national of the Empire's individual member territories, thereby creating their own differentiation over whom they recognized as a genuine British subject. This effectively created a sub-category of British subjects, those who, as nationals of a specific state or territory, were entitled to privileged treatment.

In Canada's case, this definition started with reference to the Immigration Act, which stipulated that, with a few exceptions, all British subjects throughout the Empire could enter and settle in the country. Once they took up residence, people became domiciled and thereby qualified as Canadian nationals—in effect, British subjects who'd chosen Canada as their home and primary home-identity. Speaking in the Canadian par-liament three decades earlier, the then-justice minister, Charles Doherty, had set down the definition of a British subject as it applied to Canada. "A British subject," he explained in 1921, "is a man [sic] who owes allegiance to, and who is entitled to protection as a subject of the British Crown. Our Canadian nationals will be the kind of British subject who is in a special manner subject to and owes obedience to Canadian laws as administered through Parliament and the Government and, ultimately, His Majesty, he being King of these dominions just as he is King of Great Britain and the entire Empire."[126]

It was not until 1948 that Canada formally created a citizenship of its own, but even then it gave preference to British subjects. It was this issue members of the Negro Citizenship Association had in mind when prepar-ing their brief for the federal government. As a result, every British subject in the Empire had the right to enter, vote, and stand for parliament in any country in the Empire. But while this was the ideal, it was not the practice, particularly in Canada and other white British dominions. Indeed, it was the opposite for non-white immigrants. To be allowed into Canada, sub-jects from the British colonies in the Caribbean, for example, would first have to be classified as white, and to show that by a white lineage they were

British subjects arriving in Canada indirectly via the Caribbean. This categorization had intrinsic contradictions about who was authentically white in a region like the Caribbean, which was marked by liberal mixing of peoples of all complexions from around the world. It also meant that under such a policy there were two distinct categories of British subjects in the Caribbean: those who were white and therefore welcome in Canada, and those who were Black and prohibited.

With very few people qualifying as white, the result was negligible migration from the Caribbean to Canada—the policy's undisguised intention. Those British subjects classified as Black or Negro were pointedly excluded, not so much by law, but by administrative collusion. Hypocritically, the exclusion also occurred amidst strong proclamations by Britain about its commitment to respecting and protecting the rights of equality among Empire subjects of all colours and ancestries.

The exclusion of Black British subjects occurred despite complaints by the dominions, the Empire's white parts, that Britain was not doing enough to increase migration to their colonial outposts, even as the numbers of preferred white immigrants dwindled. Potential immigrants were not in short supply across the entire British Empire. The problem was that there was an overabundance of possible Black immigrants, who were therefore considered inferior. These races did not qualify for establishing and maintaining white dominions. On the matter of immigration and the issue of preferred citizens, the Empire was sorely divided and appeared to speak with two voices. The first, which included Canada, as the leader of predominantly-white dominions, demanded that the exclusion of immigrants along racial lines be recognized and formalized into constitutional practices. The other was the voice of a somewhat torn mother country. While Britain identified with its dominions and their desire to build and expand exclusively white states, it was also trying to accommodate the aspirations of the non-white populations in its colonies and dependencies. Even as the delegation was arriving in Ottawa in 1954, the growing presence of non-white immigrants from the colonies in England was a matter of increasing concern in London and throughout the Empire.

As members of the same union, Canada and Britain were supposed to be speaking with a single voice and following the same path in terms of human rights and policy developments for British subjects in the Empire. When Britain spoke at international forums on such issues as immigration and the self-determination of colonized people, it was supposed to be speaking for an indivisible Empire, united in its allegiance to the monarchy. When the British attorney general Sir Reginald Butler declared, in the UK House of Commons, for example, that British justice did not take into account the colour of a person's skin, this was assumed to be the Empire's position, too.

"It would be deplorable if it were supposed that the application of the law in this country depends on the color of a person's skin," the attorney general told Parliament on December 13, 1954, rebutting a London judge's argument that Black colonials living in Britain should be sent back to their native lands if they broke the law.[127] According to a report in the *Toronto Star* the next day, the attorney general's statement was "the latest move in a growing controversy over the status of Negroes arriving here from British colonies, chiefly the West Indies. As British subjects, they are beyond the control of immigration authorities."[128]

But in practice such acceptance, as the UK attorney general himself suggested, wasn't the case for all the dominions. From the beginning of the twentieth century, and especially from the 1920s onward, Canada asserted its independent right to limit its sources of immigration, even in defiance of the policies Britain was adopting for the Empire. Indeed, soon after this statement, the Canadian defense minister, George Pearkes, said the opposite about immigration to Canada. "Before permitting a flood of immigrants, I think that we have the right to establish controls and to refuse to accept too many Asiatic or Africans," the England-born minister argued at a 1957 press conference. "It is up to us to decide if certain ones are to be allowed in the country and if others are not to be allowed enter."[129]

These approaches to immigration were unmistakably whites-only in preference, even though the British government at times confused their intentions by arguing against race-based immigration between and within British-affiliated countries except when it came to immigration between white member states; for those countries, it was acceptable to bar Black subjects. The result was that white subjects could visit and even live throughout the Empire, while Black subjects were effectively limited to visiting and staying in Black states. Indeed, partly to avoid this confusion in international forums, Canada and the white dominions wanted the ability, when necessary, to indicate that some British policies and pronouncements did not apply to their territories. From the 1920s onwards, when pressed on the issue, the British Colonial Office and British Commonwealth officials insisted, in international forums such as the League of Nations and its successor the United Nations, that by law all British subjects were equal in all respects in any territory within the British Empire and Commonwealth of Nations. As the British delegation to the League of Nations claimed in 1937: "It is the practice of the United Kingdom not to make any distinction between different races in British Colonies as regards civil and political rights, or the right of entry into and residence in the United Kingdom."[130]

If this was indeed the case, then policies to restrict Black British subjects from moving among the British-aligned countries would obviously be racist. It would also be contrary to claims by British and allied governments about respecting the human rights of all British subjects. This was why, from the beginning of the last century, especially on matters of population and immigration, Canada readily asserted its independence from the United Kingdom and indicated that it had an exclusive right to decide what type of British subject could become a Canadian national and, ultimately, a Canadian citizen.

The result was a two-sided immigration policy involving British subjects from the dominions, one which encouraged white immigration within the Empire, while discouraging the movement of the non-preferred races. A pamphlet titled "Are you thinking of emigrating to Canada?" published by the Canadian government—which was circulated in Europe at the time to help recruit the desired British subjects—made this expectation clear in a section on frequently asked questions by immigrants. "To be admitted to Canada they [British subjects] need only satisfy the Immigration Officer at the Canadian port of entry that they are of good character, are in good physical and mental health, and have sufficient means to enable them to become established (or are proceeding to relatives or friends able and willing to receive them)."[131] The assumption was clear: the government imagined that the readers of this pamphlet would be white and European, and more than likely from the British Isles.

The trick to keeping Black people out of the dominions was to refuse British passports to applicants that, as Empire subjects, were theoretically entitled to them. Non-white people were also often denied other government-issued documents, such as birth certificates, which might otherwise be offered up as evidence that they were British subjects. But refusing to issue passports was the main weapon in reducing Black immigration. Countries in the Empire had standardized arrangements which stated that a British passport was required for admission into a member state to which the traveller was not native. Without this proof, every territory or nation of the Empire had the right to refuse entry. Administrators across the Empire, working under a governor, usually from Britain, issued British passports locally.

At the behest of the Empire's white member states, there was a standing agreement among governors to issue passports only to exceptional non-white persons. Without a passport, even while theoretically in possession of the right of movement in the Empire, applicants could not travel outside of their homelands. This approach was buttressed by a concerted propaganda campaign, coordinated by the old dominions with the connivance of local administrators in non-white colonies, telegraphing how difficult it was for non-white people to survive in places developed for differently racialized people and cultures, and in extreme climates like Canada's.

These campaigns suggested, with a surprising lack of subtlety, that it was in fact in the best interest of non-whites to spare themselves the challenge and inevitable failure of trying to exist in societies so obviously hostile to their nature and inclinations. They used flattery in their emphasis that any-one rational and educated enough—hence exhibiting the main markers of the vaunted progress that Britain boasted was its gift to the less-advanced peoples in the Empire—would recognize it was unnatural, and even irratio-nal, to go to places where their presumed natural proclivities would make them foreigners in a hostile and alien setting. Of course, this flattery was directed primarily at educated non-whites who had absorbed the theories then dominant in the social sciences and the humanities, such as those by Robert Knox and his acolytes, on race and racial profiling.

For example, in 1906, fearful that western Canada—but especially British Columbia—was on the verge of receiving a marked increase in British subjects from India, the Canadian government pressured the British Colonial Office to intervene through its India Office. The British Colonial Office responded that "the Government in India is asking the viceroy to publicize the difficulties of life in British Columbia, the harshness of the climate, the lack of employment, and the consequent danger of becoming a public charge and of being deported."[132] The Department of Commerce and Industry, the division of the Indian government with jurisdiction over emigration, subsequently pushed this message out within its territory.

When these messages failed to have the desired effect, colonial gov-ernments instructed shipping lines and agents to refuse to sell passenger tickets to Black people in the Empire for travel to the old dominions. At the same time, the law common within the British Empire allow-ing the receiving states to refuse entry or deport British subjects to their native land if they fell into a universal list of undesirables was strongly enforced. The Canadian Immigration Act of 1910 placed on the prohibited list "anyone belonging to any race deemed unsuited to the climate or requirements of Canada, or of immigrants of any specified class, occupation or character."[133] This proved an effective way of barring Black British subjects from the West Indies. As native to the tropics, they were deemed unsuited for the Canadian climate. In an act aimed primarily at the Chinese, the government also imposed an onerous head tax of $200 on every Asian immigrant. Applicants from South East Asia and Africa also had to contend with a clause stipulating that they had to arrive in Canada on a continuous, direct journey. This meant migrants had to arrive directly from their homeland to qualify. Since there was virtually no direct travel to Canada from these colonies, very few Indians and Africans visited, or attempted to settle, in Canada.

This restrictive approach to immigration was in keeping with a decision that the old dominions—Canada, Britain, Australia, New Zealand, Newfoundland, the Free Irish State, and South Africa—had codified into an agreement thirty years earlier to "redistribute" white British subjects among themselves or within what was considered to be the emerging British Commonwealth. This gave the old dominions a way to assert their independence and separate themselves from the rest of the Empire, which really meant separating themselves from peoples of colour.

The decision to populate the dominions through a redistribution of British subjects was first made at the 1921 Imperial Conference, one of the intermittent meetings of the leaders of the so-called "mature" members of the British political family around the world. Dominion prime ministers used the meetings to make collective leadership decisions and to discuss the future direction of the British Empire. Membership was effectively restricted to natives of the British Isles—particularly England—and their descendants, and hence white.

If the entire Empire were viewed as a club or family, the leaders at the 1926 Imperial Conference would have formed the paternalistic executive that made the decisions that mattered. Historically, the conference is most often noted for its official recognition of the white British dominions as legislatively independent from Britain, yet they still remained elite members of the global British order. The dominions were the adults of the British civilized family. "They are autonomous within the British Empire," the conference statement said, "equal in status, in no way subordinate to one another in any aspect of their domestic or external affairs, though united by a common allegiance to the Crown and freely associated as members of the British Commonwealth of Nations."[134]

The older dominions had given themselves the best of both worlds when it was advantageous to them, such as demanding preferential rates on their exports to Britain and fellow colonies. They remained members of the Empire, just like any other colony, except when it was expedient not to be. In those cases, they were separate and distinct from all other colonies in the Empire. As a result, there were now, in practice if not fully in law, two different groups of British subjects: those from the newly recognized Commonwealth of Nations or dominions; and those from colonies of lower standing—such as those in the West Indies, Africa, and Asia—which were construed simply as British Empire possessions.

Justice Minister Doherty had anticipated this development while piloting a new law, whose purpose was to define Canadian nationals, in the Canadian House of Commons on March 10, 1921. At the end of the First World War, Doherty had led the Canadian delegation at the international meetings preceding the establishment of the League of Nations a year earlier. In this forum, the differences between British subjects, and who spoke for which side of the Empire's divide, had to be confronted. It was decided that Canada and the dominions would have separate memberships in the League from the United Kingdom. In addition, some policies pertaining to Canada's performance in international bodies such as the League would be decided solely from the standpoint of Canadian nationality or interests, as opposed to British subjecthood. Asked by a fellow parliamentarian to explain the difference between a British Empire national and a Canadian national under his proposed arrangement, Doherty suggested that while both were British subjects, the main difference lay in what part of the Empire the Canadian came from and resided in. This implied that there were times when Canadians, as British subjects, needed to be recognized as distinct from British subjects from other colonies and dependencies. The 1926 Imperial Conference would formalize this understanding. It marked the beginning of the stripping of Black British subjects, especially those from the Caribbean, of recognition in Canada as British subjects.

Commonwealth status was viewed as higher than mere membership in the Empire and could only be claimed by those territories that had graduated from colonial status to independence and self-rule. As such, India occupied an ambiguous position. While its prime ministers attended and participated in Imperial Conferences, the colonial possession—now known separately as India, Pakistan, and Bangladesh—was not a dominion but rather a special type of colony on its way to becoming the next independent country in the British Commonwealth. Even after the territory called India gained independence in 1947, the resulting countries of Pakistan and India would not immediately make dominion status, confirming the perception that "dominion" was a synonym for whiteness. Dominions had become key to the creation and preservation of white British enclaves around the world.

The 1926 Imperial Conference was also important for another thing that would undermine the notion of the universal equality of British subjects: it established immigration policies for British subjects, especially to the "empty" British states like Canada, Australia, and New Zealand, which needed to increase their populations with people loyal to the reigning monarch. Not only did the conference confirm the existence of a de facto British Commonwealth separate from the rest of the Empire, it also painted these groups, respectively, as white and Black. This difference is still implied in the determination of Black and Blackness in today's Britain and its former colonies: Black people are not only those with Black skin or African ancestry, but former colonial peoples who aren't nationals of the white dominions. This is a nuance of the perception of Black and Blackness in the Americas where, as both an ethnic and racial determinant, the concept is an indication of skin colour of all non-whites.[135]

Prior to the conference, the dominions had scrambled to get immigrants from the British Isles. Not getting enough white settlers was a problem, but having too many Black immigrants was potentially another. Without white British settlers, those Commonwealth countries were considered "empty," and desperately in need of population. When it came to the creation and preservation of European-style states, the Indigenous people who'd traditionally lived on the land didn't count. "The Conference is of the opinion," the conference statement said, "that the problem of overseas settlement, which is that of a redistribution of the white population of the Empire in the best interest of the British Commonwealth, is one of paramount importance especially as between Great Britain on the one hand, and Canada, Australia and New Zealand on the other. The conference notes with satisfaction that the desired redistribution of population is being accelerated."[136] Under this agreement, Britain subsidized the transportation of

British migrants to the dominions and also met some of the cost for recruitment, transportation, and settlement.

When J. W. Noseworthy questioned Canada's immigration practices in Parliament, the agreement to redistribute white people and the practice of favouring white immigration were well in place. But there was dissatisfaction with the practices and with the white dominions' failure to deliver the right immigrants in large enough numbers to meet growing demand and sustain economic development. Writing in the wake of the announcement at the Imperial Conference, a British commentator in *The Contemporary Review*, a popular magazine, indicated that the resettlement commitment was both unworkable and the wrong policy at the wrong time for the development of both the dominions and Britain alike.

"As is well known," analyst Charles McCurdy wrote,

> the British Empire contains a population of 463,000,000. Of that total, 65,700,000, or a little more than the population of Germany, are of European stock. And of the 65,700,000, no less than 46,000,000 people are squeezed into the British Isles. Not one Dominion of the Empire holds a population equal to that of greater London. Let us present these vital statistics from another angle. The British Empire contains more than one-fourth of the world's land surface and more than one-fourth of the world's people. Yet under the British flag, outside Great Britain, there are not twenty million people of our race.[137]

Adding to this lamentable situation, McCurdy said, the mismatch between population demand and supply was showing up in another way: Canada and other dominions wanted agricultural workers to bring land under production, but the populations in the British Isles were now largely industrial, and had little interest in returning to an agricultural past. If Canada wanted people to homestead, as was its policy, it should not be looking to the British Isles. Besides, Britain itself needed its industrial workers to help expand global trade and, as a result, had a prior claim on the qualified population. Even in the dominions, immigrants from the British Isles were deserting the countryside for the industrial cities and, particularly in Canada, were crossing the border in large numbers to live in the United States.

> In former days when the Empire was in the making, it did not matter much that few white men settled in its distant territories. But to hold is far more

difficult than to make an Empire. The first requisite is population [....] The smallness of the white population within the Empire is serious enough. But when the statistics relating to the occupational distribution of the white population are examined the outlook becomes still more confusing. Forty-six millions out of sixty-five millions live in these isles, and of these forty-six millions four-fifths are engaged in industry, and only one-fifth in agriculture [....] It is urgently necessary that the dominions be populated; it is urgent also that they should be populated with British stock and with the best of the British stock too! But where are these ideal settlers to be found in sufficient numbers?[138]

Population redistribution had become a drain to Britain, both in terms of money and available bodies to meet its own needs. Canadian officials often cited Britain's cutting back of transportation services as a reason why Canada had not attracted British immigrants in the numbers its government would've liked. Poor immigration numbers were also partly blamed on Britain not living up to the promises it had made, such as the agreement at the Imperial Conference. As a result, Canada was in turn hindered from attaining its full potential.

The intention of the immigration policy developed at the Imperial Conference had been to co-ordinate the dispersal of white people in the colonies, effectively concentrating this ethnic group in the whites-only British Commonwealth. This approach aimed to achieve two main things: 1) to provide exclusive homelands within the Empire for mainly British whites who wanted to escape their native land to seek fortunes and livelihoods in what were considered to be empty countries awaiting European civilization and development; 2) and to offer places of refuge for the colonial whites scattered across the globe who found themselves in colonies agitating for self-determination and majority non-white rule (e.g., the Caribbean). In the second case, these expatriates feared the former colonials. Should they escape the strict tutelage of their masters, these oppressed peoples might exact retribution on whites for their bondage. This fear made colonial whites believe they needed to move to a country under the control of, and exclusively for, whites like them.

Black people in the Empire generally, and in Canada specifically, argued that these practices disadvantaged them and robbed them of social equality, thereby creating superior and inferior categories of citizenship. A royal commission into civil unrest in the British West Indies in the 1930s argued that the dire economic situation that had spawned the disturbances could be alleviated by giving these colonies self-government, similar to that in the dominions, and by reducing high unemployment levels through immigration.[139] Because they were relatively close compared to Australia and New Zealand, Britain and Canada were the likely candidates to receive this excess population, except that the immigrants would be Black.

The sleeping car porters and their allies exploited this contradiction over policy and the authenticity of British identity. By the time they confronted the Canadian government, the delegation had support from a new group: British Caribbean governments, politicians, and trade unions, who were pushing for a new order of equality where colonies still considered part of the British Empire would be elevated to the higher status of British Commonwealth members. These leaders were disrupting the older order, first, by advocating for self-rule at home and, ultimately, for political self-determination for the majority populations in the British West Indies. Second, they were agitating for the opening up of new international markets for Caribbean peoples and their products within the relatively small Caribbean diaspora in metropolitan centres. They petitioned for a more open world, which included freedom of movement for British West Indians and the ability to live and work in any part of the world. Gaining access to the markets of Canada was a priority, in part because it was a country with which the British West Indies had long had both economic and cultural ties. In anticipation of the British West Indies becoming fully independent, Canada was also being presented as a model of how to be independent and still undoubtedly British.

Caribbean governments were already successfully resisting practices that favoured white colonies, to the point where British immigration and human-rights policies were beginning to diverge from those of the old dominions. Caribbean leaders and activists had helped to bring about this change by rallying under the identity of British subjects. Thousands had flocked to England to join the military during the Second World War, after Britain issued an appeal for all British subjects to come to its aid. The call was answered swiftly, even in the small islands of the Caribbean, and volunteers quickly assembled to fight for Britain. Several had passed through Canada, where they received advance training as Royal Air Force pilots, navigators, and bombers under the British Commonwealth Air Training Plan. They fought proudly under the British flag common to all parts of the British Empire and Commonwealth.

By 1952, the Colonial Office in London had noted that the war and the defense of Britain and British ideals had given West Indians a sense of entitlement as British subjects. "Over 5,000 men from the West Indies were recruited into the Royal Air Force," the Colonial Office recalled in a booklet about British dependencies in the Caribbean since the beginning of the war:

> Women were recruited for the A.T.S. [Auxiliary Territorial Service of women volunteers in the colonies attached to the British Army] and also served in the United Kingdom. West Indian seamen served in the Merchant Marine in dangerous waters and a large number gave their lives. In addition many men and women made their way to Canada or Great Britain and joined the armed forces. Those who served as aircrews were of very high quality and earned many awards for gallantry.
>
> In addition to direct defence services, the people of the West Indies, Bermuda and the Bahamas gave generously for various purposes. Some £750,000 was raised for general war purposes, nearly £400,000 for war charities, and over £425,000 for the purchase of aircraft for the Royal Air Force. Their governments and peoples lent over £1,500,000 to the United Kingdom Government free of interest. War charities benefiting included the Red Cross, St. John's Ambulance, King George's Fund for Soldiers, St. Dunstan's, and Aid to Russia. Mobile canteens presented by the West Indies served in London and other cities during air raids, and funds were also contributed for the "Queen's Messengers," the mobile food convoys which helped to feed the peoples of bombed towns. Many tons of surgical and hospital supplies, comforts, clothing, honey and preserves were also sent. The Bahamas War Children's Committee took charge of a party of children sent from England to escape air raids. When the civilian population of Gibraltar had to be removed, many of them were housed until the end of the war in a special camp in Jamaica.[140]

When the time came for the porter delegation to meet in Ottawa, Donald Moore emphasized this sense of joint loyalty, arguing forcibly that Black people—particularly those from the West Indies—had long fought for Canada and the British Empire:

> Our memories are still fresh with the acts of sacrifice and gallantry performed by Negroes in 1914–1918. Our hearts have presently been saddened by the

death of Canada's first quadruplet amputee of that Great War. I speak of none other than our Curly Christian. In this war the Negro had two battles to fight, first we fought to get in the Army, then we fought the Germans. In the Second [World] War, 263 West Indians volunteered in the West Indies for service in the Canadian Army—men who in some instances had never seen Canada. The Negro in Canada was conscripted, but like the first war, we had two battles to fight. We had to fight to get in the Air Force, and then we had to fight Hitler. We paid the price.

At this point in his deputation, Moore turned to highlight the presence of one of his fellow delegates, Edith Holloway, whose twenty-one-year-old son Humphrey had been killed in the European theatre. "In this very delegation today," he said,

sits a Mother wearing a Silver Cross [the medal Canada awards to mothers, wives, husbands, or the next of kin of fallen military in active duty]. That heart is proud, for she willingly gave her son to defend our beloved country. But that heart is saddened, because the country for which he fought and died has refused to let his brother [in Barbados] to enter therein. In fact, the Government is virtually saying to her, take off your Cross, your people can never become integrated into the Canadian way of life.[141]

If he'd wanted to, Moore could have also pointed to a veteran soldier of the Second World War to emphasize his point—Stanley Grizzle was a former infantryman. He could have also pointed to another delegate, Bromley Armstrong—whose brothers Eric and Everald had left Jamaica to enlist and fight in the Canadian Armed Forces, and whose mother, Edith, was denied entry into Canada at Toronto's Malton Airport in 1953 and locked up, pending deportation back to Jamaica, when she attempted to visit her sons. It took some political maneuvering to get her released and made a permanent resident of Canada a year later.

When the Second World War ended with victory for Britain and its allies, these members of the British army, navy, and air force were expected to demobilize back home to the Caribbean. But when they did so they found the colonial regime too stifling and work opportunities lacking. Most wanted to return immediately to England, where there were opportunities for employment in the post-war reconstruction, or to move to another country in the British Empire. Many of the West Indians who served alongside the British Allies also had family and friends who fought for the US, and many of those people shared homes in both the Caribbean islands and in North American cities like New York, Boston, Miami, and, increasingly, Toronto, Montreal, Halifax, and Winnipeg. To be a British West Indian Black person was to be truly transnational, having a sense of belonging in one part of the hemisphere while being equally at home wherever one had to go to make a living. Some wanted the choice of living and working in another part of the British Empire and Commonwealth as repayment for putting their lives on the line in the war.

Many West Indians began pressuring the British government about their immigration claims, putting that government at odds with those of the white dominions. With jobs in short supply in the Caribbean, immigration activists argued Britain and the white dominions had betrayed them by looking for immigrants in Eastern and Southern Europe to fill out their workforces. The West Indians were particularly angry when labourers from Poland, Hungary, and Italy were recruited to help rebuild war-torn England and to augment the supply of immigration to the colonies in light of declining migration from Britain. The more-than-plentiful supply available in one part of the Empire was being overlooked in preference for non-subjects from outside the Empire. The only possible explanation for this was that West Indians were Black.

At the same time, the United States exacerbated the employment situation in the British West Indies by drastically cutting back on the importation of Caribbean labour that had been so badly needed during the war for agriculture and munitions factories. With US consent, the Caribbean governments paid the transportation costs for nationals seeking temporary work in America. But with the war over, the United States was returning to a policy of restricting immigration from the Caribbean, even for those with valued guest-worker visas. A further tightening on Caribbean immigration to the US was anticipated with the introduction of the new McCarran-Walter Act of 1952. Also known as the Immigration and Nationality Act, it shifted emphasis away from temporary migrants to permanent residents—away, that is, from what had originally attracted many West Indians to the US—leaving them without status. Annual immigration to the United States from the British West Indies was now limited to one hundred persons from each colony. To compensate for this curtailment in the exportation of labour, British West Indians began looking to Britain and Canada.

West Indian politicians found an effective way of pressuring Britain and the white dominions: by issuing British passports to Black subjects. In the region, local governors began to give in to pressure from local politicians on the issue of British passports. Almost overnight, British officials started to issue more passports, while also publicizing that colonials in the British West Indies were entitled to passports that would allow them entry across the Empire. The British government and the dominions tried without success to get the governors and politicians to comply with the traditional practice on passports and to discourage Black islanders from travelling. But the power dynamic between the old dominions and members of the British Empire had changed fundamentally after the war. If Black people were good enough to fight and die as British subjects, it was argued, they should have the rights and protections common to all British subjects regardless of colour or race.

West Indian governments in particular were most vocal on this point. "Almost from the beginning of the decade 1945–55, the rate of increase of Asian and Black populations (in Britain) was considered to be a cause for concern," Ian R. G. Spencer writes. "Unlike the governments of India and Pakistan and the colonial governments of West Africa, Caribbean governments did not co-operate to any great extent with the restrictive measures proposed by London, and it was the rapid build up of the numbers of Caribbean migrants that precipitated the 'crisis' of 1954–5" in the United Kingdom. This "crisis" was the arrival of Jamaican immigrants to Britain.

The Jamaican government, to take one example, rejected arguments from the Colonial Office with the purpose of stemming the flow of migrants out of the island, and refused to budge from this position even when Britain sent top officials to bring them back in line. Instead, for the first time, the colonial masters found they had no way of imposing their wishes on the people. Even the white governors in the islands were in favour of more liberal regimes. "Because of Jamaica's advance to self-government," Spencer states, "the British authorities could not compel its government to legislate or take other actions to prevent the movement" of Black Jamaicans first to England and then elsewhere in the Commonwealth.[142]

In 1948, the passenger liner *Empire Windrush* returned hundreds of Black West Indian members of the British military from the West Indies to London, marking the start of the Blackening of Britain, something the Jamaican lyricist and humourist Louise Bennett described as "colonialization in reverse." Other islands soon followed Jamaica's lead. Barbadian premier Grantley Adams would become the first and only prime minister of the British West Indies Federation, the political union of a majority of the British West Indian countries, from 1958–62. In preparation for the federation, Adams visited Canada and met with members of the Negro Citizens Association, as had his counterpart Norman Manley, the then-premier of Jamaica. Both leaders advocated for Caribbean immigration to Canada and for a deepening of Canada's relationship with the British West Indies due to their common British colonial heritage.

The porters-led delegation to Ottawa, with support from J. W. Noseworthy and his parliamentary allies, were ready to exploit the divergences and contradictions in Canadian immigration policy. Their aim was to prove that Canada was out of step on the issue, including internationally, with respect to the new limits and boundaries placed on prospective citizens arriving as immigrants.

As if to reinforce this point, Walter Harris' counterpart in the British House of Commons, Henry Hopkinson, minister of state at the Colonial Office, declared in 1954: "As the law stands, any British subject from the colonies is free to enter this country at any time as long as he [sic] can produce satisfactory evidence of his British status. This is not something we want to tamper with lightly [...] We still take pride in the fact a man can say *Civis Britannicus Sum* [translated: I am a British subject] whatever his colour may be and we take pride in the fact that he wants and can come to the mother country."[143] The perception of who had an inalienable right to enter and live in Canada was finally beginning to change.

However, not everyone accepted this. Canadian politicians kept a close eye on the growing numbers of West Indians settling in Britain, and many did not think the development encouraging or exemplary. "Color Bar at Gate? A Question in Britain," trumpeted a headline in *The Economist* that was reprinted in the *Globe and Mail* on December 6, 1954. "British subjects are not statistically distinguished by color, but immigration from the colonies—mainly from Jamaica—is increasing. A short time ago, when the 'problem' first began to cause comment, the inflow was only 3,000 a year. It is expected to amount to 10,000 this year, when the total number of colored residents in Britain may reach 80,000. If arrivals grow in the same proportion, another 15,000 would come in 1955." As a result, there was growing resentment against Black and West Indian immigration, the editorial said, with critics claiming that Britain was importing unemployment from the Caribbean by admitting mainly unskilled labourers with strange cultural habits, and that the increased immigration was leading to housing shortages and the creation of slums. "In short," *The Economist* said, "if their skins were white there would be no problem. What trouble exists is mainly racial; it is the color problem that has come to Britain—or at least to Brixton, to Birmingham and to Ipswich. Unfortunately, the very reluctance that most people feel to admitting that they are motivated by color prejudice makes it hard to pinpoint just how much of it is there, and who feels it."[144]

The message to Canadians watching the situation in Britain was that increased immigration from the colonies would bring to Canada something the country had always tried to avoid—a Black problem.

PRESSURING PARLIAMENT
A New Kind of Canadian Citizenship

As THE DELEGATION WAS PREPARING to take their message to Ottawa, their trusted ally, J. W. Noseworthy, the Toronto parliamentarian for the opposition Co-operative Commonwealth Federation, continued to raise the Black community's concerns in the House of Commons. Returning yet again to the question of Black immigration on April 24, 1953, fully a year before the delegation's arrival, Noseworthy reminded the House that a year earlier he had asked the minister of immigration, Walter Harris, to investigate a special case that had been brought to his attention.

It was about "a Mr. Brathwaite," he said,

> ...a coloured Canadian citizen, a former employee of one of the railway companies, a man against whose character as a Canadian citizen there was no blot, a man who had lived a fairly exemplary life in his community, who wanted to bring his granddaughter from Barbados. I wrote the minister and in his reply the minister said: I have had the case reviewed by the immigration branch to ascertain whether some grounds could not be found for extending favourable consideration. It is quite evident, however, that Miss Brathwaite does not qualify for admission under present regulations and in the circumstances no encouragement can be offered.[145]

In his papers, Grizzle would identify the porter as John A. Brathwaite, and his granddaughter as Una Jessamy Brathwaite. In his memoir, Bromley Armstrong said Brathwaite had worked on the Panama Canal before settling in Sydney, Nova Scotia, in 1911, then moving to Toronto in 1926, "where he became a popular community worker and civil rights leader." Armstrong said Braithwaite's fight against the immigration policies "received wide attention in Toronto's Black community and brought critical support from the CCF."[146]

Using research by the Brotherhood of Sleeping Car Porters, Noseworthy made the point that Canada's immigration policy was anti-Black, then proceeded to pick apart the minister's argument against Black immigration. In an effort to undermine the long-held Knox doctrine which stated that certain races did better in specific climates, a position codified in Canadian immigration policy, Grizzle had written to leading medical universities and heads of hospitals in North America asking for any research or evidence they had that Black people did not thrive in cold-climate countries. There was no such evidence, and Grizzle shared this widely, most notably with his union—which continued to dash off petitions and telegrams to the federal government berating its immigration policies—and with Noseworthy, who did the same in Parliament.[147] On this occasion, when Noseworthy rose to speak up for the cause of Blacks in Canada, he was armed with the research the union activists had been compiling for years. He used this information to lampoon the government's standard answers for restricting Black immigration and indirectly curtailing the rights of a specific group of citizens.

Noseworthy dissected Minister Harris' response, explaining the rationale for turning down the retired porter's application for his granddaughter. Noseworthy began by reading form the minister's letter about the grandfather's application:

one of the conditions for admission to Canada is that immigrants should be able readily to become adapted and integrated into the life of the community within a reasonable time after their entry. In the light of experience, it would be unrealistic to say that immigrants who have spent the greater part of their life in tropical or sub-tropical countries become readily adapted to the Canadian mode of life, which, to no small extent, is determined by climactic conditions. It is a matter of record that natives of such countries are more apt to break down in health than from countries where the climate is more akin to that of Canada. It is equally true that, generally speaking, persons from tropical and sub-tropical countries find it more difficult to succeed in the highly competitive Canadian economy. It would be quite contrary to fact, however, to infer from this that coloured immigrants are debarred from Canada. As in the past, favourable consideration is given in cases where the exceptional qualifications of the applicant offer reasonable assurance that he will find a satisfactory level in the Canadian community or where refusal would constitute an extreme hardship on humanitarian grounds.

The Minister had offered the traditional argument so routinely supplied in response to questions about Black immigration matters since the beginning of the century. But this time his opponents were ready to strike back.

"So," Noseworthy said,

judging by the minister's statement, people from the British West Indies—British subjects from the British West Indies—are not considered to be suitable immigrants to Canada on the grounds that they cannot readily adapt themselves to the climactic conditions of our country or stand up against the competition of modern life in Canada, and that they are not likely to remain healthy in Canada. In order to find out just what the records were, because the minister in his letter said it is a matter of record, I put some questions on the order paper.

Putting questions on the order paper was a parliamentary practice where questions were written to ministers, and then researched by the relevant departments, so that more detailed answers could be provided to the questioner. Noseworthy next proceeded to read the questions and answers into the record of the debate:

1. How many persons of British West Indies origin are at present living in Canada?

    The answer was: *Information not available.*

2. How many persons have entered Canada from the British West Indies during each of the five years 1947–1951, inclusive?

    The answer was: *Statistics are not available as to the number of persons who have entered Canada.*

3. How many applicants for entry to Canada from the British West Indies have been refused entry during each of the five years 1947 to 1951, inclusive?

    The answer was: *Statistics on rejections are not maintained by country of origin.*

4. For what reasons were these applicants rejected and how many were rejected for each of these reasons?

    The answer to that question was: *See answer to No. 3.*

5. How many students were admitted to Canada from the British West Indies for the purpose of studying in Canada during each of the years 1947–1951, inclusive?

   The answer was: *Students admitted to Canada from the commonwealth countries are shown as British subjects and are not listed by country of origin. It is not possible, therefore, to give the number of students coming from the British West Indies.*

6. How many of these students tried for permanent residence in Canada?

   The answer to that was: *Information not available.*

7. How many of the student applicants were granted permanent residence in Canada?

   The answer was: *Information not available.*

8. Are any statistics available to show how immigrants to Canada from the British West Indies compare with immigrants from other warm climate countries in the following respects: (a) health records; (b) wages or salaries earned; (c) unemployment records; (d) professional occupation followed; (e) public liabilities?

   The answer was: *Statistics not available.*

Taking the responses into consideration, Noseworthy said, "I gather from the answers to these eight questions—every single one of which was answered by the statement that statistics are not available or that records are not available—that, when the minister states in his letter to me that it is a 'matter of record,' someone was judging the case on the basis of some theory that has probably been laid down by the department of immigration for some time rather than by any actual statistics or records."[148]

Noseworthy said he had sent a copy of the minister's letter to Brathwaite, who had forwarded the letter to his union, the Brotherhood of Sleeping Car Porters and the president of its Toronto division, Stanley Grizzle. Well documented in Grizzle's papers are the letters he wrote to officials in Canada and the United States seeking information to the eight questions. The union gave its own response in an editorial in the Brotherhood's newspaper, *Black Worker*, which was published in March 1952 under the headline "Immigration by Discrimination." "It is often interesting for us to see ourselves as others see us," Noseworthy told Parliament, "and I want to call to the minister's attention what the editor of the official organ of that union has to say regarding the minister's answers." In all likelihood, he was now quoting an editorial written by Grizzle, the main Canadian contributor to the union's New York-based newspaper. The language of the editorial is typical of Grizzle's writing.

> First, the minister says: I have had the case reviewed by the immigration branch... it is quite evident, however, that Miss Brathwaite does not qualify for admission under the present regulations [...] The editor says: Think of it! Here is a citizen of Canada who cannot even bring his granddaughter to Canada to see him. Why? Not because she is a communist or a subversive of any stripe, who might plot and conspire against the government; not because she is indigent and may become a charge upon the government; not because she possesses some contaminating and contagious disease; but solely because she's a negro living in the West Indies!

Put more succinctly, Noseworthy would argue, the granddaughter did not meet any of the criteria listed in the regulations that would result in her being denied entry or labelled an "undesirable."

In reply to the minister's statement that an ability to adapt and integrate into the life of the community be a condition for admission to Canada, the editorial asked:

> What about the negroes already in Canada who came from the West Indies? We have heard no sound claim made to the effect that they have failed in adaptation or integration into the life of the community. If a census were taken of the negroes in Canada and from the West Indies, it would be found that percentage-wise, they will compare favourably (1) as law abiding citizens; (2) as reliable and dependable workers; (3) as persons of good health; (4) as citizens non-dependent upon charity; (5) as citizens answering the call of their country to arms; (6) as church-goers, with the white citizens of the Dominion of Canada.
>
> The editorial goes on to point out that there are a great number of people from the West Indies living in Canada and occupying prominent positions; some are in the professions and some are active in the trade unions. The article makes a fairly good case of the charge that, apparently, there are few facts to support this statement with which the minister justifies his policy. The writer concludes that the policy followed by the department is pretty well a case of discrimination against British subjects on the basis of colour.
>
> There are no statistics available in Canada, for instance, to show that the people from the West Indies do not do as well in this country, so far as health

is concerned, or that they do not become integrated into the life of the community as well as do people from southern Italy, where the climate is very much the same, or people from Florida, where the climate is not too different.

There is abundant evidence to show that in Chicago, and other northern cities of the United States, where the climate is not so very different from that of Toronto, these immigrants have not been affected, nor has their health broken down by reason of climactic conditions. At a time when the Department of Labour has before us a bill outlawing discrimination by employers on the ground of race or colour, it ill behooves the department of immigration to pursue a discriminatory policy on that basis, particularly in regard to other British subjects. In the world today there are about two billion coloured people who are not yet communists. History may well turn upon whether or not these two billion coloured people throw in their lot with the western world or with the communist world.

In light of the attitude of these coloured races of Africa, Asia and India towards the western world, and in light of their present attitude towards white people generally, I suggest that the minister revise his policy, particularly at this time when a number of people in Canada are contemplating the possibility of the British West Indies becoming a part of our Dominion. I suggest to the minister to give some attention to that revision and the present policy regarding immigrants from the British West Indies.[149]

Almost word for word, Noseworthy's statement was the same as that given by Stanley's brother Norman Grizzle, a Toronto dentist and leading member of the Negro Citizenship Association, when the delegation met with the federal government a year later.

But the citizenship debate in Canada wasn't just about the suitability of immigrants from the Caribbean for Canada. There was also the concern about so-called Asiatic people, particularly Chinese, Japanese, and Indians. Here's what George. R. Pearkes, the British-born Conservative representative for Nanaimo—who would soon become Canada's minister of defense when the government changed in 1957—had to say:

While I am not in any way advocating any general increase in the amount of oriental immigration, yet for anyone who lives, as I do, in close proximity to a number of our Canadian Chinese, it is not hard to realize that anguish which parents suffer because they are not able to bring their children from Communist China to this country; and that statement applies also to other people who have close relatives in communist China and cannot get them out. When I am at home I do not think a week passes that some Chinese Canadian does not come and visit me and ask me if I can do something to help him bring his child, or an aged parent or some other close relative to this country.

Ironically, once in power Pearkes was adamant that Canada and the Empire's other senior dominions had the sovereign right not to have their countries overrun by Asiatic immigration.

"Very much the same factors apply to our East Indian citizens," he said on this occasion:

They have been granted citizenship rights but of course they do not enjoy all the citizenship rights in so far as bringing their close relatives into this country is concerned. The East Indians live in fairly substantial numbers around Victoria. They have made their contribution to the economic and cultural life of British Columbia. They are law-abiding, hard-working citizens, and they feel very keenly that they are not permitted to bring in their close relatives.

Pearkes went on to query why Canada could not even fill the meagre quotas from Asia, urging the minister "to give consideration to those who are eligible to come to this country and that the full quota be admitted."[150]

Parliamentarian William Thatcher, representing Moose Jaw for the Co-operative Commonwealth Federation party, said:

Certain remarks have been made in the house today that we have to watch unemployment. Of course that is sensible, but I repeat what I have said earlier, that every time a person picks up a daily newspaper he finds not columns of "help wanted" advertisements but page after page [of advertisements]. I have in my hand at the moment today's *Toronto Telegram* and there are six or seven pages of help wanted advertisements seeking brick-layers, electricians, painters, domestics, unskilled workers, shippers, service station attendants, teachers, chauffeurs, bookkeepers and so on.

In my opinion, no matter what city you mention, there is an acute and all-pervading labour shortage today. Many schools in my province are closed, and I believe also in other provinces, because teachers cannot be obtained. We have hospitals that are having great difficulty

in carrying on operations, because they cannot get nurses and attendants. As has been mentioned [...] many farmers cannot get farm help.
Factories have had to curtail operations because in some cases they cannot obtain skilled workers.

I think there is room in Canada for thousands of domestics. I believe
there is also room for a great many more unskilled workers. The way
our industry is expanding today, there are not even enough workmen
for those industries that are past the blueprint stage, let alone enough
men for future expansion. Suppose the Minister of Defense Production
decides this year that the nation is going ahead with the St. Lawrence sea-
way. Where would we get the men to build it? What would happen if the
Minister of Agriculture decided to go ahead with the South Saskatchewan
river project? Where would he get 10,000 workmen to build it? What if
our gold mines should open again? Where are we going to get men to
operate them?

Thatcher called for at least 300,000 immigrants annually, an increase from
162,000 in 1952, although his implication was that most of them should
be Europeans:

The number of emigrants from Great Britain to this country fell down very
badly last year. We only brought out 44,000 people. There are two reasons
for that. The first is that the minister has withdrawn a good deal of the
assistance on transportation, which was formerly provided. The second is
that the British government will not allow emigrants from that country to
take out sufficient money. I think the minister should be more generous
with assisted passages. At the same time the government should approach
the British authorities to see if some system cannot be worked out whereby
their government will permit emigrants from that country to bring more
money to Canada.[151]

The implication of these statements was that Canada preferred British subjects, who were no longer coming to Canada in meaningful numbers. The
decline in preferred immigrants was a cause for worry among policymakers and
those advising them. In a submission to the Canadian Standing Committee
on Immigration and Labour in 1946, the Canadian Congress of Labour had
asked whether sustainable immigration was indeed possible for Canada. "The
Congress is very doubtful whether suitable immigrants will be available in any

large numbers during the next few years," said the congress president, Aaron R. Mosher, known through the years for his anti-Black racism:

> Plenty of Europeans may want to come here but most Europeans countries will be anxious to keep exactly the types of people who would make the best immigrants. The Congress submits, therefore, that it would be very unwise to base immigration purely on the assumption that we can get as many suitable immigrants as we may want, or that we have only to reach out and take our pick of the world's population. Even if we are prepared to pay substantial amounts for assisted passage, we may find it very hard indeed to get any appreciable number of the kind of people we want.

However, a second category of British subjects—those not on the preferred list because of their racialization—was barred from entering the country. As the Canadian Congress of Labour suggested in its brief, undesirables should continue to be strictly controlled to ensure Canada did not create pools of unskilled workers, further increasing unemployment and decreasing the standard of living. "We do not want immigration used as a means of getting cheap and docile workers and breaking down the standard which organized Labour has built up. We do not want it used to provide employers with a pool or reserve of unemployed workers who will be taken on when the employer can make more profit by using extra hands, laid off and maintained at the taxpayers' expense when he cannot, and used as a big stick to keep Labour in its place."[152] Apart from the racially coded language, such as the reference to "docile workers," it's difficult not to notice that Mosher's prototype for unwanted immigrants was right there in his own union, the Canadian Brotherhood of Railway Employees, in the form of the railway porters whom he purportedly represented. Mosher had been instrumental in helping to craft Canadian policy that created pools of "docile" reserve workers for the railway, the same workers he was now afraid white Canadians—and the few desirable immigrants attracted to the country—would be turned into.

The result of this citizenship and immigration debate was the widespread opinion that Canada had a "slanted" immigration law. As the *Toronto Star* argued in its editorial of February 16, 1955,

> The department has refused admission to West Indian Negroes with education, training and skills. It has barred also children of some West Indians

who have become Canadian citizens. A quota system is observed in respect to Asians. Hon. Walter Harris, the former immigration minister, reported that no more than 150 are annually admissible from India, 100 from Pakistan and 50 from Ceylon. There is also a quota on Negro immigration to Canada of about 200 a year. Since the end of the war, more than a million immigrants have been admitted to Canada, mostly British and European whites. Of the Europeans, the most favored groups have been Germans, Italians, Dutch. There can be only one interpretation of such a selective policy, namely, that it reflects a belief in "white supremacy." And contradicts Parliament's endorsement of the Universal Declaration of Human rights.[153]

With growing numbers of allies in parliament, the media, unions, churches, and other non-governmental organizations like the Negro Citizenship Association, sleeping car porters were ramping up the pressure on the Canadian government.

IN THEIR OWN VOICES, MEMBERS of the Negro Citizenship Association would build on J. W. Noseworthy's work in their own meeting with Minister Harris in 1954, for it was through people like Noseworthy that the impenetrable fortress of white racism was first truly broached on their behalf in parliament.

"Because of the youthfulness of our organization, our inexperience in appearing before official bodies, and especially before high representatives in the highest form of government," Donald Moore said in his opening remarks before presenting the association's brief to Harris, "we approach the task undertaken with a great deal of humility. However, sir, after forty years, having integrated some semblance of the Canadian spirit, I have learned that our Government will give a listening ear to the cries of the people, and will unhesitatingly take steps to right any apparent wrong." He would beseech the minister not to continue to jeopardize Canada's democratic standards and good name internationally by continuing to deny equal treatment to all British subjects and citizens of the Commonwealth. That invoked "good name" relied partly on the perception that the government in Ottawa was always willing to listen to reasoned petitions, especially ones that spoke to its relationships with British subjects in, and from, the Caribbean, an area of the world with which Canada always had favourable ties. Even before the Canadian federation's 1867 inception, an endless number of official and unofficial West Indian delegations had arrived in Ottawa to appeal the way their country's subjects were treated.

Canada always seemed to listen, though it also always stopped short of taking action on issues related to Black immigration and the idea of merging with British possessions in the West Indies into a single political union.

The Negro Citizenship Association delegation, led by West Indians living in Canada, and with the blessing of governments in the British West Indies, was reminding the minister of the idealized perceptions of Canadian fairness and loyalty that were so central to its fraternal tradition. "In our appearance before you today," Moore said as he ended his presentation, "we bring no sword, no gun, no explosive, our only weapon is that of reason, justice, and love. We know that you will give ear to our requests, for our requests are reasonable, our cause is just, and the love of mankind surmounts all difficulties."[154]

But Stanley Grizzle was not so diplomatic when his turn came to speak. Boldly, he pointed out to the minister what he called "weaknesses" in Canada's immigration laws.

The members and officials of the Negro Citizenship Association and the Toronto C.P.R. Division of the Brotherhood of Sleeping Car Porters will continue to fight unremittingly for the right of all peoples of this planet to enter Canada and become its citizens without penalty or reward because of their race, colour, religion, national origin or ancestry. Yes, we take the uncompromising position that what appears to be premeditated discrimination in Canada's Immigration Laws and policy is utterly inconsistent with democratic principles and Christian ethics.[155]

Unlike Moore, Grizzle consistently referred to the Ottawa visit as a protest, a remonstrance by political agents against their government and its unjust policies. For him, the delegates were not begging forbearance. They were citizens demanding a specific action based on their democratic rights. Grizzle quoted recent statistics to back up his charge of discrimination through policy: total Negro immigration to Canada 1925–53: 4,122 people; total immigration to Canada 1945–53 alone: about 900,000 people, or 112,000 annually; total Negro immigration to Canada 1945–53: 1,417 or 177 annually; total Negro immigration from British dominions and colonies 1945–53: 728, or 104 annually. In the latter group were immigrants that could be classified as Black British subjects. With the quota on immigrants from South East Asia in mind, Grizzle indicated the situation was just as bad for Japanese immigration to Canada, which totalled only

93, or 12 persons annually between 1945 and 1953, and for the Chinese, whose numbers were 7,908, or 988 annually over the same period. To reinforce his point, Grizzle also showed statistically how European populations had grown in Canada from 1771 to 1951, while non-white groups had decreased, most markedly for Black people.

Grizzle represented a side of Blackness feared in some colonial quarters: that of the Black masses refusing to be quiet and acquiescent and demanding by right to be recognized fully as human. This perception of the resistant Negro had long troubled Canadian elites, who'd advocated for deeper commercial relations and even political union with the British West Indies, but who'd balked at having to contend with Black people asserting citizenship rights, including the democratic right to subvert the existing Canadian social order. In Grizzle and Moore, the Canadian government was faced with the enduring yin-yang of the two main embodiments of Blackness—one a militant, uncompromising demand for human rights; the other persuasively appealing to reason and justice in arguing for inclusion and recognition of citizenship rights; one captured in the history of such activists as Frederick Douglass, Marcus Garvey, and other militants in the emerging Civil Rights Movement in the United States, the other by earlier representatives in the same movement, such as Booker T. Washington, W. E. B. Du Bois, and, now, A. Philip Randolph of the Brotherhood of Sleeping Car Porters.

Grizzle saw their struggle and what was happening in Canada as part of a wider global social movement. He was not interested in improving conditions just for Blacks, but for all humanity. He believed Canada should open its doors to immigrants from around the world; that it should be multiracial and mirror the rest of the world demographically. In his presentation were the seeds for a Canada that would idealistically blossom forth as genuinely multicultural and inherently diversified, with all Canadians representing the entirety of the human race, living their social existence as authentically full citizens.

"I fail to see the consistency in asking China, Japan, India, Africa, or the West Indies to take a seat at the Council table," Grizzle said,

> if Chinese, Japanese, Indians, Africans or Afro-West Indians are unfit to live side by side with a Canadian. Mr. Minister, the Western races hold the predominance in material wealth and power. They evince in a hundred ways a determination to assert their superiority, and to keep other races in

a position of subordination and inferiority. It is against this very attitude peoples the world over are in revolt. But these people are rich spiritually, and justice will be exacted.

It is dangerous, strange and unfortunate that, under the terms of the Canadian Immigration Regulations, the term "British subject" does not include persons born or naturalized in British dominions or colonies of India, Pakistan, Ceylon, British West Indies, British Honduras, British Guiana, Bahamas and Bermuda. Is the reason because the total coloured population of these British territories is about 80 percent?"

To this last, rhetorical question, Grizzle quickly answered, "All indications point in that direction."

Canada could not sincerely believe, he said, that it would win friends and allies among the free nations of the world with a strategy that maintained the country for white men only.

In the interest of national and international welfare and security, this "Jim Crow Iron Curtain," which exists in Canada's Immigration Policy, must be eradicated immediately. This policy has long been established. It has not been confined to any single political administration—although this Government has religiously followed the program of Immigration by Discrimination. Although this administration cannot be held wholly responsible for the shameful policy of excluding from Canada desirable Black people who have been classified in the same group with undesirable reds, but this Parliament has the moral right and Christian duty to lift the hopes and aspirations of millions of the world's citizens of colour by welcoming them to become citizens of Canada and share with us the wealth which happens to be here.[156]

The reds Grizzle was referring to were the communists, who were not welcome in Canada, although he might also have been punning on the exclusion of Canada's Indigenous peoples as the "red men" of Canadian folklore.

Grizzle pointed out that different governments had followed this same immigration policy. The most recent iteration had occurred seven years earlier, when then-prime minister Mackenzie King, in a 1947 statement about immigration policy, said that Canada was open to immigration, indeed could not get enough immigrants, but that it did not want certain people as immigrants and would continue to keep them out in spite of the urgent and existential need for a larger population. Grizzle, obviously, had this speech in mind when drafting his statement, as several copies of it, with Grizzle's nota-tions, can be found in his archival papers. "The policy of the government," Prime Minister King had said on May 1, 1947, "is to foster the growth of the population of Canada by the encouragement of immigration. The gov-ernment will seek by legislation, by regulation and vigorous administration, to ensure the careful selection and permanent settlement of such numbers of immigrants as can advantageously be absorbed in our national economy."

Canada could not get enough immigrants from Europe, the prime min-ister had stated, because it was in competition with other countries for the same immigrants and there was not sufficient transportation available out of Europe. "The shortage of shipping means that Canada cannot secure more immigrants simply by changing laws and regulations. Since those persons we would be glad to welcome will not be able to come, the short-age of shipping also means that we have to decide to which immigrants prior opportunity to come to Canada is to be given," he said. This excuse about transportation had been cited consistently since Britain and the white dominions set up the arrangement in the 1920s so that Britain could defray the cost of transporting white immigrants mainly from England to the dominions. Despite its best marketing efforts in Britain and then west-ern Europe, Canada was not attracting white British subjects, or preferred Europeans, in desirable numbers. Under criticism at home, the government of the day claimed the main reason wasn't that people didn't want to come, but that there weren't enough ships available to bring them.

But Canada needed a larger population, and King's immigration policy was conceived to achieve this. The prime minister said that with a population of 12 million in 1948, Canada could expect, without immigration, to grow to only 14 million by 1971: "Apart from all else, in a world of shrinking distances and international insecurity, we cannot ignore the danger that lies in a small population attempting to hold so great a heritage as ours." Some people feared that increased immigration would lead to lower living stan-dards, but this shouldn't be the case with proper immigration planning, King said. "A larger population will help to develop our resources. By providing a larger number of consumers, in other words, a larger domestic market, it will reduce the general dependence of Canada on the export of primary products. The essential thing is that immigrants be selected with care, and that their numbers be adjusted to the absorptive capacity of the country."

This desirable rate of absorption included retaining the entry controls in place for non-white immigration, it being Canada's right to discriminate among immigrants and to maintain racial balance in the population. "There will, I am sure, be general agreement with the view that the people of Canada do not wish, as a result of mass immigration, to make a fundamental alteration to the character of our population," Prime Minister King said in what would become part of the oft-quoted doctrine behind Canadian immigration policy for the next generation, regardless of the ruling party.

"Large-scale immigration from the Orient would change the fundamental composition of the Canadian population," King said. "Any considerable Oriental immigration would, moreover, be certain to give rise to social and economic problems of a character that might lead to serious difficulties in the field of international relations. The government, therefore, has no thought of making any change in immigration regulations which would have consequences of the kind."[157] Moore, Grizzle, and their fellow Negro Citizenship Association delegates wanted government to disavow this racist policy forthwith.

"Honourable Minister," Grizzle ended his statement poignantly, "do not be recreant in facing your responsibility."[158] Indeed, it was doubtful other Black Canadians had ever spoken face-to-face with a government minister so forcefully and so directly. Undoubtedly, Grizzle's experience as a negotiator for the sleeping car porters—in which he found himself dealing with highly racialized issues confronting authority—had given him the gumption and audacity of a so-called *uppity Negro*. Grizzle knew the role history had handed him and he did not shirk from it. He wanted a new, inclusive citizenship for a new Canada.

Grizzle had sent copies of his speech as well as relevant newspaper clippings to A. Philip Randolph, his mentor in the trade union movement, who responded in a letter on January 13, 1954: "I want to congratulate you on this sound and progressive position. Unless people of color fight uncompromisingly for the status of complete equality in their community and country, no form of progress they make will be secure."[159] Grizzle was the prototype of a new kind of Canadian citizen: he was Black and he spoke back to power to hold it accountable.

THE MEETING BETWEEN THE DELEGATION and the minister took place six years after Canada had ratified the Canadian Citizenship Act of 1947 that formally established Canadian citizenship for the first time. Until then, Canadian citizenship technically didn't exist as a fact in law. People who identified as Canadian were, instead, legally British subjects born or naturalized in Canada. This gave them the right to live in Canada and to leave Canada and, as British subjects, to enter and live in Britain or any of its other colonies and dominions and to participate as freely as they wished in the social life of the new country.

In order to assert its sovereignty and self-determination, Canada had decided as of 1948 that it needed to cultivate an identity largely independent from its previous status as a British colony, and the Canadian Citizenship Act was an important part of this."[160] It had shown, using international law, that its citizenship was intended only for people of European ancestry, those born in the country and deemed native born, or those who were born elsewhere and immigrated to Canada, where they were naturalized as citizens. In this regard, Canada was taking a cue from its special partner in the British Commonwealth, the Union of South Africa, and from Australia, with its whites-only immigration policies. As a dominion, South Africa too had imposed racist limits on immigration and citizenship. Expatriates from the newly independent India living in South Africa had protested the social and political limits placed on them by South Africa's apartheid regime. India had protested on behalf of its citizens in South Africa, thereby creating disharmony in the British Commonwealth regarding the acceptance of immigrants from member countries and colonies. These were the "serious difficulties in international relationships" that Prime Minister King averred, and which Canada wanted to avoid by keeping out immigrants from Asia. Following South Africa's lead, Canada maintained annual quotas on immigrants from South East Asia, and, through government regulations, severely limited immigration from these countries.

As Donald Moore explained in his autobiography, the discovery of the orders-in-council prohibiting British West Indians as official government policy had come as one of several surprises for members of his Negro Citizenship Association. It is possible this discovery was made though Grizzle since, in his papers, there are several pieces of correspondence between himself and the government requesting copies of the regulations or explanations of their limits. With time, activists would rely heavily on Grizzle to ferret out such information from the government when it was needed to mount a campaign to stop routine deportations of Black West Indians. Even as a youngster in his native Barbados, Moore was indoctrinated to accept he was a British subject. That he was not considered a true British subject when he arrived in Canada was the "first shock [that] blasted the once proud boast of the West Indian: With head held high, as he smote his breast, he proclaimed to the world, 'I am a British subject, respected by all I meet.'"[161] It was a body blow to his perception of himself. Indeed *civis britannicus sum* was the proud identity of all in the empire, even, and some would say especially, those in the colonies.

This discovery of regulations limiting the rights of Black British subjects was all the more shocking given that residents of the British West Indies, who collectively boasted ancestral roots from around the world but mainly from Africa, had always proudly considered themselves to be loyal British subjects. In recalling the historic quote about what it meant to be a British subject, Moore was demonstrating the impact of British traditions on someone like him: a Black man living in the Empire who was psychologically British. He could call up, by memory, British iconography and myth as easily as any person who actually lived and was schooled in the mother country. After all, he was born and spent his formative years in Barbados, "Little England" in the lore of the Empire, an island whose people loyally identified with Britannia's trident and who were sometimes said to be more English in their traditions than England.

While British West Indians had a strong view of who they were, Canada's elites had strong opinions of people from the West Indies, with little room for reconciliation. As a result, the relationship between people from the British West Indies and Canadians were often complicatedly contradictory—at times viewed as potential fellow citizens and fellow British subjects; at others rejected as people of predominantly African ancestry who were too barbaric to be equal to white Canadians. As British subjects, didn't West Indian brothers and sisters have something in common with Canadians? Weren't they part of an alliance of British colonies and possessions in the Atlantic? In making their presentation, the members of the Negro Citizenship Association undoubtedly came armed with an appeal to history and civic perceptions. They were also ready to exploit the contradictory standings of West Indians and British subjects. First, however, the delegation had to confront the questions that continued to bedevil the relationship between Canada and the British West Indies: Exactly who were British West Indians? What should such British subjects look like? And how should they behave?

The delegation maintained pressure on the government even after it returned home. The Negro Citizenship Association and the Toronto division of the Brotherhood of Sleeping Car Porters continued to send letters and telegrams to petition the government to support their cause. Their allies also kept up the pressure, with J. W. Noseworthy continuing to question the minister of immigration for a response to the delegation's brief. Another ally putting pressure on the government was the Canadian Congress of Labour, which devoted an entire issue of its newsletter, *Comment On*, to Canadian immigration. The issue drew attention to the treatment of West Indians who did not qualify as British subjects under immigration regulations and who could not gain unimpeded entry into the country. "For immigration purposes, the privilege of a 'British subject' has been extended to [white] citizens of the United States, Ireland and France—but not to citizens of the British Commonwealth," columnist Gordon Milling wrote in the newsletter:

> Particularly in the case of the British West Indies this colour-categorization has produced considerable hardship. Each year a number of well-qualified persons from this region—Jamaica, Trinidad, Bahamas, Barbados—have entered Canada to pursue technical and professional courses in Canadian schools and universities. Under the present policy, their freedom while in this country is heavily circumscribed. They are prohibited from accepting employment in order to finance their education; an application for permanent residence invariably brings a deportation order, regardless of the individual circumstances; and every door but the port of exit is thoroughly blocked.[162]

Organizing the resistance to these issues would fall to Grizzle, who, in identifying as both Canadian and West Indian, exemplified the new Canadian. While born in Canada, Grizzle identified as West Indian because of his parents. Historically, Canada had always had a problem integrating and pacifying Black West Indians, who, as Moore suggested, proudly saw themselves as Black British subjects and were ready to fight for this recognition. As such, it was perhaps not surprising that a majority of the Ottawa delegation was West Indian—Canadians who proudly embraced both sides of their identity.

West Indians were traditionally viewed as a headache for Canadian social planners because they were believed to be incapable of assimilation. Even though they were socialized and educated as British, their skin colour made them incapable of becoming authentically Canadian. But once it was accepted that a Canadian citizen did not have to be white or European, a new ideal of the modern Canadian began to emerge. Individual citizens could now all be equally Canadian while maintaining their attachment to separate communities, cultures, histories, and identities. West Indians had known this way of living since the beginning of modernity, and theirs was the kind of approach Grizzle and his cohorts wanted for the future of Canada and Canadians.

A CREOLIZED COUNTRY
The Black British of the West Indies

STEEPED IN THE TRADITIONS OF British colonialism, West Indians perceived themselves as British. When Britain went to war, West Indian soldiers took up arms to fight alongside white and mixed-ethnic British subjects for the Empire's honour. They delighted in speaking the King's English and proudly practised English cultural norms. West Indian parliaments and social orders were based on the British Westminster system and jurisprudence, and in the case of Barbados and Jamaica even instituted parliamentary and legal precedents that were later incorporated in Canada and other British dominions. It was with pride that Barbados considered itself the Empire's Little England. West Indians played the English national sport cricket as passionately and as well as the English themselves. Stanley Grizzle, for example, proudly recalled his prowess as a cricketer, despite being born in Toronto and spending most of his life in the city.

West Indians were the products of the much-vaunted British education system; their intellectuals studied with and patterned themselves after the leading British academics, politicians, and moralists. Working-class West Indians from the turn of the twentieth century had been organized by trade unions patterned after the leftist British Fabian socialists, who made social welfare the hallmark right of citizenship in the mother country, and those unions later helped form durable political parties patterned on those in London. As was the case with Canada, several West Indian nations chose political independence as a confederation of islands, or even individually, while retaining British status as members of the Commonwealth. Elite West Indians fancied themselves as managers and administrators trained in the

British systems and they valued their British education, which they considered to be the best in the world. They were also used to living in multi-ethnic societies, where people of different ethnicities lived together as British subjects equal before the law, a prototype for what would later be called multiculturalism. In schools, churches, union halls, and mass political meetings, West Indians discussed the burning political and social issues of the day. Of central importance was how Black people—especially those whose ancestors were slaves—should be recognized as free men and women living under, and contributing to, the democratic government of their making—an ideal to which Canada aspired. They treated, with utter disdain, the idea that Canada would dare strip them of this essential part of their identity.

Barbados-born Austin Clarke arrived in Toronto in 1954 in the midst of this political activism and would write about the period in his fiction and non-fiction on his way to becoming one of Canada's most celebrated authors. But as a contemporary of Grizzle and the members of the Ottawa delegation, Clarke would always caution that, though a Canadian, he was ultimately a Barbadian, particularly a Black Englishman, as he was taught and socialized to believe when he was growing up in the Caribbean. Writing specifically of Barbados, he noted in his memoir *'Membering* the sense of self and ambition that were inculcated in his generation in the 1940s and even earlier in high school:

> We were the new leaders: boys being turned into men. We knew that each of us would be in the vanguard to lead the Island, a Crown Colony into independence, would be the constitutional lawyers to trade intricacies with the colonizing English up in Westminster, would be the permanent secretary to guide the files in the right direction to keep their secrets confidential, would be the headmaster to guide the coming generation following our 'example.' Or, with the choice and cockiness of ambition, could, if we wanted to, become the most notorious murderer, thief, criminal, gambler throwing dice under a tamarind tree, in any neighbourhood; or be a seaman, or stoking furnaces in a broiler room on a merchant ship, roaring like the fires of hell, but making 'good money' from it; or, going to America and Panama and becoming a stowaway when faced with the majesty and promise of the Statue of Liberty.[163]

And, of course, becoming sleeping porters in Canada too.

Clarke was describing the construction of the quintessentially modern Enlightenment Man, rootedly rootless, independent of mind in an independent society of his choice and making, transnational in spirit, tied not to history but to the present and the future, and above all self-made. Not only were Clarke and his classmates going to make themselves into creatures of their own likeness and imagination, the essence of self-determination, they would do the same for the world itself. And what was true for the boys and men was equally true for the girls and women. Here in these new human beings were the good and bad of European and African histories, reconciled into a spirit that opened up vistas of choice and opportunity to the one who dared. Clarke shared this view with his friend Derek Walcott, born in the neighbouring British island of St. Lucia, who also spent time in Toronto on his way to the Nobel Prize in literature for a body of work that celebrated the modern specimen of humanity that was the West Indian.

"Our possibilities began at the top of the scaffold of ambitiousness," Clarke wrote in his Barbadian cadence, deliberately. "And these possibilities swarmed over each step on the ladder of social and moral decorum in the Island. The Island is the Island of Barbados. A Crown Colony. 'Bimshire' Little England." It was not coincidental that Clarke capitalized the first letter in Island, for it was common to capitalize the letter when talking about the British Isles, and for him there was no real difference, save for location, between the two places. The possibilities for Clarke not only included rising to acclaim in Canadian and British Commonwealth literature, but, after a spell at such American universities as Yale, to be counted among the pioneers of what came to be known as African-American or Black Studies.

"The irony in the last two names, 'Bimshire' and 'Little England,' stamped us, for life and made us act like black Englishmen: in our upbringing, in our attitude towards one another, and towards other West Indians [...] We were English, British. Britannia ruled the waves. This was our virtue. And it became, through our indoctrination, our ideological and moral liability. We were loved and disliked in equal proportion of intensity, by other West Indians, because of these two 'virtues'."[164] With this attitude, Black West Indians believed that in the British pecking order they were already as good as, or even ranked higher than, Canadians, for they were as good as the top-ranking British themselves.

West Indians also saw themselves as politically mature as any other educated British subject, and those in government and the upper classes put themselves on par socially with fellow subjects in white dominions like Canada, New Zealand, Australia, and South Africa. West Indians were above all loyal British subjects, with the exception perhaps of those who'd migrated to the United States over this same period and joined the struggle for civil rights and African redemption. But even then, because they were West Indians, it was still assumed they retained a British allegiance beneath their Americanism. In all facets, British West Indians were proud to be part of the so-called British civilization and often pointed to themselves as examples of the Empire's redeeming values on non-Europeans.

West Indians, though predominantly Black, thought themselves a special breed of people. Cultural critic and anthropologist M.G. Smith captured this feeling in *The Plural Society in the British West Indies*, his pioneering book on pluralism in the Caribbean.

> The British Caribbean culture is one form of Creole culture. The Creole complex has its historical base in slavery, plantation systems, and colonialism. Its cultural composition mirrors its racial mixture. European and African elements predominate in fairly standard combinations and relationships. The ideal forms of institutional life, such as government, religion, family and kinship, law, property, education, economy, and language are of European derivation; in consequence, differing metropolitan affiliations produce differing version of Creole culture. But in their Creole contexts, these institutional forms diverge from their metropolitan models in greater or lesser degree to fit local conditions. This local adaptation produces a Creole institutional complex which differs from the metropolitan model.

This raised the question of who was an authentic West Indian, and what to make of that identity, especially within the imperial Commonwealth of Nations:

> Without explicit recognition of this fundamental Negro-white combination within the Creole complex, it is difficult either to specify the distinctive features of West Indian life and culture, or to understand how other ethnic groups and traditions fit into it. The Negro-white complex which has been formative for the West Indies diverges sharply in its racial and cultural components. In this area Negroes outnumber whites markedly, and have done so for centuries; but European institutions and cultural models predominate. The Creole configuration that reflects the particulars of this association is so unique because of this imbalance and historical depth. The West Indian-bred white is not culturally European, nor is the West

Indian-bred black culturally African. Naturally, in view of its predominance, the European component in Creole culture has undergone less obvious modification than its African counterpart; but it has been modified, there can be no doubt [....] It is only with this multiracial Creole complex that West Indians can identify as West Indians. Whatever their racial affiliations, self-declared West Indians implicitly refer to this amalgam in which the basic racial and cultural elements are white and Negro, and society is that mode of their association to which important elements from other traditions are selectively accommodated.[165]

The place of British West Indians in the British Empire and Commonwealth and the rights they could claim as British subjects—as opposed to British *objects*, mere colonized peoples without recognition, rights, or privileges—was for a long time part of the narrative of nationhood and state formation in the Americas. As products of European Enlightenment, these people of predominantly African descent living in the New World believed themselves to be as much the epitome of the liberal dream of manhood as any other European. Jamaican intellectual Louis S. Meikle wrote, just after the turn of the twentieth century, about West Indians searching for a place in the civilized world and of the need to consider their own nationhood. His book *Confederation of the British West Indies versus Annexation to the United States of America* was popular and provocative. The book was a response to the open secret that Britain was considering withdrawing from the British West Indies, leaving a vacuum that many experts at the time felt would be filled by one of the three potential regional behemoths, Brazil, the United States, or Canada, as the new colonial masters. Among other things, it argued for the recognition of the British West Indies as a politically viable nation state that could take its place in the hemisphere beside Canada, the United States, Brazil, and other Latin American countries.

In this regard, Meikle was riffing off a suggestion that had been gaining currency toward the end of the nineteenth century: that Britain had produced a unique type of subject, "Black British" in the Caribbean who were capable of ruling themselves. These subjects had evolved enough to be socially responsible and to claim the same parliamentary system that Britain eventually offered to Canada and the other dominions. But at that point, the dominant social order seemed to be in flux. Canada was still an evolving federation, with the provinces Alberta and Saskatchewan yet to join. Newfoundland and Labrador and the British West Indian possessions were separate colonies. Throughout the British Empire, particularly in debates in the United Kingdom, it was argued that if Britain were to withdraw from directly administering its Atlantic colonies—the introduction of the Monroe Doctrine in the US that was the catalyst for this discussion opposed British colonialism in the region—it would be best to confederate them into one state.

Others before Miekle had raised this as a possibility, such as C. S. Salmon, a top British colonial figure. "The point aimed at in this book is to show the fitness of the black British subject in the West Indies for admission into the communities of the British Empire by allowing them together with the white races in these colonies to share in the privileges of British subjects everywhere—by having a full share in their local government," wrote Salmon, a former president of the West Indian island of Nevis, in 1888. Salmon had served in several roles as a British colonial administrator, including stints as colonial secretary and administrator of the Gold Coast and chief commissioner of the Seychelles islands. In retirement, he became a prolific and much-read commentator on British colonial matters. "Where the machinery of local self-government does not exist, in accordance with British ideas it is useful that the same be at once set up. It is recommended to unite the whole British West Indies into one confederacy."[166]

The units of this confederacy would be Antigua (with Barbuda), the Bahamas archipelago, Barbados, Dominica, Grenada (with parts of the Grenadines), Guiana in South America, Honduras in Central America, Jamaica (with the Turks and Caicos Islands), Montserrat, St. Kitts-Nevis (with Anguilla), St. Lucia, St. Vincent (with the remainder of the Grenadines), Tobago, Trinidad, and the Virgin Islands. While the confederation's population would be predominantly Black, its member states would be white in "specialization" or orientation and socialization.

"It is impossible to dissociate the black British subject in the West Indies from the kindred races of Africa," Salmon said to emphasize that this confederation would be exceptional in the Empire—it would be African and Black.

What one may be the other may be. If the British people and their Government fail to place their black fellow subjects in the West Indies on an equal footing within the Empire with the white races, they will be using their position to perpetuate a wrong, or rather to prolong it, for in all human probability to perpetuate it they will not be able. They will be prolonging a social and a political blunder. By giving the black subjects of the Crown some of those rights they themselves enjoy, the British people will be using for a good purpose that position of vantage they now possess; a position which enables them to do that which will be an honour to themselves and a profit to the Empire.[167]

Although they weren't united by membership in a single country, British West Indians were perceived as singular in attitude and social philosophy—and it was all because of their Britishness. This was particularly true of those British West Indians who lived in the United States, especially in Harlem, where many joined the vanguard of the Civil Rights movement. "To the average American Negro," wrote W. A. Domingo at the height of the Harlem Renaissance in the first quarter of the nineteenth century, "all English-speaking black foreigners are West Indians, and by that is usually meant British subjects. There is a general assumption that there is everything in common among West Indians, though nothing can be further from the truth. West Indians regard themselves as Antiguans or Jamaicans as the case might be, and a glance at the map will quickly reveal the physical obstacles that militate against homogeneity of population; separation of many sorts, geographical, political and cultural tend everywhere to make and crystallize local characteristics."

In this separateness or insularity, Domingo argued, lay the strength of these transplanted West Indians. They were accustomed to leadership positions because their smaller island societies required good management from people of all social strata and racial background:

> Social gradation is determined in the islands by family connections, education, wealth and position. As each island is a complete society in itself, Negroes occupy from the lowliest to the most exalted positions. The barrier separating the colored aristocrat from the laboring class of the same color is as difficult to surmount as a similar barrier between Englishmen. Most of the islanders in New York are from the middle, artisan and laboring classes. Arriving in a country whose every influence is calculated to democratize their race and destroy the distinction they had been accustomed to, even those West Indians whose station in life have been of the lowest soon lose whatever servility they brought with them. In place they substitute all of the self-assertiveness of the classes they formerly paid deference to.

As a result, West Indians were industrious, calculating, and self-assertive—distinctly British traits. This meant, wrote Domingo, that

> coming to the United States from countries in which they had experienced no legalized social or occupational disabilities, West Indians very naturally

have found it difficult to adapt themselves to the tasks that are, by custom, reserved for Negroes in the North. Skilled at various trades and having a contempt for body service and menial work, many of the immigrants applying for positions that the average American Negro has been schooled to regard as restricted to white men only, with the result that through their persistence and doggedness in fighting white labor, West Indians have in many cases been pioneers and shock troops to open a way for Negroes into new fields of employment.[168]

This was in addition, Domingo added, to starting their own businesses and seeking to buy homes in traditionally white neighbourhoods.

In Louis S. Meikle's conception, there were no real racial distinctions between West Indians, for they were all British subjects living in the British West Indian possessions as the colonies were then called. And by "West Indian," Meikle pointedly meant the "children of immigrants, both white and black, and their offspring born in the West Indies—the aborigines being mostly extinct." This confederation would be noted for its special people, who by definition would be Negro or Black but of such a mixing of cultures so as to make its population unique. Having benefitted fully from British civilization, this confederation of islands would help advance civilization within the existing British Empire. "We want to be looked upon as part and parcel of the British nation," he wrote. "We want to equip ourselves as to be in a position to take up our share of the burden of the defence of the Empire."[169]

But Meikle also understood that life was not easy for West Indians outside of the British West Indies, primarily because the majority of West Indians were racially African but also mixed with other races and ethnicities, resulting in questionable ethnoracial authenticity. As Meikle said at the time of his writing, 90 percent of British subjects in the West Indies were "of negro descent and consequently, of mixed blood. Their freedom of action and liberty have gone on unrestricted for generations." Then there were those, according to Meikle, that the Americans described as "West Indian Whites," those who "have taken up the guise and demeanour of the Europeans, with the title of 'white' to boot. And imitating the 'jackdaw in peacock's feathers,' they 'strut along' among the illiterate under the garb of 'white men.'" This was a social practice commonly referred to as "passing," where people that otherwise would be classified as Black under dominant social standards were treated as if they are white. According to this classification, a "Jamaican white" might not be fully European. "These 'West Indian Whites,' were they to be told that they are negroes, with a view of circumscribing their sphere of action or social standing, would be rudely shocked at the seemingly uncalled for remark, that they would actually have to stop and look at their hands before they would realize what was really meant".[170]

Added to this mix were West Indians whose backgrounds included ancestors from places like China, South East Asia, and other parts of the world. Together, they formed the first modern societies not defined by an exclusive ethnicity, race, or nationality. The West Indians that emerged from this hodgepodge had one thing in common: a non-differentiable British subjecthood. In a somewhat ironic twist on the meaning of the coloured line, Meikle argued that "the West Indies have no colour question of any moment to solve, in the broad sense of the term."

Any real difference among British subjects in the West Indies, he argued, was based in class, not race. Without saying it directly, Meikle was intimating that the British West Indies was, like Canada, avoiding a Negro question.

[I]t must be borne in mind, that the people of the Dominion are not entirely different in sentiment from the people of the United States on the race question," Meikle wrote. "It is a common occurrence for East Indian and Japanese immigrants to be mobbed in Canada, and at times the situation has become so critical that military force has had to be summoned to quell the disturbances. The Negro in Canada is not exempted, and comes in for his share of outrage, notwithstanding that the strong arm of the law is always ready to protect everyone; but as the Dominion, like the United States, is essentially a white man's country, it is not possible to avert such eventualities.

Meikle's knew that life was not easy for Black people in Canada.

Quite recently (June 1910) two coloured students of medicine—British subjects from the Island of Trinidad—were refused admittance to a public anatomical show, held at Montreal, on account of their colour. They were kicked and beaten for no other reason than that they had the courage to go up to the ticket window and ask to be sold tickets for admission. These instances suffice to illustrate, in absence of any other, that the white people of the Dominion are no less drastic on the race problem than their American neighbours, the only difference between the two is, that your legal rights are recognized and treated impartially in the law courts of the former. While in the latter the Negro has no legal status.[171]

Canadian elites knew that any political union with British West Indians would not only force Canada to confront its own Negro problem, but would encourage the emigration into the country of the wrong type of Black people: those who were crass and uppity enough to think they were as good as whites. As Domingo had stated: "The outstanding contribution of West Indians to American Negro life is the insistent assertion of their manhood in an environment that demands too much servility and unprotesting acquisition from men of African blood. This unwillingness to conform and be standardized, to accept tamely an inferior status and abdicate their humanity, finds an open expression in the activities of the foreign-born Negro in America."[172] Given the dominance of this narrative about British West Indians, it was no surprise that Canada would, in 1923, formally strip them of their Britishness, thereby denying them the automatic right granted to other British subjects to immigrate to Canada.

When the Ottawa delegation met with Canadian government officials in 1954, it was common knowledge that the rights and freedoms of West Indian British subjects had already been regularly raised as a question of social justice. In the international racialized hierarchies of ethnicities, nationalism, and civilizations, British West Indians saw themselves as occupying the same high rung as Englishmen. In fact, elite Black West Indians saw themselves as Black Englishmen who could seamlessly fit into any British social order. That status was conferred on them by the social influence of British civilization, which, they boasted, was noted for its perfect mix of benevolence and the fear of the colonial whip.

Ironically, in the mind of British West Indians, this placement not only positioned them socially ahead of all other groups and races in Africa, Asia, and North America, but ahead of all those Eastern and Southern Europeans who, in the dominant British narrative, were inferior to the English. At the same time, this socialization and the resulting attitude—often described as arrogant—left British West Indians open to special teasing from other Blacks, who called them King George Negroes, Banana Eaters, Monkey Chasers, or Monkey Eaters. These sentiments were also expressed by Black Canadians, who either borrowed the inter-ethnic animus from Black

Americans or from their own interactions with West Indian immigrants, who were generally viewed as self-centred, pushy, uncivilized, uncouth, and lacking in understanding about their adopted society. The porters helped to spread and also battle these inter-tribal sentiments across North America, but because of the conditions faced by all Black people, and the opportunities the railways gave for different Black groups to coexist, these differences were usually held in abeyance, primarily through the influence of the unions.

By the early 1950s, West Indian Blacks believed they were full British subjects with the right to Canadian citizenship. The demand for the right of entry to Canada came not only from Blacks still in the Caribbean but those who had migrated to the British Isles and, on second thought, decided to move on to Canada. Both groups found their paths into Canada blocked by government regulations. In stark contrast, a West Indian of proven and pure European ancestry had no difficulty moving to Canada. To rectify this situation, members of the Negro Citizenship Association and the Brotherhood of Sleeping Car Porters turned to their government allies.

Leading members of the Negro Citizenship Association and the porter unions in Canada were British West Indians or their descendants. They were multi-generational British subjects with extensive roots in the British Empire. For generations, the Canadian railways and shipping lines had recruited Caribbean Blacks as porters and seamen, with the workers often spending part of the year working on railways and their down time on the ships.

Because of this connection, many West Indian porters in Canada became prominent union organizers. Arthur Robinson, who hailed from St. Kitts, established the Order of Sleeping Car Porters, the first union of Black workers in North America and the forerunner of the Brotherhood of Sleeping Car Porters, which organized Pullman porters across North America, with its Canadian branches under the direction of A.R. Blanchette, also a native of St. Kitts and a relative of Robinson's. Charles Ernest Russell, a native of Barbados based in Montreal, was organizing porters on the Canadian Pacific Railway at the same time. Both Robinson and Russell—reportedly working independently of each other, although that was unlikely in such a small industry—were lobbying the iconic Black labour leader A. Philip Randolph to set up branches of the sleeping car porters union in Canada. When Randolph did establish the new branches, Blanchette was the main Canadian field organizer, a position he held for almost four decades.

Indeed, scholars such as John Walter argue that the unionization of Black workers in North America was primarily the effort of West Indians, including the triumphs of the Brotherhood of Sleeping Car Porters under Randolph. Walter points out that while Randolph is known as the founder of the union, "Upon close examination, it is evident that Randolph was aroused as a result of contact with a number of West Indian immigrants. The first to influence Randolph was Hubert Harrison, who justly deserved the title 'The Father of Harlem Radicalism,' which had been conferred upon him by W. A. Domingo. As Harlem's earliest and most influential street corner orator and union organizer, he persuaded Randolph and his partner, Chandler Owen, to join the Socialist Party in 1914, and soon thereafter Randolph himself appeared on the street corners espousing Socialist doctrine."

Harrison, born in 1883 in St. Croix, the Virgin Islands, was a leading member of the West Indian community in Harlem, where much of the political and communal life revolved around the Association of West Indians clubs. Although it was dominated by British West Indians, the federation was open to all associations representing the peoples of the Caribbean. But because of his parentage (Harrison's father was a Barbadian), and because he was born before his homeland became part of the US Virgin Islands in 1917, he was also a British subject, a situation shared by many Blacks in the Virgin Islands whose parents hailed from the Anglophone Caribbean. But in promoting socialism for Black people—a prominent position in the West Indies, where trade unionism was on the rise—Harrison was openly at odds with the two dominant camps representing the aspirations of American Blacks: the National Association for the Advancement of Colored People, led by W. E. B. Du Bois, and the less radical disciples of Booker T. Washington.

"Randolph's first two major areas of influence on the political scene were his magazine, *The Messenger*, and his leadership of the Brotherhood of Sleeping Car Porters, Workers, and Maids," Walter writes. "In both of these ventures, West Indian immigrants played the initial and essential role. Between 1917 and 1923, Randolph and Owen started more than half-a-dozen political and trade union organizations, all of which failed within a short time. When asked, however, by two West Indians, Ashley Totten and Thomas T. Patterson, to head up the Pullman Porters Brotherhood, Randolph became a success."[173]

The porters' struggle was seamless, in spite of the national borders separating the workers and organizers. As historian Winston James says in *Holding Aloft the Banner of Ethiopia: Caribbean Radicalism in early Twentieth-Century America*, "one of the most intriguing sociological and historical facts about American radicalism in the twentieth century has been the prominence and often pre-eminence of Caribbean migrants among its participants."[174] This was true in Canada as well, with the struggle for civil rights and social acceptance often occurring in a transnational space that bound the Caribbean, the United States, the UK, and Canada in the same struggle for liberation. Usually, it was the migrants from the West Indies who were most likely to cross these different national spaces in their search for a better life and to find a permanent home free of the memory and residue of chattel slavery. For them, the struggle was the same regardless of location, an attitude that undoubtedly infused the Black railway porters and seamen circulating across North America and linking the Caribbean, Latin America, and North America into a potential homeland for Black hemispheric peoples.

So the key questions were not only who was a British subject, but also who, or what, was a West Indian. The delegation to Ottawa suggested that the cultures and even passions of West Indians and British subjects were inseparable, and as British subjects they were as qualified as any other European group to become good Canadian citizens. And there was no doubt that the delegates had the backing of the governments of the British West Indies in taking this message to Ottawa.

Four years after the delegation arrived in Ottawa and Grantley Adams officially became the prime minister of the Federation of the British West Indians, he and other political leaders were free to more openly press their case for greater Canadian and West Indian cooperation, including easier immigration from the region into Canada. In an address to the Empire Club in Toronto on October 23, 1958, days after meeting Prime Minister John Diefenbaker in Ottawa, Adams said he hoped the two federations would forge a relationship that extended far beyond the standard protocols and trade duties, one that would lead to a renewed British Commonwealth family. Importantly, he wanted the two nation states to see themselves as equals based strictly on British values, not ethnic racialization.

The West Indian prime minister, preparing his audience for the crux of his speech, said:

So far I have been speaking in terms of politics, constitutions, trade and economics. However, I am far from unmindful of the fact that your Club is closely concerned with Commonwealth affairs. Indeed, I understood that its official purpose is to advance the interests of Canada within the strong ties of the British Commonwealth. It is therefore only right that before I close I should say something about the Commonwealth link that binds our two countries together. Unlike the former American Colonies which, as the United States of America, achieved independence in defiance of Britain, British West Indians have united, and are on the threshold of self-government, under British guidance and with Britain's blessing. The West Indies, like Canada, have for generations followed the British way of life, and the Commonwealth tie is as strong with us as it is with you. We have the same respect as you for British traditions of parliamentary democracy and the supremacy of the Courts of Justice. Thus the constitutional advance, which is now taking place in The West Indies, will serve to strengthen our attachment to the Commonwealth. An association, which is now taken for granted, because of our colonial status will become a conscious, and therefore more valuable, act of deliberate choice. It is on this, I might almost say, spiritual plane that we think that the West Indies can make a positive and unique contribution to the Commonwealth ideal.

But even then, Adams had to acknowledge that West Indians were enigmatic, sometimes even to themselves. They were colonial people, but different from most others elsewhere; the majority of the people were descendants of slaves, but their schooling and culture were different from other slave descendants in the Americas. And unlike others who had suffered slavery and colonialism, West Indians had become nation founders and nation builders—without having to resort to armed conflict. "As you know," Adams said,

we constitute one of the most remarkable multiracial communities in the world, and it is no accident that we have chosen as a motto for our new Federation a phrase that epitomizes the Commonwealth ideal: 'To dwell together in unity.' Our people have their origins in Africa, in Europe, in India, and in China, to an extent that today a West Indian cannot say, 'I am a European or an African;' he can only say 'I am a West Indian.' The very existence of The West Indies is a refutation of the myth of racial superiority, and we pride ourselves that we can bring to the Commonwealth community a successful demonstration that race and colour are matters of no significance in the context of human dignity and endeavour.

The new nation led by Adams was a paragon of diversity, one founded by different ethnic and racial groups based on equality of citizenship and a common sense of belonging, despite historic differences. He said:

> In the first place, since the Napoleonic Wars, these islands have all been British Colonies, with the British Government and the Colonial Office serving to maintain common patterns of administration and holding out the ultimate aim of self-government within the British Commonwealth. In The West Indies we all have the same respect for British traditions of parliamentary democracy and the supremacy of the courts of justice. When we say that we wish to break away from colonialism and secure the right to order our own affairs as we choose, we are all thinking about the same thing—the creation of a free society based on respect for one another. There is no danger of independence bringing with it the emergence of violent inner conflicts, which, in some other parts of the world, have come to the surface with the removal of imperial government. In the second place [...], we are linked together by a common faith in our ability to create a nation in which race and colour cease to have significance. We are well on the way to being a truly multi-racial community, a people with diversity of racial background but with identity of outlook and purpose.[175]

This was not the only time a West Indian leader had brought the message of a state built on racial harmony to Canada. Premier of Jamaica Norman Manley had painted a picture of the creation of a new country in the Americas that transcended all languages, ethnicities, racialization, and any other categorization used to discriminate among humanity. Manley and Adams were among a group of West Indian leaders meeting in 1957 at a conference at Mount Allison Summer Institute in Sackville, New Brunswick, to discuss with Canadian political and business leaders how a West Indian federation could work and how Canada could support the fledgling union. But at the same time, the British West Indies provided Canada with the model of an organic multiracial society, where peoples of the world could live together and where issues of tolerance and acceptance were taken for granted. Dominance and privilege based on ethnicity would have no place in such a society; everyone, regardless of background, would be treated as a citizen with the same opportunities as any other citizen.

"Today we are a mixture of peoples drawn from all over Europe," Manley said, "from Africa, and in later days from India and from China. We truly represent one of the most remarkable multiracial communities in the world and that in itself is a bond of association and familiarity between us all." This was a lesson the West Indies could teach to other parts of the world.

> I dare to say that the West Indies has travelled hundreds of years ahead of large parts of the world in solving the problems of how people of different races and origins can live together in harmony. One has only to look around this room to comprehend that we have completely exploded the myth of racial superiority, and we are rapidly progressing to a higher level in that field than most countries know because with us it is ceasing to be a matter of tolerance, for tolerance itself supposes that there is something to be tolerated. And it is ceasing to be a matter of acceptance because acceptance in itself supposes that there is some problem to overcome and some difficulty to be accepted.

Through its social evolution the British West Indies was rapidly becoming a community where natural differences had no social importance and where the liberal value of tolerance was more than just a word. "We are truly learning to be part each of the other without consideration of anything except natural human feeling, affection and respect," Manley concluded. "And that is a very great and significant achievement."[176]

Many of the delegates visiting Ottawa in 1954 saw no reason why Canada could not, like the West Indies, refute the myth of white racial superiority. This message of universal brotherhood resonated with Grizzle and Blanchette, who wanted Canada to adopt the same ethno-racial model as the British West Indies. Even the American civil rights leader Martin Luther King Jr. saw the British West Indies as a place where much of what he described in his "American Dream" speech had already been realized.

In a sermon at Ebenezer Baptist Church in Atlanta, Georgia, on July 4, 1965, King spoke about how the American Dream he proudly described only two years earlier had become a nightmare. But even then King again gave his listeners a very concrete reason for why he still had hope and why they should too. He told his congregation a story of having visited a better place, one in which the American Negro could only dream of living:

> The other day Mrs. King and I spent about ten days down in Jamaica. I'd gone down to deliver the commencement address at the University of the

West Indies. I always love to go to that great island, which I consider the most beautiful island in all the world. The government prevailed upon us to be their guests and spend some time and try to get a little rest while there on the speaking tour. And so for those days we traveled all over Jamaica. And over and over again I was impressed by one thing. Here you have people from many national backgrounds: Chinese, Indians, so-called Negroes, and you can just go down the line, Europeans, European and people from many, many nations. Do you know they all live there and they have a motto in Jamaica, "Out of many people, one people." And they say, "Here in Jamaica we are not Chinese, we are not Japanese, we are not Indians, we are not Negroes, we are not Englishmen, we are not Canadians. But we are all one big family of Jamaicans." One day, here in America, I hope that we will see this and we will become one big family of Americans. Not white Americans, not black Americans, not Jewish or Gentile Americans, not Irish or Italian Americans, not Mexican Americans, not Puerto Rican Americans, but just Americans. One big family of Americans.[177]

This was the message of fraternal well-being based on the elimination of racialization and the acceptance and recognition of the diversity of humanity that the sleeping car porters embedded in their statement to the Canadian government. What Adams and Manley wanted for the British West Indies, the delegates wanted for Canada: a recognized creolized country that was proud of its colonial history and its multiracial and multilingual population, where representatives from all over the world would live in fraternal harmony, where individual citizens would not simply describe themselves as African, European, Indian, or Chinese, but as Canadian.

None of the members in the delegation to Ottawa believed he or she— nor any other person classified as a Negro—was fully a Canadian citizen even though they were British subjects. Still, they were proud Negroes, people who believed in what they called Negro Pride, even to the point of engaging the queen's publisher in Ottawa in 1955 in a debate demanding the capitalization of the first letter in Negro as a sign of respect. This is a fight they lost initially, but *Hansard,* the official report of parliamentary debates, would eventually capitalize the first letter in Negro, even if by then the term was falling into disrepute before being ultimately banished from polite conversation. What Black people clearly were not was "niggers," a term designating a class of people who were considered subhuman and unworthy of citizenship. More than asserting this pride and showing themselves worthy of the accepted descriptor of being a credit to the race, those who were Black British subjects were a special type of Negro. For it was their "Britishness" that would make them the equal to all other Canadian citizens, who were, ultimately, fellow British subjects.

As their statement to the federal government made clear, the Ottawa delegation aimed to bring full citizenship not only to Canadian Negroes but all ethnic and racial groups who would later be lumped together under the term "visible minorities." At the time, that designation included not only the Blacks, Chinese, and South East Asian communities, but several European ethnicities not yet fully assimilated into Canada's dominant Anglo Saxon or French Canadian identities and cultures. The aim of the delegation was to force the political powers to examine the dialectics of history that had brought Canada to this specific point in time, and then to determine what lessons could be learned for the future. Canada was called upon to determine which historical practices were no longer acceptable and ought not to be repeated. The country also had to choose civic practices that could lead to a brighter collective future. The railway porters' brief in Ottawa spoke to the conscience of Canada, reminding the nation state of its racist past but also calling upon Canada to forge a new national identity, one constructed with, and out of, a diverse community of people from around the world.

A PARALLEL AWAKENING IN BLACK communities across Canada also informed the delegation's mission. Three years earlier, the Negro Citizenship Association had been formed to address the frustration of Blacks who realized their lives did not fully matter in Canada. The association's founder, Don Moore, was frustrated by the lot of Black West Indians and their complaints about unequal treatment, especially with regard to immigration. "By 1950," he recalled, "the unequal treatment of Black West Indians seeking entry into Canada became public knowledge. Close relatives and visitors of Canadian citizens were refused entrance and a few who had managed to get in were detained under house arrest or held in the (Toronto) Don Jail. A few were deported to their native lands."

> It was quite distressing to me to listen to the many sad stories I heard over the counter of my (dry cleaning) store from customers and from those directly affected personally and financially by such circumstances. When I began to give the matter a closer look, I discovered no one knew who appeals should be addressed to. No one knew on what grounds the refusal

was made other than the patented reply: 'Your application has been care-fully reviewed but I have to advise you that it does not meet the require-ments of the Immigration Act and regulation. I regret to inform you that no further action can be taken with your application.'

The saddest part of all was that so many in the community had become fatalistic, dismissing these incidents with a shrug of the shoulder and the oft-repeated phrase: "Those white people don't want Negroes in their country."[178]

Harry Gairey, another founding member of the association, saw the frus-tration arising from the unequal treatment at his own place of employ-ment. "The chief aim (of the association)," he recalled, "was to try and break up this immigration problem, because I knew that it was discrim-inatory. Working around (Toronto's) Union Station as I did, I saw all of the immigrants coming in, but no Blacks, not a trickle. I saw a number of immigrants from countries that we'd been fighting, Italy, Germany, all over. The Europeans were coming in, but no Blacks."[179] Clearly, in Gairey's eyes, those immigrants were not as deserving as those from the Caribbean, whose loyalty to the British Empire could never be questioned.

But as Moore said, the frustrations and silent grumbling were nothing new. What was new was the decision by the Black community to work for change. The timing was right. Blacks in Canada were maturing politically, and much of this maturity could be traced directly to the lessons porters had learned after five decades of fighting to better their working conditions. Some of the best Black thinkers—those who aspired to become profes-sionals, artists, academics, and intellectuals—were numbered among the porters, but they had been held back because of their skin colour. But these restrictions increased rather than curbed their desire for the knowledge and learning that would set them free.

The railway porters were uniquely positioned to the take temperature of the times. They discussed the news of day on the trains and back home in their communities. In their minds, they would resolve international and domestic disputes alike, rationalizing the greater meaning of life and the destiny of human kind. The followers and practitioners of every academic discipline and profession could be found amongst the porters and the wider Black community. In spite of this, Blacks in Canada did not enjoy the dig-nity of being human and the opportunity to improve their own positions and give life to their dreams. They were not free to enjoy the social mobility that would allow the next generation to better itself, bringing a familial improvement in status, prestige, and even wealth. Instead, they were confined to living what might very well be described as unexamined lives. Mentally, they were never free. Even more stultifying was the awareness that those of a different skin complexion were free to chase their dreams and to enjoy social mobility, even if their abilities and training were inferior. Freedom of opportunity was not open to them as Black Canadians, and as a result they were denied social justice and equal opportunity. Complicit in this oppression was the nation state, which the porters and other Blacks expected to deliver protection and advancement in return for their loyalty and responsibilities as good citizens.

THE STRONG PERSONALITIES AND CHARACTERISTICS West Indians often exhibited did not always aid the cause of Black unity in Canada. From the 1950s onwards, several attempts to establish a national body representing Blacks in Canada—somewhat similar to the National Association for the Advancement of Coloured People or the Student Nonviolent Coordinating Committee in the US—failed because of differences between West Indian groups and the so-called "indigenous Blacks" who claimed a longer ancestral presence in the country. Questions about power sharing between the newcomers and the historically embedded Black people in Canada bedeviled community affairs, just as they had in the US. Even when the Negro Citizenship Association was leading the fight for improved non-white immigration to Canada it was beset by internal problems, some of which alarmed their allies in the human rights community.

Gordon Milling, executive secretary for the Toronto Labour Committee to Combat Racial Intolerance, wrote to Montreal-based Kalmen Kaplansky, director of the Jewish Labour Committee, in a confidential letter on March 2, 1953, a month before the delegation presented its brief in Ottawa:

> The Negro Citizenship committee is not getting along too well. [...] It is the only group I have been able to locate which cuts across denominational and national lines; however, I think the preoccupation with immigration cases has reduced its constituency to mainly Jamaicans. We might be able to get them going on F.E.P. [Fair Employment Practices]—we talked over the federal bill—but it will take more than that to enable the group to recover its momentum.

Anticipating a leadership vacuum in the organization, Milling wondered "if Blanchette of the Sleeping Car Porters could be interested in stimulating some increased participation in this kind of work among his Toronto Membership. I believe his headquarters are in Montreal, so I'll leave the idea with you to work on as and when you see fit."[180] Blanchette would take on a leadership role mainly at the national level through the Canadian Congress of Labour, with much of the organizational work falling to Grizzle, in the division of the sleeping car porters in Toronto, and Lee Williams, a porter on Canadian National Railway and head of a Winnipeg local of the Canadian Brotherhood of Railway Employees.

PERMANENT RESIDENCE
Social Identity and the State

THE QUESTION OF WHO WAS a West Indian—or an East Indian or Asian for that matter—was not always clear. On September 17, 1953, eight months before the Negro Citizenship Association delegation arrived in Ottawa, Harry Narine-Singh and his wife Mearl Indira arrived in Toronto on vacation and decided to extend their visit indefinitely. While staying with his uncle, Harry, a British subject, decided to sign up for a three-year stint in the Canadian Army. Singh's thinking was not unusual since for decades British subjects from the West Indies had served in the Canadian armed forces, which were seen as an extension of militaries based in England or the Caribbean. During the Second World War, several West Indians who later emerged as prominent leaders in the region— including Jamaica's Michael Manley, Barbados' Errol Barrow, and St. Vincent's Milton Cato—received military training in Canada or served in the Canadian forces.

When Narine-Singh, then a twenty-five-year-old draughtsman, tried to enlist, he was told he needed to change his status from non-immigrant to immigrant, a routine condition for British subjects prior to 1947. He would also need to be interviewed. Unbeknownst to him, Narine-Singh claimed, the interview was not with the Canadian military but with immigration officials. It's possible that, like many other British subjects, Narine-Singh was not aware of the changes in military registration that came into effect five years before his application. He said he told the interviewers he did not want to become a Canadian citizen, nor to stay in the country permanently; he merely wanted to serve in the Canadian

Army for three years without worrying about his status expiring before returning to his homeland.

He and his wife did not hear about their case until immigration officers showed up at his uncle's house early one morning. They were told they were to be deported on the grounds that Narine-Singh did not meet the regulations that allowed British subjects to migrate to Canada. They were then whisked away to the infamous Toronto Don Jail where—as was usual with immigration detainees until the Negro Citizenship Association had the practice banned—they were held pending deportation and treated like the criminals housed there. Family and friends secured their release following an application of habeas corpus to the courts. Having lost an appeal against the deportation order before an immigration tribunal, the couple turned to the courts for a final resolution.

The question for the immigration department was: What was the real national identity of Narine-Singh and his wife, and into which racial quota for prohibited groups should they fall? Their case would highlight the contradictions and even absurdities in Canadian immigration policy, all of which would be pointed out to the government by the Negro Citizenship Association, the sleeping car porters, and their allies. Undoubtedly, this case was on his mind when Stanley Grizzle made his deputation to Minister of Immigration Walter Harris almost a year later, when he spoke of the deportation of West Indians and the limited quotas for spouses and families of people of immigrants from India, Sri Lanka, China, and Japan who were already living in the country.

By referencing their last names and other traditional ethnic markers although they had Anglicized first names, immigration officials classified the Narine-Singhs as Asiatic—Indians from, and native to, Southeast Asia—one of the prohibited classes of people. However, if the applicants were to be deported to their native land, meaning the land of their birth, they would have had to be sent back to Trinidad, one of the British possessions in the Caribbean. So the question to be decided was whether the couple was West Indian, as they claimed, or Asiatic Indian, as the immigration officials declared. The answer would determine which pool of prohibited immigrants they would be slotted in amongst.

This led to a series of questions: How free were the Narine-Singhs? Were they free to choose their own racial and ethnic identity? Were they free to reject an identity that had been imposed on them? Were they free to have no racial and ethnic identity at all? Was their primary social identity freely chosen and self-determined or ascribed by others—such as government officials—based solely on immigration policy? Could they change this ascribed government identity if necessary?

According to the government's thinking, even though the Narine-Singhs hailed from the Caribbean, a region that had taken in Indian immigrants in sizeable numbers since the emancipation of African slaves, in the Knoxian sense they were Asiatic Indians, no matter where they were born.

"I have never in my life been in Asia or anywhere except Trinidad and Canada," Harry said in his affidavit, as was reported in the *Globe and Mail* on May 2, 1954. "My parents and grandparents have both, to the best of my knowledge, lived all their lives in Trinidad. I am informed by them and believe that their ancestry is at least in part Indian." But he implied in the sworn statement that, even so, that did not make all his ancestors fully Indian. "In Trinidad," he says, "are people whose ancestors went to Trinidad 150 years or more ago, but they do not form a separate group in the population, but mingle with the people of other origin and extraction, and are Christian in religion."[181]

The question of whether ethnicity and race were the same thing was at the heart of this case as it made its way through the courts. Andrew Brewin, the couple's lawyer, argued in the Supreme Court of Ontario that racial discrimination was odious and that there was no clear definition in Canadian law of what made a person ethnically and racially Indian. According to the *Toronto Star*, Brewin argued that because there was no clear definition in Canadian law of the word Asiatic and, by implication, the word Asia, immigration authorities had no authority to "go into the racial background" of anyone to determine their racial category. Rather than signifying race and ethnicity, Brewin claimed the words Asia and Asiatic signified a geographical area and a geographical-based identity that could not be applied to his clients because they did not come from Asia or India.

But the lawyer failed to persuade the court with his argument. Justice Henry Aylen ruled that in the absence of a specific definition, immigration officers had to make a pragmatic interpretation of the law. Upholding the deportation, the judge noted that there was no such thing as a single Asiatic race and that the region contained a "bewildering pattern of races," the *Toronto Star* reported on July 10, 1954. The judge said it made no sense to interpret the law as if it were singling out people solely from a specific region.

In making this ruling, the judge indicated there was no doubt that racial differences based on universal group characteristics were to be taken into consideration when applying the law.

Furthermore, he concluded that, from a practical stand point, immigration officials "cannot be expected to deal with pure Indians or pure Mongolians or pure Chinese or pure examples of the many Asian races," but to apparent variations of these ethnicities.[182] They had to rely on their experiences handling such matters; they had to continue trusting such factors as the geographical origins of the applicant, race, and any other matter such as intermarriage, and to make a decision based on the applicant's predominant characteristics.

This was not the only case of this type before the government and courts. One case turned on the question of whether the wife of an applicant for immigration to Canada, who was an Indian living in Holland, was Dutch, one of the groups of Europeans favoured for immigration to Canada. As the *Globe and Mail* reported on December 8, 1955, an unnamed white man had been denied permission to emigrate from Holland because his wife, a citizen of the Netherlands, "was of Dutch East Indian origin." Immediate members of the man's family were already Canadian citizens and wanted him to join them under the government's family reunification provisions.

"Immigration Minister Pickersgill has said that no bars exist against any national or racial group, and in formal fact that may be true," an accompanying *Globe* editorial stated. "There is a joke applied against people of Southwest Asiatic origin in that they are only to be allowed entry if they have come from their country of origin to a Canadian port by one continuous trip. Direct travel facilities from that area to Canada are almost nonexistent, so the technicality serves as a barrier. It may be that this is being used in the present case." The absurdity of this practice meant that people deemed to be Indian who resided elsewhere—in the Caribbean or Europe—would first have to return to India and book a passage on a carrier travelling directly to Canada.

But there was a second hurdle that they would also have to overcome: even if the applicant travelled directly from an Indian port, it might be debatable as to whether they would be essentially Indian. Put another way: if they were deemed not essentially Indian, would there be any way around these hurdles barring their entry?

"The question is fundamentally altered by the fact that the East Indian woman is a man's wife, and she now lives in Holland. It is incredible that if a man is fully acceptable under our laws as an immigrant his wife is not equally acceptable under the same regulations, no matter where she might have been born," the *Globe and Mail* opined. "Does the Canadian

Government dare to insist that any foreign-born citizen or potential citizen may pick a wife only from the white race? It is an intolerable proposition."[183]

By the time that the Liberal government, with Harris and Pickersgill as succeeding immigration ministers, was replaced by the Conservatives, the government had many similar immigration controversies tied to the new citizen legislation to deal with. One such case, according to the *Toronto Star* edition of June 15, 1957, was that of Adwin Akan, who lived in Trinidad with his family and wanted to join the Canadian army so that his family could live in Canada. One of the applicant's close friends was Jerome Flanders, who had served in the Royal Canadian Regiment for twenty-one years. When Akan applied to immigrate, Canadian officials turned him down because he had no immediate family in Canada. "But Flanders, who says he sold Akan on life in the Canadian army during a visit to Trinidad," the *Star* reported, "maintains that many from the British West Indies are allowed to migrate to Canada without having first-degree relatives here. But as Flanders says, these people, unlike Akan, happen to be white."[184]

Apparently, despite the new citizenship laws, many in the British possessions in the Caribbean believed that enlisting in the army was still an avenue to gain admission to Canada. The Negro Citizenship Association had to regularly clarify this change to people from the Caribbean. In a letter to a Wilberforce Maxwell, of Marley Vale, St. Philip, in Barbados, Donald Moore could only hold out faint hope that his application to join the army would be successful. "Since 1947 it has been the policy of the Government to admit to the Canadian Army only persons with Canadian domicile," Moore wrote in a letter dated January 28, 1956. "To obtain this status, a British West Indian must be sponsored by a close relative such as father, mother, brother or sister who is a domiciled Canadian or a Canadian citizen. Unless this regulation has been recently changed, the offer of our organization to assist you in getting established would not materially help nor satisfy immigration requirements."

"In our experience we have found that there is no blanket rule handling all applications," he continued so as not to leave the applicant hopeless. "While some are successful, others in similar circumstances have been refused. You may feel free to use the name of the Association as having offered to assist you in becoming established [...] Write me as soon as you have had a definite reply from the Immigration [department] and if you should require other information, I shall be only too glad to give it."[185]

Numerous other examples of the arbitrariness of the Canadian immigration system as related to racial and ethnic considerations abounded.

A similar case to that of the Narine-Singhs was the application by Ethel Brown-Owen of Jamaica, who wanted to remain in Canada after she completed her training as a teacher. Brown-Owen was already a qualified teacher, having been trained at Bethlehem, one of the leading teacher training schools in Jamaica, and having worked for seventeen years as a teacher in her native land. Upon completion of her training at the Toronto Teachers' College, she returned home with several job offers to teach in Canada, which was at the time suffering from a shortage of teachers, especially those with Brown-Owen's primary school specialist training. She wanted permission to enter Canada along with her eight-year old daughter and her husband, an accounting clerk who, according to her, was "desirous of pursuing further studies of the profession."

When her initial application was rejected, Brown-Owen turned to the Negro Citizenship Association for help and in turn was invited for a meeting at the office of the Canadian Trade Commission in Kingston, Jamaica. She was there advised to submit additional information in the hope of changing the department's decision.

As with the Narine-Singhs, the Brown-Owen family indicated that they did not plan to remain in Canada forever. "I should like to make it understood that we have no intentions of taking lifetime residence in Canada," she wrote. "Primarily our sole intention was based upon having a few years overseas experience which is so much a necessary feature among progressive people. [...] It is requested therefore, that this be not taken in the literal sense of 'Permanent Residence.'" This was not an outlandish claim, as many Caribbean visitors to Canada genuinely believed that they did not want to grow old and die in the cold, preferring instead to retire back in the tropics. Many assumed they would stay in Canada five to ten years, in the process saving enough money to improve their living standards when they returned. It was only after they settled and started families that their dream of returning home would be put on hold, first presumably until the children born in Canada were grown and independent, but most times, by happenstance, forever.

"Lastly," Brown-Owen argued, "I should like to state that I have received cable graphic communications from Schools in Canada requesting my early assignment to duty. Apparently they are unaware that any such hitch would be occasioned by your department, and in replying I stated the true position and expressed the hope of an early and favourable decision. Wouldn't it be an unfortunate breach in human relations if I were deprived the privilege of doing service where it is so greatly needed?"[186]

But the government determined in the end, for reasons known only to itself, that Brown-Owen was an Asiatic from India and therefore prohibited from immigrating to Canada. "With respect to the question raised concerning the length of time you plan on spending in Canada I may say that any person coming forward with the intention of seeking or engaging in employment in this country must be regarded as an immigrant and, therefore, upon applying for entry must comply with the requirements for permanent residence," the Department of Citizenship and Immigration wrote her on January 12, 1955. "In this connection under existing regulations the admission of any Asian, including person of East Indian race, is limited to the wife, and the husband, and the unmarried children under 21 years of age of any Canadian citizen living in Canada, who is in a position to receive and care for his dependents."

"It is clear," the department bureaucrat concluded, "from the information furnished in your application that you do not come within the admissible categories described above. In the circumstances I very much regret to inform you that the admission of yourself and family could not be authorized."[187]

Upon returning home from their meeting in Ottawa, the porters and their allies ramped up their lobbying to get Ottawa to change its policies on immigration and to enforce fair practices in employment across the land. The delegates concentrated their lobbying on three main areas: among international and domestic unions, at the grassroots level through meetings and discussions—where they received the active support of West Indian governments—and in churches and the print media.

A GATHERING OF LABOUR AND union delegates met at a special convention in Toronto on April 23, 1956, that was to change the institutional face of labour in Canada. Delegates from members of the Trades and Labour Congress of Canada and the Canadian Congress of Labour were to meet at the Coliseum of the Canadian National Exhibition in Toronto to merge into a single umbrella organization called the Canadian Labour Congress. The meeting was called in part to end a schism in the labour movement that had begun in 1926 over the role of international unions in Canada. The foreparent of the Canadian Congress of Labour, at the behest of the powerful Canadian Brotherhood of Railway Employees leadership, Aaron R Mosher, had at the time taken a nationalist slant on the issue, initiating the schism. Since the 1920s, Mosher's wing of the Canadian labour movement was adamantly opposed to US-based unions—such as Randolph's Brotherhood of Sleeping Car Porters—participating in Canadian politics or social affairs.

As Stanley Grizzle and members of the Brotherhood of Sleeping Car Porters prepared for the event, they lobbied union officials across the country and drafted and approved four resolutions on Canadian immigration that they wanted adopted at the founding convention. Grizzle was a delegate for his division but the main representation for the porters occurred at the union's national level. Representing the Brotherhood of Sleeping Car Porters would be A. R. Blanchette, Canadian field organizer for the international union and an ally in the struggle against discrimination. Months after his appearance as a member of the Negro Citizenship Association before the Minister of Immigration in Ottawa, Grizzle and his allies among the porters at the Canadian National Railway had pushed the Canadian Congress of Labour (C.C.L.), to which the Canadian Brotherhood of Railway Employees union was affiliated, to go on the record criticizing Canada's immigration policy. Every year organized labour would petition the government on an array of issues, including the labour supply and what types of immigrants were needed to build the country. They also called on the government to set up a permanent advisory committee—with members representing labour, industry, farming, social welfare organizations, and other bodies—to overhaul the country's immigration policy. In particular, the C.C.L. resolutions condemned Canadian immigration policy as discriminatory "against coloured persons, particularly from Commonwealth countries, and threaten[ing to] civil liberties through [its] arbitrary deportation for a variety of grounds, including acceptance of public welfare."[188] Grizzle and his union were also working feverishly with the Trades and Labour Congress of Canada, to which his union was affiliated, to pressure the provincial and federal governments to enforce fair practices legislation, with the aim of outlawing discrimination in employment, accommodation, and restaurants.

But as the date for the special convention approached, other trade unionists kept mentioning their plans for the meeting to Grizzle, none of which had been formally conveyed to him. So, on March 21, 1956, only a month before the convention, Grizzle wrote to one of the organizers, Gordon Cushing, his representative as general secretary-treasurer of the Trades and Labour Congress of Canada. "It is my information that some delegates to the Founding Convention of the Labour Congress have received a copy of the proposed Constitution of the C.L.C.," he wrote. The main business of the convention was the adoption of a constitution, the election of officers, and the discussion of resolutions, messages and petition. "Since I have *not* received a copy of this proposed Constitution I am wondering if you would forward same to me at your earliest convenience."[189]

Grizzle and Blanchette were concerned that the merged entity—the Canadian Labour of Congress—would actually make it more difficult to pursue their causes. They understood that the amalgamation, which would merge the Trades and Labour Congress of Canada and the Canadian Congress of Labour, whose name it would all but take over, was more than just a simple name change. Even worse, none other than Aaron R. Mosher, the president of the soon-to-be defunct Canadian Congress of Labour and the man whose Canadian Brotherhood of Railway Employees helped to ins-titutionalize Jim Crow-style practices on Canadian railways by negotiating the contract that limited Black workers to employment as porters, would be influential in the new Canadian Labour Congress (C.L.C.). Mosher was to be named honorary president of the C.L.C. at the convention, while being elected to the Labour Hall of Fame. As it turned out, largely because Blanchette's influence on the new organization's human rights committee, the C.L.C. emerged as a trusted ally to the porters. Grizzle, Blanchette, and their allies would also join with several Jewish activists to push the congress to aggressively champion immigration and human rights reform.

Grizzle's suspicions about the meeting proved to be justified. While he had led his Toronto division in drafting the convention resolutions, he discovered at the last moment that the resolutions had to be signed by a union executive and not merely a division head like himself. Also, for the resolutions to be discussed, they had to be submitted to the organizers sixty days before the meeting. By the time Grizzle and his allies were informed of these rules, that submission date had passed. There was still one other way to introduce the resolutions at the convention, but it required the resolu-tions' authors to win a two-thirds majority approval from the convention delegates. This started a mad scramble, with Grizzle formally asking his immediate superior, A. R. Blanchette, for support and Blanchette hastily writing to union president A. Phillip Randolph in New York for permission to submit the resolutions.

Randolph responded seven days later. "If Brother Grizzle wish [sic] to have the resolutions of the Toronto Division introduced, I would suggest that you go ahead with the plan to have them introduced since I think there would be no difficulty in acquiring two-thirds of the delegates to agree to the introduction of the resolution."[190] Blanchette dashed off copies of the resolutions to organizer Gordon Cushing immediately.

The resolutions submitted by Grizzle stated that the merged Congress would establish a standing committee on human rights; urge the federal government to liberalize Canada's immigration policy with regard to coloured British subjects and persons of colour; and set up an advisory committee with the federal government, which would include representation from labour, farmers, management, and other interested groups to help administer Canadian immigration policies. Further, the government would crack down on deportations by limiting how municipal governments recommended the deportation of immigrants on welfare. Finally, in recognition of their human rights, immigrants would have the right to a public hearing and to legal representation when faced with deportation.

There was another reason Grizzle and Blanchette suspected that there had been an attempt to shut them out of the discussions. Convention organizers had blocked off a number of rooms at the Royal York Hotel in Toronto for delegates. In a letter to Grizzle on March 15, 1956, Montreal-based Blanchette shared his experience of trying to book one of these rooms. "My having some two weeks ago been advised by the Convention's convener that my request for Single Room accommodation at the Royal York Hotel had to be denied since all rooms had already been taken, and that they reserved in my name a Double Room at the King Edward Hotel, which I would have to share with a Brother from Quebec since no more Singles were now available and all remaining delegates, yet to be accommodated, would consequently have to "double up." I instructed the Convenor to cancel the said reservation, and told him I would make other suitable arrangements myself." As a result, Blanchette told Grizzle that, outside of immediate business at the convention, he expected to be free and that "it will be a joy indeed for me to have the opportunity to see as many of the fine Brothers and Sisters of the Toronto Division and Auxiliary as possible, during the convention week."[191]

Union lobbying had been successful in raising the visibility of anti-Black discrimination in Canadian immigration. In February 1955, speaking at the annual convention of the Ontario Federation of Labour, which represented 200,000 workers, the legislative representative for the Ontario United Steel Workers Union, Eamon Park, called Canada's immigration laws a "disgrace" and claimed that the act was based on the same principles supporting racial supremacy in apartheid South Africa.

The convention approved a resolution by Grizzle condemning Canada for limiting its definition of British subjects for immigration purposes to whites born in Britain, Ireland, Australia, New Zealand, the US and South Africa. "These sections enable the immigration department arbitrarily to exclude from Canada because of their color or racial extraction, particularly prospective British West Indians, and thus give the lie to our professions of brotherhood with the rest of the British Commonwealth, and also increases suspicion of Canada's democratic ideals among the non-white people of Asia and Africa."[192] Later that year, trade unionists in the C.L.C. met in Winnipeg to discuss Canada's immigration policies and to call on the government to change its policy so that immigrants would not be used as cheap labour and could enjoy higher standards of living. According to the *Winnipeg Free Press* of October 3, 1955, the convention passed four resolutions: Canada needed a larger population to expand its industrial base; the government should set up an advisor committee on immigration; immigrants should have all traditional civil rights; and the Immigration Act should exclude all discrimination based on race, creed, colour, nationality, or religion.

Similarly, in a meeting of its synod in Edmonton on September 7, 1955, the Anglican Church of Canada adopted a resolution asking the federal government to allow greater immigration from the British West Indies. Canon W. W. Judd, the general secretary of the Church's council, said that Canada should increase British immigration, including more Black immigrants from the West Indies.

In the meantime, the porters and the Negro Citizenship Association kept up the pressure on the government through their lobbying and community involvement. In particular, they strategically focused on the deportation of West Indians and Black people from Canada, a move that would eventually cause the West Indian governments to raise the matter directly with their Canadian counterparts. In early 1956, Grizzle continued to bombard officials in the Department of Immigration for information on the number of Negro immigration applicants over the past three years, how many had been refused entry, and how those numbers compared with those for other racial groups. A letter from the department's director, C.E.S. Smith, dated February 27, 1956, said that, "the Department does not maintain by ethnic origin statistics on the number of applicants for admission to Canada, nor do we maintain by ethnic origin statistics on the number of applicants who have been refused admission to Canada."[193] In response to a request for information to the Vancouver branch of the United Nations Association of Canada regarding Canada's policy of barring Black people from the country, Grizzle wrote to Blanchette on March 12, 1956, and said that, from his research, "at least 25 Negroes have been denied entry into Canada. These have been men who are tradesmen being skilled as machinists, carpenters, painters, chemists, accountants, stenographers, electricians, diesel engineers. These persons who have been refused entry into Canada during the last six months have all been able to pay their way to this country."

The same rules governed Black immigrants arriving from Britain. "Concerning West Indians living in Great Britain," Grizzle wrote,

> no matter how long they have lived there when they apply for admission into Canada they are treated as if they were applying for admission from any B. W. island. You see it is my understanding that there is no such (thing) as citizenship, as we know it, in Great Britain. Also on record are several cases (number unavailable) of persons from the W. Indies having completed courses at educational institution [sic] in Canada, then have been offered a job and still [they] are compelled to return to their homeland.[194]

Examples of students studying in Canada who were then forced to leave or deported were regularly reported at the time in the mainstream media. One example involved thirty-two-year-old Messa Dencha, an Ethiopian student who had been studying in Canada for eleven years. Dencha had come to Canada at the invitation of a missionary, who had met him at a school in Addis Ababa. Along with a friend, Dencha was granted a scholarship to the Prairie Bible Institute in Three Hills, Alberta. After three years of high school, Dencha remained at the school for another four years to take missionary Bible courses. His guardianship was taken over by the Toronto Baptist Seminary after it acquired the institute and Dencha studied theology there for another four years. After his studies were completed, the federal government said he had to leave the country. The *Toronto Star* reported that Dencha wanted to enroll at the University of Toronto to become a chemist because he now felt that he could do more good in his homeland as a chemist than a missionary. As the *Globe and Mail* reported on July 6, 1957, "he was also told he was not eligible for Canadian citizenship, said Dencha, because Africans and Asians are not in a class of persons admitted to Canada." In addition, he did not have any family in Canada to sponsor him. "Dencha feels it is not just 'that a person should be denied only on racial grounds, if he is of good character," the article said. "Dencha said he knows West Indians who have overcome the problems by marrying Canadian citizens. 'That is not the right basis,' he says. 'I would like to feel that my appeal perhaps may help someone else as well as myself.'"[195]

The next month several newspapers reported that the immigration authorities had told students from the West Indies who were studying at the University of Toronto and Queen's University that they should prepare to leave the country upon the completion of their studies. The situation with the West Indian students made the news when the premier of Barbados and future Prime Minister of the West Indies Federation, Sir Grantley Adams, arrived in the country to speak at a conference on Canada's relationship with the new federation. "There is one thing we have against Canada—I won't say it is a matter of ill feeling but rather one of regret—and that is the matter of your immigration laws," Adams was quoted as saying in the Globe and Mail on August 7, 1957. "They are worse than the McCarran Act of the United States, which at least allows 100 nationals of each country in the West Indies to enter the US."[196] Adams was reiterating the plea made by his minister of labour, Mencea Cox, at an international labour confer- ence two months earlier. Cox was quoted in the Toronto Star on June 15, 1957, as calling for Canada to "open her doors both to skilled and unskilled workers from the British West Indies on terms at least similar to those existing in the United States."[197] Eventually Adams would lobby the Prime Minister of Canada directly when, on a visit to Ottawa, he met with John Diefenbaker. "We are all British subjects," he said in a report in the Toronto Star on October 25, 1959. "Some people say Barbados is more English than England," the report continued,

> though in Canada at a time when several West Indians are fighting depor- tation orders, the premier was guarded on the controversial subject. He emphasized, perhaps tactfully, that he has not yet heard anyone in the West Indies suggest 'discrimination' against West Indians seeking to enter Canada as immigrants. But Sir Grantley made it clear he feels more of his people should be allowed to immigrate to Canada. The great majority of West Indians, he said, 'are no different in their outlook than Canadians. They have the same way of life, and the same religion.'

Rather, he suggested that Canadian immigration practices open access to some people from foreign countries "who don't know western ways."[198]

But if it was not diplomatic to call the policies discriminatory, as the Prime Minister said, the Black activists did not feel governed by the same constraints and did not hesitate to describe the policies as discriminatory and racist. The example of the railway porters, whose very job descriptions were the result of racial discrimination, would figure prominently in these arguments.

DEMERITS AND DEADHEADING
The Rail Companies' Unreasonable Demands

ON CHRISTMAS EVE 1954, CANADIAN Pacific Railway porter John K. Crutcher reported for duty at 7:30 p.m. at Toronto's Union Station. Assigned to Tourist Car #360, which was scheduled to depart at 10:25 p.m. for Winnipeg, Crutcher did his mandatory inspection to make sure his car, as the company demanded, was spic and span. He had to be very careful: should he ignore any regulations, his job could be in peril. The employee handbook referred to a range of demerit points that, should an employee reach a total of sixty, would lead to automatic dismissal. "For each repetition of a similar case, the number of demerit marks will be doubled if [an] employee's record is not clear of demerits and when sixty demerit points have been accumulated against an employee's record, his service will be dispensed with," the company instruction booklet read. However, demerit points would also be removed from a porter's record at a rate of twenty points for every year of good service, which was at least some small consolation.

Some infractions led to automatic dismissal regardless of the state of the employee's record. "Disloyalty, dishonesty, immorality, insubordination, incompetence, gross carelessness, untruthfulness, concealing facts concerning investigations, drinking on duty and showing signs of having been drinking prior to reporting, will result in employee being subject to dismissal." On the other hand, the instructions promised that "good judgment" in emergencies and meritorious conduct would entitle employees to merit marks.[199]

As a seasoned porter with seniority and his own scheduled runs, Crutcher nevertheless still had to work these holiday shifts. Upon arriving, Crutcher's duties would largely involve re-checking the work of the previous porter, who was expected to leave the car the way he would want to find it—or else. Indeed, the checklist provided to trainee porters by Canadian Pacific had twenty-one items to which a porter needed to attend:

1. Toilets clean, sanitary and equipped with toilet paper at all times.
2. Passageways and Smoking Room and Ladies Room mopped regularly.
3. Carpets properly swept—use Small Broom and Dustpan.
4. Window and Woodwork kept dusted at all times.
5. Washbasins and Mirrors kept clean.
6. Make sure before passengers rise that cold water is drawn off so that water will be hot for washing.
7. Keep aisles clean of Baggage and Passengers effects.
8. Keep drinking water tanks supplied with ice.
9. Washrooms supplied with clean towels and soiled regularly removed.
10. Constant removal and disposal of refuse.
11. Vestibules swept and walls dusted.
12. Handrails wiped down before receiving and discharging passengers.
13. Keep Dixie cups containers well filled.
14. Equipment stored in proper place when not in use.
15. Cuspidor and ashtrays kept clean.
16. Matches in ALL ROOMS and ROOMETTES, none in Ladies' Room.
17. Check to see soap plunger working properly. Supply Individual Cake Soap in rooms and roomettes, not ladies rooms.
18. Clean water glasses displayed in rooms where paper cups dispensers are not available.
19. Coat Hangers and Folders in Room and Roomettes.
20. Maintain proper Ventilation and Temperature Control.
21. Clean personal Appearance at ALL Times.[200]

But as Crutcher went through his departure ritual and dutifully positioned himself by his car at ten p.m, he discovered that—maybe because it was Christmas—he would have nobody to serve on the way out to Winnipeg, and possibly beyond and back. Instead of the partially full load of passengers Crutcher and his colleague James Ewing on the neighbouring car had expected, their trip was going to be one of those dreaded "deadenders" or "deadheaders" porters hated. When Crutcher and Ewing had called the reservation office the day before, they had been told that Ewing would have three passengers and Crutcher two, but they'd hoped these numbers would have picked up by departure time. Now that Crutcher would be servicing an empty car, management wouldn't even consider Crutcher to be working, which meant that he would not be paid for his time even though he would be required to remain in uniform. Prospects were just as poor regarding tips, which meant that he did not even have enough money to pay for his meals and regular upkeep away from home.

Crutcher asked Ewing to spot him a small loan to cover his expenses while working, but, as Ewing recalled, "I had enough (only) for myself."[201] Crutcher then decided to chance it by making a quick trip home, or to a friend's, to borrow some pocket money, hoping to make it back to work before the scheduled departure. As he later conceded, he knew he would be breaching the rules, but what else could he do since he needed to feed himself while working. Plus, with only two passengers to welcome and get settled before the train pulled out, no one should even realize he was gone. His buddy could cover for him. The widespread fear among porters was a shift with no tips at the end of the journey, a frightening enough prospect to force an experienced porter like Crutcher to take such a chance.

As Ewing attested in a report to management and the union, "At approximately 10:25 p.m. Porter Crutcher apparently made up his mind to go home and obtain additional funds. He had on his uniform at this time, but put on his civilian overcoat and hat, and asked me if I would look after his car and the entraining of his passengers until he got back." Unfortunately, due to the weather and a shortage of taxis, Crutcher was delayed. Realizing he would be cutting his arrival back at the station tight—if not entirely missing the departure—Crutcher decided to call ahead and alert his supervisors. This was the beginning of a six-month struggle by Crutcher to save his job.

Platform inspector S. Gilmore was well into his inspection of the departing train, which commenced at the back and moved toward the front. He found a lack of menus in the Dome coach and returned to the office to get more. At eleven p.m., just before he was to leave again, "the telephone rang and on answering it (I) found Porter Crutcher on the other end of the wire," the inspector stated in his supervisor's write-up, which started the dispute. "Knowing that he was supposed to be on his car I questioned him as to his whereabouts. He advised me that he was at his fiancée's home, and on asking him his reason for going there, he avoided the question, and replied he had a taxi at the house and could catch the train at the West Toronto station," a minor stop a few miles west. With the inspector signaling to him, a conductor quickly called a standby porter to the track and both of them made a dash for Crutcher's rail car. "But the train had already departed before he (standby porter) reached the platform," inspector Gilmore recalled. Still on the phone with Crutcher, the inspector told him "to get the taxi and make sure he got on his car at West Toronto."[202] Crutcher called him back at 11:20 to report that he was at the station and the train had not yet arrived. In a statement, given six days later, Ewing confirmed that Crutcher "boarded his car at West Toronto where he was standing on the platform when the train arrived."[203]

As a result, Crutcher was docked fifteen demerit points for desertion and leaving his car without permission and was suspended from service. Desertion was one of many dismissible offences. Days later Crutcher was hit with an additional charge of drinking on duty, even though he had not done so and his co-worker Ewing attested to as much in his statement. It fell to his union, the Brotherhood of Sleeping Car Porters, to try to save Crutcher's job.

Conditions of service for porters left no room for infractions big or small. Everything was measured and standardized. Porters departed from those standards at great peril, for the railways made sure porters were aware of the regulations by issuing a relentless stream of circulars on every aspect of service. At the beginning of a run, conductors received a diagram of the entire train with the names of every worker, type of service offered, and the train's occupancy. The circular from the Division of Night Watch instructed that conductors should always keep a check on porters, even indicating when they took breaks for rest, to eat, and to sleep.

The circular specified that when a porter was allowed to rest during the day, "the space reserved on [the] tourist car diagram must be used, but sleeping car porters should only be allowed to occupy such space when it will not interfere with [the] rest of tourist car porters." In other words, porters could sleep in the smoking room, as long as there were no passengers there. The instructions also indicated how and when a porter could take a rest or have meals. "While porters are in dining cars, it is the duty of conductor to frequently patrol cars, and attend to the wants of passengers during [the] porter's absence. Conductors must make it a practice, when guarding cars by patrolling, to inspect [the] annunciator [a device signaling the train is passing a specific point on the track] in each car and respond to any calls which may be found registered, and [to] keep cars in proper condition."[204] Under these rules, it was in the conductors' best interest to limit the rest and meal breaks of all porters in order to reduce the time the conductors had to fill in for them.

The same circular from 1938 stipulated how porters must always watch over their train cars. For example, on the first night of a transcontinental express train from Montreal to Vancouver, the porter had to be on guard all night, with specified times allowed for rest. Porters could rest for short periods between 1:30 and 5:30 a.m. on the tourist car but had to be awake and outside the train when it stopped at the stations. The same was true between 11:20 p.m. and 8:15 the next morning for the second night of the trip from the Ontario towns of White River to Port Arthur. On the third night, starting at Winnipeg at 9:30 p.m. and arriving at 8:20 the next morning in Moose Jaw, Saskatchewan, car porters were permitted to have a short rest between 11:30 p.m. and 3:30 a.m. Porters on the tourist car, however, had to be on guard for another night, taking a rest when conductors allowed them during the day. All sleeping car employees had to be on duty when the train pulled out of a station along the route. For the fourth night, between Calgary and Revelstoke, B.C., between 11:05 p.m. and 8:15 a.m. porters on the sleeping car were on guard the entire time, while those in the standard car were allowed to take a break between midnight and four. On the Calgary to Vancouver Observation car, the rules stated that the porter could "rest from midnight, provided all passengers have retired, until 4:15 a.m."[205] The work schedule was so detailed that porters, and to a lesser degree conductors, were often severely sleep-deprived, especially near the end of a run.

A similar pattern for night travel occurred on the train leaving Vancouver for Montreal, which required a fifth night of travel with little rest for the porters, except for those who worked in the tourist car, where they were allowed to rest between 11:15 p.m. and 3:15 a.m. Other runs, such as interprovincial ones or shorter services across Canada, had various detailed instructions regarding rest breaks. The rulebook stipulated that conductors were "responsible for the actions of porters" and porters were required to follow conductors' orders unquestioningly.

One other rule was clear: porters could never be conductors, even if there were no conductors supervising the train. When the most senior porter undertook a conductor's duties, he became the porter-in-charge, but he could not be referred to as a conductor. Conductors were also deemed superior to porters by being allowed to eat with passengers while porters could eat with neither passengers nor conductors. "Conductors are the only train employees permitted to take meals with regular passengers," the company specified in an instruction booklet to employees.[206]

"THE COMPANY'S WORLD-WIDE REPUTATION FOR service," Canadian Pacific Railway stated in an updated set of instructions to its workers, "is built up by the efficiency of its employees, and no employee can be efficient unless he combines courtesy with service."[207] These new instructions, issued in 1964, just before Canadian Pacific went out of the passenger rail business, were to replace the previous rule book, first issued in 1921. All porters' jobs depended on these rules that, for half a century, were considered oppressive by the employees.

Over those years, the book was divided into the same three sections: instructions for conductors performing "In Charge" duties and which clearly stipulate to porters who were their superiors at work; directions detailing the precise steps of the job, specifically for porters who worked in sleeping, parlour, observational and buffet cars; and sanitary guidelines for all employees, but which were largely directions on how porters should handle such things as cases of communicable diseases, flies, and mosquitoes, or how to provide screens or ventilation and heating in the cars. "Courtesy is not more than considerate behaviour towards others, or [a] duty performed in a kindly, polite manner," the booklet informed the readers. "Employees who are obliging and courteous, alert to anticipate the wants of passengers, and cheerful in executing their orders, will help maintain the high standard of service and earn the goodwill of our patrons."

To be courteous and efficient, employees had to be knowledgeable about their work. Porters were encouraged to "study how they may best help patrons to enjoy the maximum benefits of all facilities offered for their comfort and enjoyment." Porters also had to know how to speak to passengers: "In addressing passengers, the term 'Sir' or 'Madam' should be used." Under a section titled "Special Instructions to Sleeping Car Porters," the railway detailed its expectations for delivery of onboard service. First, the rule book said, it was important to call passengers at the time specified on the call card attached to each berth, unless the train was late.

The porters were also instructed on such things as how to conserve energy, day or night ("use a minimum of light when making up berths. As soon as most passengers retire, ceiling lights should be turned out and floor lights turned on"); how to turn down beds ("a minimum of light should be used and each bell and berth lights should be tested to make sure they are in working order"); how to store beds and tables ("when putting away bed please remember the comfort of passengers still asleep and avoid making any noise"); how and when to mop ("Clean with water and soap powder. Rinse out mop after each use of mop wringer, detach from handle and place on edge of mop pail to dry"); purchasing supplies en route ("do not accept money from passengers to leave car to purchase supplies of any kind"); how and where they should position themselves to receive and discharge passengers; and when to use a step ("conductors and porters on duty must place a stepping box outside at all stops, handrails must be wiped clean"). Upon embarking, the rules said the porters must

> call out car numbers and indicate a willingness to be of assistance [...] When discharging passengers, make sure baggage is dusted and put off before passengers detrain [...] Exercise the greatest of care to see passengers detrain on station stops en route are discharged on STATION SIDE); and how and when to announce train arrivals and departures (porter should make announcement, such as "CHAPEAU, TEN MINUTES STOP— THIS WAY OUT" [...] When a train is running late, it does not always remain at a station for the full period advertised in the time folder and to eliminate danger of passengers wandering off and missing their train, they should be advised that train will leave as quickly as it can be serviced.

Some procedures received extra attention, such as those for shining passenger shoes. "Porters are required to clean and polish the shoes of all passengers in their cars, including those of the car conductor, each night," the instructions stated, using capital letters for emphasis. "This work is to be done in the smoking room, with the porter taking not more than TWO PAIRS AT A TIME and marking the soles to indicate the space from which they were removed. The better the shine, the better the impression gained. When returning shoes to the proper space, place [...] under berth with toes pointing inwards. Porters should indicate to room passengers, locations of [the] shoe door."

The booklet also offered another useful tip for polishing shoes: "Protect white coats when shining shoes as polish stains are very hard to remove and may result in permanent damage to the white coat." A stain on a porter's coat would be a violation of the dress code; damaging the coat was not only against the rules, but would result in the porter having to purchase a replacement coat at their own expense.

On top of these and other duties, porters were also expected to police the cars, ensuring there were no disturbing noises, especially at night, and so had to "avoid slamming car doors, trap doors, etc." They should also inform the conductor of any objectionable behaviour by passengers, such as making noise or smoking in prohibited areas. Porters were to remind passengers that "smoking rooms are provided on cars for this purpose [and] when lounge cars [are] operated on [a] train, passengers may be directed to that car, where they may relax, smoke and enjoy a good library book or other reading material."[208]

By 1964, changes to the manual had been made, largely because of two decades of union challenges. While the booklet stated that the company was eager to receive suggestions for service improvements from all employees, by the 1960s the commitment seemed much more serious and the manual indicated that the company would be holding discussions with employees at locations across the country. By then porters were finally being paid for deadheading and could purchase food on board at half price.

"Conductors and porters deadheading on company's service will be furnished with a trip pass, half-rate meal order, and order to cover sleeping accommodation," the booklet said. But some things had not changed, including the stipulation that, "Under no circumstances must any deadhead employee be furnished accommodation without proper authority. Sleeping car porters when deadheading must be suitably attired in uniform trousers, fresh shirt, tie and suit coat. Employees in deadhead service must not occupy Lounge or Dome observation facilities." And even though porters were now permitted thirty-minute breaks for meals, they still had to eat behind a screen so that passengers could not see or mix with them.

The railway had also not changed its attitude toward tipping. "Employees must not solicit or act as though appearing to solicit gratuities from passengers."[209] Waiting in anticipation with an upturned palm was technically illegal. Tipping was only considered a breach of the rules if the porter asked for the gratuity. The railway continued to turn a blind eye to the tips that came without begging, demanding, or coercion, choosing to assume such gifts were made in appreciation of service and were an incentive to make porters try harder. Not all passengers were happy with tipping, however, a fact that porters to remain mindful of.

AT A MEETING OF JANUARY 19, 1954, Stanley Grizzle successfully argued that Crutcher should not be dismissed and that the charge of desertion be reduced to a lesser but unspecified offence. Crutcher lost his seniority status and was relegated to the spare board to work on an as-needed basis, a position to which he did not go easily. Crutcher ended up with few shifts and had to fight management's claim that the quota of in-charge porters was full.

This would not be the last time the company would hear from Crutcher and the Brotherhood of Sleeping Car Porters. Crutcher would soon take the unprecedented step of applying to become the first Black railway conductor in North America. Because he had been disciplined for leaving work without permission that Christmas day, Crutcher failed to qualify. But his attempt helped break down the barriers of employment for Black porters and improved social mobility for all Black Canadians.

AN UPHILL BATTLE
Pushing for Policy Changes

FOLLOWING THE PRESENTATION OF THE brief in Ottawa, the porters and their fellow delegates lobbied intensively to extend and enhance citizenship rights. Black Canadians were firmly at the forefront of this struggle. Newspapers across the country took note of the Negro Citizenship Association Negro Citizenship Association' unprecedented lobbying efforts. Their message was beginning to receive nationwide attention.

The *Globe and Mail* reported the next day news of the meeting under a headline *Group Present Views to Harris- Lift Bars on Negro Immigration, Ottawa Urged.* The minister's evident lack of enthusiasm was apparent in the report. "Mr. Harris said later that he promised to give the brief serious consideration to see whether it would be possible to widen the present category of admissible mothers and wives and children of Canadian residents." This was typical of government responses, and clearly indicated to the porters and their allies that little would be done about their brief beyond sticking it in a file and forgetting about it. The minister highlighted the fact that "the delegation had been unable when asked to suggest what proportion of the 100,000-odd immigrants brought in (to Canada) annually should be Negro. Entries each year are held to the number the Government considers can be absorbed without upsetting the economy." Moore and Grizzle and the rest of the delegates found this comment ominous, as it meant that the minister had not been persuaded by the presentations.

Still that the visit to Ottawa happened at all was a victory, and would long be a subject for conversation and commentrary, both within the Black community and the larger country. *Globe and Mail* columnist J. V.

THEY CALL ME GEORGE

McArea, in an editorial titled *Black and White* and published on July 2, 1954, fulminated:

> Nothing more disastrous could happen to Canada than an immigration flood of 5,000,000 Negroes, unless it might be a flood of 5,000,001. Thanks to many factors, our climate for one, Negroes do not thrive in Canada as they do in the United States. Why should any sane Canadian want to help establish in this country the terrible race problem that has grown up in the United States. This is said with no ill will to any Negro or to colored people as a whole. It is not said to suggest that the blacks are not as good as the whites, given equal opportunity. We wish them all well, but we do not think it be a good thing for their numbers to be appreciably added to Canada. Once here we say they ought to have the same rights as a white person; but they ought not to be encouraged. The basic truth is that whites do not naturally intermarry with blacks, and a good rough test of an acceptable immigrant would his likelihood of being accepted as a husband by the average Canadian girl, or vice versa.

But in the Black community and among the delegates, spirts remained high. Whatever the opinions of McArea and other like him, progress was being made.

The day after their presentation, the Negro Citizenship Association delegation to Ottawa returned to Toronto as conquering heroes. Harry Gairey, who always had problems with his supervisors at Canadian Pacific Railway, was emboldened after the Ottawa trip to exhibit what West Indians, mainly Jamaicans, would call his *facety* or outspoken brashness to authority.

> When I came back the next day, the paper had the news that we'd gone to Ottawa and petitioned the government. And Mr. Collins, my superintendent at the CP, called me up and said, 'I see you were in Ottawa to try and change the laws of the land.' I said, 'Mr. Collins, I respect you; you are a fine man. You have treated me well. But I want to say this right now. I am Black and anything that I can do to help my Black people, and not to hurt anyone, I will do. I'm going to do all in my power to help my people, within the framework of democracy.' He said, 'I didn't mean anything.' I said, 'I know you didn't mean anything, but you shouldn't have said it.'[210]

Governments in the West Indies were quietly supportive and would eventually throw their full diplomatic weight behind the delegation's cause at top-level meetings of the British Empire and Commonwealth and in direct negotiations with the prime ministers of Canada and the United Kingdom. Later that year, Jamaican premier Norman Manley visited Toronto and, in a meeting with members of the Negro Citizenship Association he openly encouraged their activities. Direct discussions between the activists and the politicians in Caribbean capitals became more open as well. Several of these debaters in the West Indies were graduates of Canadian universities and had been trained or served in the Canadian armed forces, working as porters in the off season. Black families in the Caribbean, the US, and Canada shared in a common struggle, which ramped up pressure on Canadian politicians to make changes.

Five years after the Ottawa meeting, Grantley Adams, in one of his first acts after becoming the first and only prime minister of the new British West Indies Federation, led an official delegation to Canada, visiting Toronto and Ottawa, where he directly petitioned Prime Minister Diefenbaker to increase West Indian immigration to Canada. Adams argued that West Indians "are no different in their outlook than Canadians. They have the same way of life, and the same religions."[211] While the region had made some initial gains and select groups of workers were being let into Canada as immigrants, Adams wanted many more admissions at a faster rate. He came away from his trip with a pledge by the Diefenbaker government to give ten million dollars in aid to the federation, along with helping to improve transportation links by sea between the Caribbean and Canada.

With renewed vigour, Black community leaders and groups concentrated on four main areas, the success of which would fundamentally shake up Canada: increased immigration to Canada by non-white people, primarily Black British West Indians; the enforcement of civil rights at the provincial and federal levels to ensure the recognition of the human dignity inherent in all peoples; the passage and enforcement of fair employment practices legislation at all levels of government, along with similar legislation to outlaw discrimination in housing, places of accommodation, and restaurants; and full integration in the workplace and housing. The goal was for Black people to enjoy the same opportunities as white Canadian citizens; to be able to apply for any job with the reasonable expectation of being hired and promoted based on their abilities. The railways—with the porters in the vanguard—would be at the forefront of those battles.

It was an uphill battle as the porters and their allies fought to overthrow a system based on inherent discrimination, a social order that was supported by people who were in strategically stronger positions. The opposition of a group calling itself the Canadian Free Enterprise Committee, based in Winnipeg, was typical. "This brief is dedicated to the preservation of Canada as a free, Christian country," the committee said in a statement to Diefenbaker to protest the government agenda of expanding full human rights to all Canadians.

The brief—found among the former prime minister's papers—rehashed the views of Knox and other traditionalists, who argued that a society should only be changed slowly and with the greatest of care. "It is prepared and presented with the compliments of those who have made a long and careful study of this whole question, to business men and other Canadian citizens who have been so expending their lives working and producing to build up this nation with only a constructive mentality and viewpoint, that they have not had the time to study and prepare themselves to effectively combat the insidious forces working like termites within to undermine and destroy the very foundation of our free, Christian society."

Who were these termites, one might ask? The brief said that the fair employment practices laws were a Jewish plot imported from the United States and propagandized by "communists, socialists, labour bosses, and other groups misled by Marxist strategies cleverly disguised in the robes of 'tolerance' and 'brotherhood.'" The brief's authors decried that under the fair employment practices it would now be unlawful to: "(1) [inquire] into the original name of an applicant for employment, whose name has been changed; (2) [request] a birth or baptismal certificate; (3) [inquire about] the complexion or appearance of an applicant for employment; (4) [request] a photograph from an applicant; (5) [inquire] into the religious or spiritual beliefs or values of an applicant for employment; (6) [inquire] into the racial background or ideology of an applicant for employment; (7) [inquire] into the general military experience or citizenship status of an applicant for employment."[212]

To back up its argument, the Free Enterprise Committee quoted from an article in the January 26, 1952, *Financial Post* to make their case that fair employment legislation would be a disaster in Ontario and as further evidence that morality cannot be legislated. "Instead of outlawing discrimination against race, creed or color," the brief's author argued, "this Act […] makes it impossible to select for special positions the very people it was supposed to protect. If a negro porter, for instance, is wanted for a certain job, the potential employer cannot advertise for a negro. If a Jew is wanted to sell Jewish specialties to Jewish people, or a Frenchman to sell to Frenchmen, or a Chinese to sell to Chinese, asking for one would be classified as discrimination."[213] The quote implied that it was common business practice to hire members of specific ethnic groups to service members of the same groups. In other words, businesses were expected to respect the colour line rather than hire employees to serve customers from all social and ethnic groups.

"For a great many positions special qualification in the way of race, color, creed, language, habits and experience are valuable assets," the *Post* had editorialized.

> That point is recognized in everyday life. It is recognized in politics. But the Ontario Fair Employment Practices Act says we must not recognize it or even mention it. As a result of this ill-advised attempt to make a law do something that only education can do, employment agencies, both private and public, have been thrown into confusion.

The authors of the brief contested the argument that Canada needed to outlaw racial and other discriminatory policies to maintain its status as a member of the United Nations. They argued the UN charter allowed for a period of teaching or inducement to allow change for compliance with its human rights declaration.

> Let us assume that this same type of so-called "non-discriminatory" measure is next applied to our immigration policy. What would it mean? It would mean that we would not be able to choose whom we brought into this country. We would have to accept whomever applied or whomever the UN or a "world authority" sent. Any objection on our part, or any move to select on a basis of national origin, would constitute "discrimination."
>
> The inevitable result of such a policy of "non-discrimination" in immigration, of course, would be our destruction. Under the guise of equalizing populations and living standards, Asia's teeming surplus would stream into America, into Canada, and we would be swallowed up in a sea of colour. It would be done, no doubt, in the name of the UN, charity, humanitarianism, and the "general welfare." But it would spell the end not only of Christian civilization in Canada and America, but also the end of our high living standards [...] Such a policy, under any guise, is *suicidal for Canada.*

In conclusion, the brief fell back on the old argument against change by stating: "F.E.P. is not demanded by the public. F.E.P. is contrary to our whole concept of freedom built upon INDUCEMENT, not COMPULSION. F.E.P. is a project of Statism into the very heart of our private affairs and businesses. F.E.P. is the very antithesis of the only sound employer-employe [sic] relationship—voluntary co-operation and mutual respect. F.E.P. is in its very essence Anti-Christian and, therefore, Anti-Canadian."[214]

The fundamental disagreement between the porters and their allies and their adversaries was a question of morality and what was good for Canada and its citizens. Opponents viewed the proposed changes to Canada as fundamentally evil; the porters argued their fundamental goodness. And in such battles of morality, history has shown there is usually no reconciling radically divergent positions: only one version of what is good for the country can in the end win. Indeed, in many ways, the battle is still being waged today.

But these arguments against the F.E.P. in Canada—including the name calling—were not new. The same talking points had been trotted out over the previous decade in the United States. With the Second World War winding down and the expected return home of millions of men and women in the armed forces and auxiliary services, America was divided on the question of anti-discrimination legislation in the workplace. Supporters argued that legislation was needed to codify what had already been achieved when, at the bidding of the international sleeping car porters union leader A. Philip Randolph, President Roosevelt issued his 1941 executive order temporarily establishing the Fair Employment Practices Committee. Opponents argued that the market would regulate itself and that supporters were falling for a communist plot advanced mainly by Blacks and Jews. Although this argument had been somewhat discredited in the US, it still had power in Canada. It needed to be discredited here as well, and who better to do so than the original proponents of the F.E.P. in Canada: the porters and their brethren and supporters in their international union, the Brotherhood of Sleeping Car Porters.

ON AUGUST 30, 1944, CHAIRMAN Dennis Chavez called the subcommittee of the US Senate's Committee on Education and Labor in Washington to order hearings on proposed fair employment practices legislation. It must have felt like the eyes of the entire hemisphere were on him, but perhaps none more so than those of the Black workers in North America and the Caribbean who had a direct stake in the deliberations' outcome. Sleeping car porters were anxiously following the proceedings in the Black newspapers they distributed across Canada. "We are here to consider today a bill which was introduced by its sponsors in the best of faith and for what is considered to be the best interest of the country," the Senator said.

> [This bill] is designed to promote in peace the same national unity we have
> achieved in war, to give body to our declarations of freedom from want and
> freedom from fear, to raise the standard of living and purchasing power of

our people, and finally, but not least, to confound our enemies who hope by dividing us class by class, race by race, group by group, to snatch from us all permanent gains out of winning the war.

Earlier statements by a number of political colleagues, most notably from the Southern Democrats, must have been ringing in Chavez's ears. Those voices argued that fair employment practices legislation would upset the otherwise harmonious race relations between Blacks and whites, and that with life returning to normal after the war there was no need for the government to create instability. Chavez disagreed:

We approach the problem of discrimination in employment, therefore, from the fundamental proposition that the full utilization of manpower is just as much a problem of the peace as it is an emergency of the war, that discrimination in employment against properly qualified persons by reason of their race, creed, color, national origin and ancestry foments domestic strife and unrest, deprives the United States of the fullest utilization of its capacities for production, depresses the standard of living, cuts down the purchasing power of the population; and that it is the duty of the national Government to eliminate such discrimination in all employment relations which fall within federal jurisdiction or control. The right to work and to seek work is a basic right of every person within the United States, and [this bill] declares it to be an immunity of all citizens protected under the Constitution and laws of Congress against abridgement by any State or instrumentality of a State.

The new legislation, he argued, would make the United States more democratic:

In order to eliminate uncertainty the scope of unfair labor practices within the purview of the bill has been strictly defined. The bill takes away nothing either from management or from organized labor, which either can rightfully claim. The unfair labor practices are all prohibited; no positive action of any kind is required either of management or labor. Management is left free to set its hiring practices, adjust its internal plant-control policy, to discharge according to any standard or standards so long as there is no arbitrary discrimination because of race, creed, color, national origin, or ancestry. In the same way, organized labor is free to manage its internal affairs according to its own light, except in substance it cannot claim to organize a closed shop and exclude workers in the shop or in the same field because of race, creed, color, national origin or ancestry.

Most of all, the legislation was intended to offer equality of citizenship, especially among the war veterans who had risked their lives for the country and its way of life. "The veterans will soon be coming home in ever-growing numbers," Chavez said.

They will represent all elements of the population. There has been no favored class among them. They have shared the same risks and made the same sacrifices. Both on the casualty lists and the list of decorations and honors every race, every creed, every color, every source of national origin and ancestry is honorably represented. If we owed a duty to no other section of the population, we owe it to these veterans to see that their opportunity to work is on the same democratic base as their obligation to serve.[215]

One voice that must have been echoing in Chavez's mind was Congressman John E. Rankin of Mississippi, who rose in the House of Representatives on May 26, 1944, to denounce legislated fair employment practices. "Mr. Chairman, this is one of the most serious questions that ever confronted Congress," Rankin said.

It is one that goes to the very roots of our form of government, our way of life. This so-called Fair Employment Practice Committee, with headquarters at 1006 U Street, which is in the Negro section of Washington, and which was set up without authority of law, is one of the most dangerous communistic agencies ever created to annoy and harass the white people of this country. It has assumed the powers of a dictatorship by attempting to compel the white people of this Nation to employ people of other races, and to promote them to positions of trust and responsibility, whether they are wanted or not.

Perhaps thinking of the origins of the call for such practices and the role played by Randolph and the sleeping car porters, Rankin added: "[The committee] has attempted to force the railroad of this country to place Negroes in positions of conductors and engineers. It is attempting to force business establishments to employ Negro clerks, and even managers, and place them beside, and even over, the white men and white women they have always employed."[216]

Such an approach—one that would be copied by civil libertarians in Canada's quest for its own F.E.P. legislation—was purportedly harmful to society, as it tried to bring equality to racialized groups. "The greatest responsibility placed on mankind is too keep his race pure," John Gibson from Georgia, a Rankin ally, argued. "The greatest destroyer of civilization and Christianity is the mongrelization of races. If this bunch of moral lepers is not stopped, the depth to which they will bring our citizenry is unpredictable. God made his people as he would have them be, and if you doubt that the full plan and chart of these communistic rats calls for a full race adulteration watch the years that are to follow soon, and your complacency so abundantly enjoyed now will stand before you an ugly skeleton of condemnation."

But these views were not those of the majority at the hearings. More typical was Rabbi J. K. Cohen, chairman of the Commission on Economic Discrimination of the American Jewish Congress, who said that he was appearing

> not alone as an American interested in the principles of human dignity and economic fair play, but also as a Jew—as a representative of one of the minority groups in our multigroup society; as a spokesman for a group which has actually suffered discrimination in our economic life. A distinguished American Jew, my teacher and colleague, Rabbi Stephen S. Wise, has said: "Racial and religious discrimination in the field of employment is a denial of democracy; it is of the essence of fascism."

Rabbi Wise was a director and co-founder of the National Association for the Advancement of Colored People when the civil rights organization was incorporated in 1914.

Bromley Oxnam, a Black Methodist bishop representing the Federal Council of Churches of Christ in New York City, delivered resolutions from his council condemning discrimination as immoral and against Christian principles. "We stand for the recognition of the rights of the Negro," he said. "To this end we urge: One, the foundation within our schools and colleges of special courses and activities promoting racial understanding. Two, equal opportunity in employment, upgrading and conditions of work; in the exercise of the full right of citizenship; in excess to professional and business careers; in housing; in transportation and educational facilities."[217]

The case for fair employment practice legislation had been made at the federal level in the US and a number of states would also introduce their own legislation. This would spill over into Canada in a reverse pattern that started with the provinces and ultimately arrived at the federal level.

CANADIAN PORTERS NATURALLY KNEW WHAT it was like to be discriminated against in employment and in housing or public accommodation. Yet certain forms of discrimination still rankled. In the fall of 1952, the Brotherhood of Sleeping Car Porters decided to move its Canadian office permanently from Winnipeg to Montreal. A. R. Blanchette, the top Canadian officer of the Brotherhood, was tasked with finding a space to house the union's operations. In a letter on October 25, 1952, Blanchette sent a report on the progress of his efforts. The letter was sent to Bennie Smith, the second international vice-president of the Brotherhood, who was based in Detroit. Blanchette wrote:

> Just a few lines to give you the information with respect to a regrettable experience I had ten days ago when I interviewed the landlord of a recently erected Office Building in Montreal, the location of which is ideal for the purpose of establishing the Brotherhood office in Canada.
>
> The office building, situated right in front of the Windsor Station, on St. Antoine Street, has many available offices at a rental of $60 to $65 per month, but the landlord stated that if he were to rent me an office, he would have to rent me the whole building since the other tenants would not appreciate the Organization's being a tenant; that he, the landlord, must be concerned about the type of tenant he has. He also asked me would there be loitering around the office, and would we be playing Poker. After I explained to him the purpose for which we desired an office, he stated that he would have to refer our application to the Board of Directors. Later in the day, his secretary phoned me, and informed me that she was instructed to advise me that the Board regretted to have to turn our application down, but they had decided to confine the tenancy to Commercial Businesses.[218]

While this was happening, the Brotherhood and its allies were documenting cases of discrimination across the country. People of colour were denied the purchases of homes, as was the case in a Capilano real estate division in 1950s Vancouver; would not be seated at leading hotels in Vancouver, such as the Waldorf Hotel Beer Parlour; were refused the rental of apartments in Toronto and Ottawa; were not served in restaurants in Dresden, Ontario, a practice that launched a celebrated civil rights court case. Former military veterans were not allowed to participate at various celebrations. Parliamentarians asked the government why West Indian civil servants were still denied rental housing in Ottawa as late as 1968, and why Black and First Nations people were still not allowed to be buried in St. Croix cemetery in West Hants, Nova Scotia. There was also the resistance of the Chrysler Corporation in Windsor, Ontario, to hiring Black employees, among numerous other cases. Simply put, racial discrimination was still rampant, routine, and systemic.

On January 27, 1953, Conservative MP Ellen Fairclough of Hamilton West, Ontario, withdrew a proposed bill, the Fair Employment Practices Act, from the House of Commons. She had doggedly tabled the private member legislation for seven consecutive sessions, but without the support of the government the proposed law went nowhere. But this time Fairclough was optimistic. By withdrawing her bill she was clearing the way for the federal government to introduce its own legislation.

"The provisions of the legislation will apply to all employers of five or more employees, excluding non-profit educational, fraternal, charitable, religious, and social organizations," Minister of Labour Milton Gregg explained. "The legislation applies to employment upon any work, undertaking or business which is within the legislative authority of parliament to regulate, to crown companies, and to trade unions composed of persons employed upon such works, undertakings or businesses."[219] Gregg's speech and the resulting debate was conspicuously absent of any reference to Black workers, although it mentioned anti-Semitic and anti-Ukrainian discrimination.

Liberal-Conservative William J. Brown of St. John's West, Newfoundland, expressed a similar sentiment:

It is a long distance from the old days about which I have heard in my own family. When immigrants went to the United States and they saw signs on the factories saying, "No Irish need apply" or "No Catholics need apply." I think every one of us in our own experiences has come across examples of prejudice either toward ourselves or toward others on account of race, religion or colour. I remember very well an example, which occurred over thirty-five years ago, and I am glad to say that I took the part of a negro, who was refused admission to a certain organization with which all others were white. I remember that I advocated that he should be allowed to enter.[220]

The Fair Employment Practices Act came into effect Canada Day, July 1, 1953, but it could not possibly end discrimination overnight. Political will and action were necessary. The Black activists needed to shift their campaign as well.

In the case of workplace discrimination, activists focused on disrupting hiring and employment practices that limited so many Black people to working as railway porters and to subvert the idea that porters could not be promoted to operational jobs (i.e., every other kind of service.) The two national railways would be the site for the struggle: Canadian Pacific over the question of whether Black workers could become train conductors; and the Canadian National Railway over practices dating back to the beginning of the century which separated Black and white workers into distinct divisions within the union, each with its own seniority lists and job opportunities. The battle for amalgamation at Canadian National Railway—in which the porters had to fight their own union—would seek to merge all workers into one unit with a single seniority list, thereby making Black workers eligible for all jobs on the government-owned railway. It also meant that portering, as a field reserved exclusively for Black workers, would also be opened to workers of all ethnicities and racial backgrounds.

The project envisioned by the Black activists was to fully transform Canada from a society privileging ethnic nationalism to a country with a mixed bag of ethnicities and cultures, where competition between individual citizens was limited to merit and natural abilities. This just society was to be a meritocracy, where race did not matter and where citizens lived together in a common humanity, a "fraternity of universal brotherhood" in the language of the day. But in order to succeed the country would have to be torn down to its very ideological foundation and rebuilt. A new Canada would then emerge out of the racial ashes of history.

PARLIAMENTARIAN J.W. NOSEWORTHY RETURNED TO the issue of Black immigration on June 26, 1954, almost exactly two months to the day after the Negro Citizenship Association brief was presented in Ottawa. There was a need to keep pressuring the government. The House of Commons Committee of Supply was examining the government's proposed annual spending on citizenship and immigration. As was his wont, Noseworthy was plying his nemesis, Minister of Immigration Walter Harris, with queries. "I have one other question to raise with the minister regarding immigration," Noseworthy said.

It is one that I have dealt with on other occasions. I am merely going to ask the minister to tell us what action, if any, the government has taken or proposes to take as the result of the brief presented to him during the latter part of April by the Negro Citizenship Association on behalf of immigration from the West Indies, those British subjects who, by regulations of the immigration department, are not British subjects and cannot be classified as British subjects for immigration purposes. What consideration was given to the brief?[221]

Before the minister could respond, Parliament was treated to another speech on the anxious concern Canadian whites were experiencing. Representing Winnipeg South Centre, Gordon Churchill marvelled at the ethnic and racial transformation taking place in Canada and wondered aloud whether or not it had been by design. Regardless, the policy implications it necessitated were profound, especially regarding what types of people should be allowed to become future Canadians.

Quoting from an article in the Canadian Legionnaires' newsletter *Legionary*, Churchill reported that

Mr. Gurton draws attention to the racial origin of the population of this country at the time of confederation, and the change that has taken place from that day to this. For example, in quoting from the census returns from 1901 to 1951, he shows that in 1901 the people of British origin in this country amounted to 57.03 percent; French were 30.71 percent; and others 12.26 percent. Then, the writer follows it through decade after decade to 1951 where the percentages are as follows: British, 47.89; French 20.83; others 21.28, indicating a decline in the people of British origin in this country of opportunity 10 percent.

Continuing with existing policies, Churchill reported that by the end of the twentieth century "people of British origin in the country will be 32 per cent; French, 20 percent and others 38 percent." The implication of these stats was that in less than 50 years, current policies would mean Canada would no longer be a white country. Similar arguments were also put forward by groups like the Committee for Free Enterprise, who said that this collective of undesirable ethnic groups would surpass the critical 20 percent population threshold for group recognition in a state.

"We are concerned not only with the numbers of people who enter this country," Churchill said. "It is not a question of whether we will have fifteen million or thirty million; rather we are concerned with the type of people who are here, and the type of citizens they may become."[222]

Churchill was highlighting a policy bind then facing Canada. At a time when leading policymakers conceded that Canada should drastically increase immigration to increase its population, the government had started to cut back on the number of immigrants coming into the country, largely because it was failing to attract the "appropriate" ones, a policy that would stay in place until 1962 when a new policy was introduced, which would pave the way for more diverse groups of immigrants. Churchill also pointed out something that would plague Canada's future national discourse. All meaningful population projections posited that both the Anglo and French communities would diminish as a percentage of the overall population of the country as the twentieth century progressed. This development would enflame French nationalism, with many Quebecois demanding a homeland of their own, an ethnically French, independent Quebec nation—and for some, a *white* homeland.

The question of how to position Blackness in this discourse became a singular test of Canada as a moral and ethical social order. In their homes, church basements, and town halls, in porter halls, on trains, and increasingly in the corridors of influence and power, Black Canadians were central to this re-imagining of what was, and who could be, Canadian. The brief from the Negro Citizenship Association was forcing white Canadian elites to consider a future in which they would have less control over the country's demographics.

"Upon receiving the brief, we studied it," Minister Harris said of the Negro Citizenship Association's document as he wrapped up the debate in Parliament.

> I examined the statistics with regard to these persons and I found that there has been a steady increase in the number of Negroes from the West Indies being admitted to Canada. If we leave the present regulations as they are for the time being I think the number will probably increase in any event and that we shall have what I would consider to be a reasonably fair representation of these people in the flow of immigrants to Canada.[223]

But the government had done more than study the brief. It was actually resisting its suggestions, with the top civil servants on the file leading the way.

Within a month of its delivery, the brief had been evaluated by the director of the immigration branch of the ministry, C.E.S. Smith, and had been rejected as implausible. "Nothing can be said regarding our policy with respect to colour and partly coloured immigrants that has not already been said,"

Smith argued in a memo to his boss, Deputy Minister Laval Fortier. "I would not advocate any change a [sic] this time." He also recommended against expanding the class of relatives to be allowed into the country, killing debate on the very case that first brought the delegation to Ottawa: Braithwaite's application for his granddaughter in Barbados to join him in Canada. Such expansion, the civil servant argued, would lead to "an increase of sponsored applications from all sources."[224] Instead, Smith made the case for maintaining the provisions under which Canada accepted Black immigrants with exceptional merit as a special group, with numbers varying as conditions dictated. Considerations might include humanitarian grounds, or anything which was at a given time deemed to be in the best interest of Canadians.

The federal government did its best to avoid responding to the Negro Citizenship Association in the months immediately following the presentation of their brief. This inactivity prompted Grizzle and his union to sharpen their language in their government correspondence, with the union passing, and then sending, on March 7, 1955, a resolution to Prime Minister St. Laurent informing him that his immigration policy "reeks with discrimination against those whose skins are not white."[225] Grizzle had also copied his letter to the prime minister to the Toronto District Trades and Labour Council, asking that it be passed on to the parent Trades and Labour Congress of Canada in the hope that the Congress "would soon support our fight." Writing in his capacity as a Negro Citizens Association member, Armstrong said: "It was evident through his ministers' lack of response that Louis St. Laurent considered immigration to Canada from the Caribbean an unimportant matter."[226]

Agitation for new immigration policies continued, creating the kind of diplomatic embarrassments that Mackenzie King had tried to avoid when he was prime minister. The policies made Canada seem hypocritical and undermined international credibility, for while they were claimed to abide by various tenets of social justice, such as the entrenching of universal civil rights, the policies continued in practice to discriminate against racialized groups. "If we are to build a democratic society in Canada," Noseworthy said once again in Parliament on February 15, 1955, "then we can ill afford to shut out from our country immigrants purely on the basis of their colour, creed or race."[227]

By then Harris had been replaced by Jack Pickersgill as immigration minister, but the jousting over the direction of Canadian immigration continued, with the Liberal government beginning to leave behind the policies that had been championed as recently as a decade earlier by Prime

Minister King and continued by his successor St. Laurent. Noseworthy continued to apply pressure on the government until his death on March 30, 1956. The Liberal government was voted out of office in June 1957 and was replaced by the Conservatives, led by John Diefenbaker, who had long been viewed as a friend of the porters and an advocate for a Canadian Bill of Rights.

On the long train rides between Ottawa and his riding of Prince Albert in Saskatchewan, Diefenbaker got to know the regular porters well. He developed a close bond with them, that grew into friendship with some. This meant that the porters, despite the regulations which otherwise permitted fraternizing unduly with clients, sometimes were able to lobby the young parliamentarian, who often showed a great deal of sympathy for their political objectives. Diefenbaker liked talking to the porters about his own hopes for the advancement of human rights in Canada and the implementation of anti-discriminatory practices, all issues that were central to his political life.

Diefenbaker's campaign for a bill of rights and its implementation in 1960 put more pressure on the immigration file. Dominant political parties realized that immigration policies were to be henceforth shaped by civil rights concerns. Canada's immigration policies must therefore line up not only with the United Nations' charter but with a new bill of rights outlawing discrimination based on race, colour, or creed. The new government promised new immigration legislation consistent with anti-discriminatory policies.

One of Diefenbaker's first official guests was Prime Minister Grantley Adams of the British West Indies. Adams came with a plan for deepening cooperation between the countries on all fronts, particularly in the areas of trade and immigration. The aforementioned loophole in Canadian immigration policy became the focus of discussions. West Indians, deemed exceptional because of their skills, were already slipping through this loophole when the two leaders met. Diefenbaker would continue to deepen his appreciation for the porters as the West Indies, eventually maintaining a cottage in Barbados where toward the end of life he spent his winters.

The porters and their allies could now claim much of the credit for negating the racist legacy of the old Canada and pointing the way toward a new, more inclusive Canada. The brief presented by the porters and the members of the Negro Citizenship Association haunted not only the federal capital but all of Canada. Under this pressure, Canada was slowly changing. Not coincidentally, so was life on the national railways, including the working conditions of the porters.

FAIR CONSIDERATION
The Porters Gain New Ground

AFTER YEARS OF LOBBYING, ON October 6, 1955, Negro Citizenship Association founder Donald Moore received a letter stipulating that the Canadian government was about to introduce legislation which had the potential to greatly increase immigration from the British West Indies. Written by W. W. Dawson, Director of the Special Services Branch of the Federal Department of Labour, it stated that the "National Employment Service in conjunction with this branch are working out the arrangements for the reception and placement of domestic workers to be brought from the British West Indies for employment in Canadian households." The first indication of this policy change had been received a few months previously on June 10, 1955, when the government had decided to allow on an experimental basis Black domestic workers into Canada. The West Indian Domestic Scheme started with the initial target of seventy-five workers from Jamaica and twenty-five from Barbados. Dawson's letter informed Moore that the first workers were to arrive by air in Montreal on November 3, 1955, after which they would be interviewed by placement officers for jobs in Montreal, Toronto, "and one or two other eastern Canadian points."

The National Employment Service is now receiving, and carefully scrutinizing, applications from potential employers and it is expected that there will be little difficulty in placing these girls on arrival in satisfactory homes. While it was intended that there would be 100 girls brought forward this fall, the supply countries have found it impossible to complete arrangements for the movement of all of them this fall. It is expected, therefore, that only twenty-five or thirty will come forward at this time and the balance will arrive in the spring.[228]

With this news, the Black community in Toronto began frantic plans to receive the women, to help them acclimatize socially and physically to Canada, and, most importantly, to educate the women as to their pioneering role in Black immigration to Canada. Their success would pave the way for other non-white women to enter the country as domestic workers, especially women from places like the Philippines and South East Asia. Once settled, these women would be able to sponsor immediate family members to join them and, one by one, every new immigrant would move Canada further away from its history as a white country.

The West Indian program was the first real application of the merit-based immigration system that the Negro Citizenship Association had recommended in its brief. Domestic servants joined nurses on the list of qualified West Indians who could help Canada with its labour shortages in specific segments of the economy. These pioneering women demonstrated how the merit-based system could work: instead of blanket general immigration, demand for labour in specific sectors was met through targeted immigration. As the letter to Moore suggested, the government felt there was no shortage of potential employers for domestic workers; in fact, there was disappointment that the full allocation of one hundred workers was not immediately available. It was not a question of the arrivals' racial or ethnic grouping, but rather if the social skills they brought with them met specific economic, cultural, or social needs. This framework would become the basis for Canada's much heralded points-system for choosing future immigrants, when, in 1962, the government formally abandoned choosing immigrants on an ethnic and racial basis and threw out the orders-in-council that granted British subjects exclusive right of entry into Canada.

Instead, Canada shifted to, as the civil servant Smith had recommended, a system of selecting immigrants based on how "they will contribute appreciably to the social, economic, or cultural life of Canada." The immigrants would henceforth be chosen because of their excellence and merit in consideration of broad public interests. No longer would new Canadians be chosen or rejected by racial criteria, but by a system that rewarded the most excellent applicants—the experts in their fields or calling—from around the world, as long as there was a stated demand for them. Excellence would be determined by criteria that rewarded applicants with points for an array of skills and abilities—education, age, languages, work experience—that made them potentially desirable citizens. The actual qualifications might change; different weights could be given to identifiable skills and abilities required by Canada at a specific moment. But the fact that decisions would be based on merit and need and not on race or colour marked a giant victory for the NCA, the porters, and for people of colour everywhere.

The idea of sending well-trained domestic workers—experts in good housekeeping—from the British West Indies to Canada began with efforts by the Barbadian government to increase immigration to the United Kingdom and Canada. In 1954, at a meeting in London with British and Canadian officials, Barbados' Minister of Labour Ronald Mapp had proposed that the island should send, on a trial basis, two hundred trained domestic servants to work in British homes. In a follow-up visit to Ottawa, Mapp suggested a similar plan for Canada, an idea that was extended to including workers from all the British West Indies. In 1966, with less fanfare, Canada and the Caribbean governments started the Canadian Farm Labour program, under which West Indian agricultural workers would come to Canada. This was similar to the HB1 visa programs in the United States, which allowed agricultural workers to work in the United States primarily during the harvesting period. These were not immigrants but guest workers who returned home after the work was finished. A major difference between these two programs was that the agricultural workers were temporary and almost exclusively both unskilled and male; the domestic servant program was for skilled women who would be given the opportunity to eventually become Canadian citizens. The women also served in Canadian homes and were integrated into the communities into which they'd been sent, while the men in the agricultural program worked out of sight of the public view on isolated farms and rarely engaged with the wider Canadian society.

The Caribbean government would undertake to train the women, making them skilled in such things as home economics and good housekeeping. As trained professionals, the domestic workers would be able to manage and take care of Canadian homes, since more and more Canadian women, in the years after the end of the Second World War, were choosing to remain in the workforce. The domestic servants would live in the homes of their employers, taking care of both children and the elderly, while performing all the necessary duties of maintaining a home. Paid a relatively small salary, the women often worked long hours and were given two days of their own weekly. They washed, cleaned, cooked, and mopped; they were maids and nannies. In many ways, they were no different from porters on the trains, especially those porters who over the years were derisively called domestics and chambermaids. It was not coincidental that the domestic servants program was modeled after the Pullman porters, since that program was widely regarded as the international standard bearer of Black labour.

Not only did porters lead the fight for increased Black immigration, they provided the model on how it should be patterned. Also, by establishing new criteria for choosing immigrants, Canada had moved toward making Canada a just home for Blackness. Yet despite this progress, the porters were still fighting for their own social emancipation and recognition.

"I CHARGE THAT I WAS discriminated against in my application for this job because I am a Negro," porter John K. Crutcher said in an explosive accusation in the spring of 1954 to the federal government after his employer, Canadian Pacific Railway, refused to hire him as a conductor.[229] With his petition to the federal government, Crutcher would act as a test case for claiming job discrimination against Black workers.

Both Crutcher and George Garraway, two seasoned sleeping car porters who had often been deputized on runs as porters-in-charge when conductors were unavailable, had responded to the Canadian Pacific Railway's call for applications for conductors, jobs traditionally earmarked for white employees. In the dismissive manner reserved for such applications from Black people, the railway had replied thanking them for their applications and politely stating that "due consideration will be given to all persons whose services are available for the positions so that the men most suitable for them will be employed." This was the typical brush off for such applications, which were promptly placed in a file never looked at again. But armed with the federal government's fair employment practices legislation banning racial discrimination in the workplace, Crutcher, and then Garraway, were up for the fight. They demanded that "due consideration" reflect a commitment toward equality for all applicants and a government review of the railway's hiring practices.

In a letter of May 21, 1954, to the director of industrial relations in the Department of Labour, ten months after the fair employment practices legislation came into effect, Crutcher said that since he had applied for the position he had learned that the company had hired ten new conductors,

"some of them without any previous Railway experience, and with less education and leadership experience than myself, and none being Negroes."
In terms of his own qualifications for a conductor's job, Crutcher said he
had "a good record" with the railway over the previous seven and a half
years, that he had a high-school education, and that he "had leadership
experience and experience supervising men in view of the fact that I was a
personal yeoman with the Navy for three years." Although he did not state
it, as porter-in-charge on trips he had done all the supervisory duties of
conductors, which meant he'd already worked repeatedly and satisfactorily
in the capacity of a conductor, without the title or the pay.

"I can only conclude," he wrote, "that the Canadian Pacific Railway is
deliberately excluding Negroes as being 'suitable' for sleeping car conductor's
jobs and has overlooked my application and my qualifications for this reason.
I would appreciate your looking into this case as soon as possible."[230] Prior
to sending his letter, Crutcher had coordinated his strategy with the Toronto
chapter of the Brotherhood of Sleeping Car Porters and with the Toronto
Joint Labour Committee For Human Rights, which was sponsored by the
main Canadian unions with the direction to fight against human rights abuses,
especially against discrimination based on race, religion, colour, or creed.

Six months after the request for a review was filed, Stanley Grizzle
finally got approval from his superiors in the US to write the government,
supporting Crutcher and Garraway's complaints. "Our Organization is of
the opinion, that, on the basis of their past experience with the C.P.R., they
would qualify for the position of sleeping car conductor especially since
they both have had 'in-charge' training," Grizzle wrote to the director of
Industrial Relations Branch of the Department of Labour.

> The apparent disregard of the complainants' qualifications and experience
> by the C.P.R. when the company chose men with less experience to fill the
> position the complainants had applied for, and the fact that none of these
> men were Negroes, strongly indicates an apparent policy of discrimination
> by the C.P.R. in violation of the provisions of the Canada F.E.P. Act. Our
> Organization unequivocally condemns such a policy of discrimination in
> employment and strongly urges the Department of Labour to fully investi-
> gate these apparent violations.[231]

The international union had been spoiling for this kind of fight, although
it had been anticipated that the matter would first be settled in the US

since that had been the first country in which the union's leader, A. Philip Randolph, had made his original call for fair employment practices laws. But from the outset, the Toronto division was out of step with the US leadership of the International Brotherhood of Sleeping Car Porters, and it was partly because of this difference that Sid Blum, executive secretary of the Joint Labour Committee for Human Rights, took the lead in helping the porters' fight. Indeed, before Grizzle could send his letter of support, he had to win an internal union struggle. Differences between Canadian and US sensibilities—and the understanding of Canadian law and political climate—caused a rift within union leadership.

Detroit-based international vice president Bennie Smith, to whom the Canadian leaders reported directly, had written Grizzle informing him that the union wanted to focus the struggle on the porters' right to be promoted to conductors. The Canadian struggle should focus on what the US leadership called the *upgrading* of Black workers, where they moved from one job classification to a higher one in the same unit. Instead, Grizzle was fighting for all Black Canadians, in this case two who happened to be porters, so that they might exercise the right under Canadian law to apply for whatever jobs they wanted without fear of discrimination. Grizzle wanted anyone to be able to apply for a conductor job, even if they weren't previously employed by the railway.

This was not the international union's position. As a result, Smith withheld permission for Grizzle to send his letter and suggested that Grizzle was picking an unnecessary and untimely fight with railway management. In his estimation, Grizzle had not done the necessary research to support his claim. "If we are to participate in the establishing of a case of discrimination," Smith wrote to Grizzle on November 10, 1954, "based upon race, creed, colour or national origin, we should do so with clean hands. I would also suggest that you inform the two men affected as to your method of approach, so that each and all may understand. May I ask who initiated this matter, we, they or the Committee for Human Rights, as I should like to think the matter through from the beginning."[232]

The internal dispute eventually ended up on Randolph's desk. "I note that you are taking the position that the C.P.R. is guilty of discrimination against the aforementioned porters," he wrote Grizzle.

> As you know, it is the position of the Brotherhood, taken in the last convention in Los Angeles, that a major effort would be made to secure the

upgrading of porters from position of sleeping car porter to that of sleeping car conductor. Of course, this does not involve the question of transfer, it involves the question of promotion. Now, are we, in this case we are developing, pushing the question of <u>promotion</u> or <u>transfer?</u> [Underlined in original] It seems to me that our grounds would be stronger for promotion than for transfer, inasmuch as the question of transfer would have to be developed under some rule in an existing agreement and we don't have any such rule, but we have plenty grounds to find for promotion.[233]

"Please be advised," Grizzle responded to Randolph on November 13, 1954,

that concerning applications of Brothers Crutcher and Garraway the main issue is based on their contention that their application which was an out and out application for the job of conductor was not dealt with fairly. And the charge is being laid by them based on the existence of the Canada Fair Practices Act. The question of promotion and transfer do not enter into the picture. Except that since both the men affected are presently employees of the C.P.R. would, if hired by another department of the C.P.R., be shown on C.P.R. records as having transferred. But this point is irrelevant.

Having explained the situation and legal implications in Canada, Grizzle ended, "I am hoping that there will not be any further delay in your approval of this local sending a letter to Mr. MacLean, Director Industrial Relations, Federal Dept. of Labour, Ottawa, supporting the investigation—and not the charge (of whether it should be a promotion or a separate application for a job)."[234]

Grizzle finally received the approval he sought and sent the letter. Within days, Grizzle received the expected thumbs up from Blum with the good news of progress in the case. "Thanks for sending me the copy of your letter on the Canada F.E.P. complaint to Maclean," Blum wrote Grizzle on December 1, 1954. "It is an excellent letter. I now expect the Labour Department in Ottawa to obtain some of the results or else order a Board of Inquiry on the complaints." Offering more good news, Blum stated, "I understand that an attempt is being made to obtain a three month trial period for the complainants. If successful, this should be the basis of a satisfactory settlement. The onus would be on the company to present <u>definite proof</u> that Crutcher and

Garraway weren't qualified for this job. I feel pretty sure that they wouldn't be able to find this proof. [Underlined in original.]"[235]

Canadian Pacific fiercely fought the complaints. It argued that the men were not qualified for the jobs of conductors and that, in the case of Crutcher, his employment history was questionable. Crutcher would not help his case much when he was charged with desertion of duty six months later. But in a letter to the Department of Labour on June 25, 1954, Crutcher said that the company was using the demerit points as a ruse against him since the demerit points had not prevented him from working as a porter-in-charge. "If these demerit points were considered seriously by the company as disqualifying me from the position of Conductor," he wrote, "they would have never put me in an 'in-charge' Sleeping Car Porter job in the two years immediately following the issuance of the demerits."

The railway also argued that Crutcher's poor English had been a consideration in his failed application. "I can only say that this appears to be both an unfounded and spurious reason for the C.P.R. to put forward," Crutcher responded. "I have never heard of the Company giving English tests to perspective candidates for Conductor's jobs. If such tests are usually given in written, or any other form, I demand that the C.P.R. produce them; prove that they actually do judge the English qualifications of a candidate by such test; and then permit me to take the test in the presence of a Department of Labour official."[236]

But with political opinion running against Canadian Pacific, the railway finally gave in, though initially only for conductors who worked out of Toronto, a clear indication of the local union's clout and the effects of the provincial fair employment legislation. On April 18, 1955, Canadian Pacific Railway hired Garraway as its first Black sleeping car conductor, and two days later William Lowe as its second. They would be hired on a trial basis for the summer season. Crutcher missed out. In a sacrifice so as not to hold up the general fight against Canadian Pacific Railway, Crutcher agreed to withdraw his application to the tribunal because of the demerit points on his record.

With an eye to public relations, Grizzle speedily issued a press release, dated April 30, 1955, and sent off a letter with the good news to the Brotherhood's head office. "A fight to end the colour bar in employment on Canadian railroads has scored its first success. Mr. George Garraway became the Negro hired as a Sleeping Car conductor with the Canadian Pacific Railway company on 16 April last and Mr. Wm. Lowe became the second Negro hired on 18 April, 1955, in Toronto, Ontario, Canada [...] Both men made their initial [journey] from Toronto to Winnipeg, Manitoba and return."[237]

This was indeed a triumph for the Brotherhood, coming eleven months after the union won the right for Black porters to apply for conductor jobs on North American railroads. The initial triumph was the Massachusetts Commission's announcement that the Pullman company had finally agreed to end discrimination for conductor jobs in the state. According to the *Pittsburgh Courier* of May 22, 1954, this precedent left it "up to the ten other states which have similar LAWS to press the Pullman Company to end its color discrimination in their jurisdiction."[238] A report in the *Toronto Telegram* of May 2, 1955, was typical of the news of the Canadian milestone. Under the headline "C.P.R. Promotes Negro Porters To Conductors," the item read, "For the first time in Canadian Railway history there will be Negro sleeping car conductors. The Canadian Pacific Railway disclosed the promotion of three porters [....] The appointments were made on the basis of length and type of service and ability, a C.P.R. spokesman said. He said there is nothing new in the promotions of Negroes to such posts 'as Negroes often hold supervisory positions.'"[239]

Randolph was quick to congratulate Grizzle. "I am very glad to be brought up to date on the developments in connection with this important and significant fight to eliminate discrimination in the employment of persons of color on the railways of Canada," he wrote Grizzle on March 29, 1955. "I want to congratulate you on the splendid fight you have made against discrimination on the C.P.R. [...] I think that the achievement of the employment of our person of color as a sleeping car conductor on the C.P.R. is a notable one and will, no doubt, help the proposed policy of the Brotherhood to upgrade porters to the position of sleeping car conductors in contractual form with the C.P.R.."[240] Randolph was so impressed with Grizzle that he ordered him to write a report detailing the successful fight for publication in the union's newspaper, the *Black Voice*, for continent-wide circulation.

But while Black workers could now apply and be hired as conductors, they still had to fight the railway and the established unions representing mainly white workers to fully enjoy the rights and privileges that normally came with such a position. When the conductors were hired they were first treated as brand new employees without any seniority, no matter how long they had previously been employed by the company. This meant they

229

risked unemployment after the end of their trial period or the end of the busy season, when the company traditionally laid off workers at the end of summer. Grizzle was alerted to this problem by Sid Blum.

"There is one difficulty," Blum wrote Grizzle March 15, 1956, "both in Mr. Garraway's case and in the case of the other five prospective applicants, that should be cleared up. Should we be successful in placing some qualified porters as conductors for summer runs, they will lose their seniority in the Brotherhood. When the summer runs are over and there is no more work for them as conductors, they will be faced with serious financial hardship." As a result of their promotions to conductor the workers would no longer be members of the porters' union—having signed up with the conductors' union—and would, therefore, be jobless and likely to be rehired again as either a porter or conductor on the dreaded as-needed basis.

"We must realize that the C.P.R. will use, or try to use, this threat of economic hardship to discourage our qualified applicants from accepting conductors' jobs," Blum said. "I have every hope that our work in breaking down the C.P.R.'s employment color bar will be crowned with success. However, all the gains will be futile if the applicants cannot accept the appointment because of the fear that because they take a summer run conductors' job, they will lose their seniority as porters."[241]

Blum and Grizzle figured out a strategy. The Black conductors would ask Canadian Pacific Railway for a leave of absence from their job for ninety days so they could work as conductors, thereby allowing the men to remain members of the porters' union while working as conductors. This way, if they did not complete the probation period or were laid off at the end of it, they could return to their old job and retain their seniority.

But even then the workers still had another hurdle to overcome. Conductors were members of their own union and in a closed shop workplace it was a condition of employment that all conductors be in the same union. The Order of Railway Conductors and Brakesmen in Canada would literally blackball the Black conductors—the process where the three-man admission committee voted on new members by putting forward white balls of approval or black ones of disapproval. One black ball resulted in a negative vote. Admission to the union required unanimous approval. On April 7, 1958, V. I. Petgrave, a founding member of the Toronto division of the union and a porter since 1919, wrote Canadian Minister of Labour Michael Starr to complain about his blackballing. "There are five of us (coloured) who are Sleeping Car Conductors and range in complexion from 'white' to dark brown and in which latter group, unfortunately I am," Petgrave said. "The other four have been admitted to membership with one having more difficulty than the other three due more or less to the natural divergence in their complexion."

Petgrave said he made several attempts to gain membership but failed each time.

> Monthly dues, nevertheless, are being withheld from my wages for the support of the union, the processing of which I am compelled to pay the costs. I have been compelled too to accept the health plan just instituted with the union directing the disbursement of benefits to its members. Not being a member I have no voice in the business of what concerns me materially. Not being a member I have no representation whatsoever whether it be a grievance of any nature, be it wages, working conditions or false accusations.[242]

Eight months later Bernard Wilson, director of Industrial Relations for the ministry, wrote Petgrave to tell him the results of the review into his complaint. "We do not think that a case has been established under the Canada Fair Employment Practices Act whereby you are discriminated against by the Order of the Railway Conductors and Brakesmen because of your 'colour,' as from the evidence other Black workers were allowed to join the union."[243]

The other unions found other ways to oppose the policy changes. Senior conductors would make harsh evaluations of new Black conductors, leading Blum to write to the company questioning the "objectivity" of the evaluators and requesting that new conductors should receive training on 'student trips' before undertaking regular ones.

The result was that Canadian Pacific Railway started to require IQ tests for applicants for conductor jobs, reputedly making it the first company in Canada to introduce such testing for employment purposes. This led to charges that the company was using IQ testing to reinforce the colour line. The IQ tests themselves were not the issue, the railway argued, but that the rejected workers failed the same test other Blacks had passed. Blum had to break this news to a number of Black applicants who had been turned down by C.P.R. One of them was Toronto porter Leo Gaskin, who Blum wrote on March 7, 1956, to report that the federal conciliation officer had ruled he "could find no evidence that the IQ tests have been used to bar coloured applicants from sleeping car conductors' jobs. The company contends that you [...]were not advanced because you failed to pass the tests."[244] Blum could only recommend that Gaskin try to retake the test.

Blum wrote to Grizzle November 18, 1955:

> I have just received some confidential information about the latest development in our fight with the C.P.R. to give fair consideration to Negro applicants for Conductor's positions. It seems that eight colored porters, and two white porters have applied this year for conductor's positions. These applicants were all given the aptitude test that the company is using. It seemed that they all flunked, or failed, in some subject or other—so that the company couldn't put them on as conductors. It also seems apparent that there is a serious shortage of conductors and the company will be forced to hire someone shortly. What I wonder is if you could find out for me some specific data on who are the eight colored porters who applied and were tested, and who were the two white porters. Also, if the company informed them that they failed to pass, and in what subjects they had failed to pass. The company knows that if they overlook these ten guys and hire people without previous railroad experience, we will be down on them immediately and force them to prove that the eight guys (or ten guys) that they overlooked didn't have the qualifications for the job. I believe that is why they are afraid to take outside guys. I want to break this set up, and get the company to start *acting fairly* in all their cases—that is why I need the information. I will be trying to get in touch with the Gaskin brothers, and others to see if I can get some more details on the case.[245]

In a moment of frustration, Blum reported to his superior, Kalmen Kaplansky, director of the Jewish Labour Committee of Canada, about how Canadian Pacific was preventing the gains under the Ontario legislation from spreading to the rest of its operations across the country. "The C.P.R. in Montreal has been pulling the same tricks as they are trying here (Ontario)," he said in a letter dated November 30, 1955.

> Unfortunately there is no Stan Grizzle there to take an interest in the situation and channel information into the Committee's office. The primary publicity angle of these cases—though we are fighting the same battle we fought earlier this year with Garraway—is that here we have Canada's largest corporation; with its huge staff of personnel people; and its principles of

advanced management; and its supposed interest in the welfare of the country and its passengers; here we have the C.P.R. evading the Canada F.E.P. act, picking less qualified men for sleeping car conductor positions, and indulging in all sorts of expensive and time consuming childish games (such as I.Q. tests) in order to bolster its discriminatory employment policies.[246]

In another letter to his superior a month later, Blum was more optimistic as he prepared for a meeting with railway management. The aims of the discussions, he wrote, were:

1. We want to get a standardized procedure established and recognized so that the likelihood of Negro applicants being overlooked simply because they are Negroes will be minimized. 2. We want to get the company to recognize that discrimination was practised in the past, and that its practice in the present and in the future is a costly foolish procedure, and will get them in trouble with the Federal govt. 3. We want to get a procedure whereby applicants who fail the test will be told specifically what sections they failed, and an informal procedure established whereby applicants who question the results will be able to have an impartial authority (the Federal conciliation officer, for instance) check the results—without the whole a machinery of the Labour department being mobilized by way of a formal F.E.P. complaint. 4. We want to get some sort of compromise agreement on the present three complaints (who I feel are qualified for the position) whereby they will be given trial periods as sleeping car conductors when such positions are open.[247]

In the end, the porters had scored a massive victory in the battle for fairness in the workplace: porters could now become conductors. They would use this victory as motivation to extend the anti-discriminatory struggles to other areas of Canadian society, such as housing, accommodation, and restaurants. But the Canadian porters still needed one more major victory, and with this one they would strike at the very heart of the structure that formally brought Jim Crowism to Canada. With this battle, the porters would finally get the chance to settle an almost fifty-year score with the Canadian Brotherhood of Railway Employees and the government-owned Canadian National Railway.

THE PORTERS' FINAL FIGHT
A Multicultural Country

WHEN JOHN DIEFENBAKER BECAME PRIME Minister in 1957, the porters believed that they finally had an ally at the highest levels of the federal government, someone who might change the employment policies adversely affecting Black workers on government-owned railways. The porters had found themselves in an acute battle with two enemies: the Canadian Brotherhood of Railway Employees and the Canadian National Railway, both of whom had maintained anti-Black labour segregation practices since the beginning of the century.

"Sleeping Car Porters Accuse Railway Firm," read a headline on April 26, 1961, in the *Winnipeg Free Press* and a number of other newspapers: "A local official Tuesday accused the Canadian National Railways and its parent union of conducting a policy of racial discrimination against sleeping car porters."[248] The charge was made by Lee Williams, chairman of Local 130 of the Canadian Brotherhood of Railway, Transport and General Workers. He was also calling out the railway and his union in a most public way—on *Eye to Eye*, a popular public affairs program on the Canadian Broadcasting Corporation, the national broadcaster.

Williams, who was born near Waco, Texas, moved with his parents to Hillside, Saskatchewan, as a young boy and spent his working life on the railway out of Winnipeg, where he joined with a strong group of porters fighting against the discriminatory employment practices of their union and their employer. Williams knew he could count on the support of Blanchette, Grizzle, and their allies in the Canadian Congress of Labour, especially now that new leadership had taken over the organization with the ousting of the Canadian Brotherhood of Railway Employees founder Aaron Mosher. Indeed, it took some time to determine the Congress' true intentions and to convince Williams and his colleagues to put their trust in the Congress. As a compromise, it was suggested that Sid Blum mediate their dispute. Blum had acquired a reputation for successfully mediating employment disputes between the railways and unions, particularly the Brotherhood of Sleeping Car Porters and the Canadian Pacific Railway. Williams and his supporters initially objected to Blum's intervention because they did not trust him to be impartial, but they eventually gave in.

In a letter to Prime Minister Diefenbaker on August 1, 1957, a little more than a month after the change in government, Williams wrote:

> We realize, Sir, that you are still very busy. But it seems we have no other course but to appeal to you. We say this as it is now more obvious than ever, that C.N.R. Management and CB of RE [Canadian Brotherhood of Railway Employees] officials are more determined than ever to make a mockery of the democratic principles of this great country, as well as the Human Rights of its Citizens under the F.E.P. Act, and otherwise if this F.E.P. Act is not sufficient to protect the rights of Citizens, it seems to us steps should be taken to protect those rights. They are using every method, and they know all the methods, to by-pass and violate the Constitution of the C.L.C. [sic] [Canadian Congress of Labour], which advocates equal rights and opportunity for advancement to all regardless of race, creed or color. Seeing this is so, we can only appeal to you to take steps to order C.N.R. management to call in CB and RE top officials with a view to have them delete the discriminatory clause in our agreements which forbids porters the right of advancement.[249]

This letter kicked off the final fight between the porters and Canadian National Railway, a battle fought for seven years against the government corporation. The main issue concerned the merging of two groups of employees into a single unit within the union and the desire for all members to have the same right to apply and to be promoted for all jobs and positions represented by the union. The Williams faction argued that with the merger, porter jobs held exclusively by Black people would be lost to white employees, who would almost certainly be given preference for the jobs. Through the merging of the separate seniority list for Black and white employees, all jobs on the railway would be opened up to all workers. Seniority, and not race, would determine who would get any job.

"Porters and colored citizens in general have reached the stage where they are fed up on C.N.R., a government institution, whose policy is to spend thousands of dollars of the peoples' money, their money, to train employees with a few years seniority to promote over Porters with twenty-five or thirty years of faithful service, who are already qualified to perform the duties of said promotion." Williams added: "Seeing these are the facts of the case, the C.N.R. are even now training Dining Car Employees for Sleeping Car Conductors, and they have men on the Sleeping Car Conductors' seniority list now who seldom make a trip, even in summer season, which is the busy season. It is very easy to see their policy is one of discrimination, as this would bar porters from an opportunity to promotion for the next twenty years, even if we were given the right to promote at this time."

Williams reminded the prime minister that officials of the Canadian Brotherhood of Railway Employees supported the opposition CCF party in the election that brought him to power, "so you owe them nothing." In fact, unlike the union officials, Black Canadians, especially the porters, supported Diefenbaker and considered him a friend. "Sir, we realize that you will have a lot of ways to handle this case that we could never think of," Williams wrote. "However, having nothing in mind at this time but consideration for you, and your position, we respectfully suggest that if your Minister of Labour was instructed to handle this matter with C.N.R. Officials, it would be to the advantage of all concerned [...] We realize that this may be a big job for you at this time, Sir, but we feel that we have taken all the humiliation over the years that any one group of people should be required to take from a government institution."[250]

A month after Williams' letter was sent, the president of the Canadian Brotherhood of Railway Employees received a letter from the assistant deputy minister in the Department of Labour, M. M. Maclean, the civil servant responsible for implementing government labour policy. In his letter of September 27, 1957, to W. J. Smith of the union, Maclean reminded him of prior conversations about porters on the Canadian National Railway. He reminded him that the porters had been pushing for revision to the contract language to allow them to be promoted and that Smith had promised him that the union was working to amalgamate the seniority lists for both Black and white members. "I shall be glad if you will give me a full statement of the present position of the Brotherhood with respect to this situation, with a copy of any supporting documents or communications which may be of value in relation to any proposals the Brotherhood may have put forward for the solution of the problem and the reaction thereto of your members in either or both of the two seniority groups concerned."[251]

Minister of Labour Michael Starr was also personally active on the file, at the behest of the prime minister. Two days before the deputy minister's letter to the union, the minister had met with a number of officials in his ministry and the union to discuss the position of porters on the railway. It had been agreed, in consultation with the Canadian National Railway, that the problems raised by the porters resulted from differences within the union itself, and that it was therefore an issue that must be resolved by the union.

In a memorandum dated October 4, 1957, describing a follow-up meeting the minister had ordered between the union and officials of his department, the union reported that it was fully aware of the problem raised by the porters and that it was proposing in response the merger of the seniority lists for Black and white union members. However, the union said there was a problem: the porters wanted to keep all porter jobs available to Blacks while at the same time hoping that porters would be promoted to jobs that had not previously been open to them. The union representative, according to the memo, indicated that "the Brotherhood was in favour of full democratic treatment for all members in hiring and promotion and he hoped that eventually the porter group would agree to the merger of the two seniority groups."[252]

The porters had achieved their first goal: getting the attention of the prime minister and convincing him to act on their concerns. The media was also paying careful attention now, which meant that it would be harder for the government to ignore their agitations. But they would find that their second objective of creating anti-discriminatory hiring practices was more challenging.

Williams was also fighting with the Canadian Congress of Labour, calling for the Congress to uphold its policy that all member-unions must disavow discriminatory hiring practices. Distrustful of the Congress from the outset, Williams was not pleased when the umbrella organization said there was nothing it could do to force the Canadian Brotherhood of Railway Employees to conform. In a letter to C.L.C. president Claude Jondoin on October 4, 1957, Williams made clear the position of his local. "Brother Jondoin," he wrote, "our case is very simple. We want the discriminatory status deleted from our Collective Agreement that denies us any right to advancement. The first word of the Fair Employment Practice Act, the word fair, means to be fair, is not to deter from advancement, or words to that effect. We therefore do not accept the stand taken by our [Canadian Brotherhood of Railway Employees] national President, W.J. Smith, that the F.E.P. Act has no bearing on our case."[253] The letter was copied to Minister of Labour Starr for good measure, with a covering letter criticizing Canadian National for maintaining its discriminatory practices against porters.

Ultimately, both parties decided in 1961 that the C.L.C. should investigate the charges Williams had brought against his union and its leadership. That investigation would be led by Blum but, again, Williams was unsure whether Blum would treat him fairly. Williams told the national media that Blum was too close to the C.L.C. In the end, Williams reluctantly agreed to Blum's appointment. Williams and his colleagues in Winnipeg received strong support from porters elsewhere, particularly from D. I. Fenton, the local chair of the union's Montreal division, who broke rank with other union locals. In a letter to Blum on the letterhead of the Canadian Brotherhood of Railway, Transportation and General Workers on May 24, 1961, Fenton bluntly stated, "It goes without saying that I am in full accord with the aspirations of Brother Lee Williams. It is also my opinion that any Porter with the lightest shred of ambition would also fully support Brother Williams."

Fenton put the blame for the lack of opportunity for Black porters on the railway, the government, and his union. "Can you imagine in this present day and age where the entire world seems to be championing the cause of Freedom and Equality for all, that one of the foremost champions would force a group of people to remain in a subservient position for his working life? Well it is allowed to happen in this great country—Canada, on its National railroad and by the C.B.R.E. & G.W."

He pointed out that under the existing collective agreement, sleeping car porters must remain in their position until retirement. So the big question was: If someone was ambitious, why seek employment as a porter in the first place? The answer, Fenton said, was that you would be resigned to the fact that "if you are coloured you *will not* be hired by our National railroad as a cook, waiter or pantry man. In other words, if you are black you are not allowed in Group 1. Now it would be extremely difficult to prove that this is a policy laid down by the Management, however, it is definitely the unwritten policy of the lower echelous [sic] of the dept. of the C.N.R., and those are the men who are responsible for the hiring of new employees. This may sound somewhat sickening sir, but believe me a little investigation would prove this to be quite true."[254]

The next day the chairman of the Toronto division of the union, A. Kamarowsky, wrote to Blum setting out the union's official position. He traced the problem over the hiring practices all the way back to the creation of Canadian National Railway in 1924. Undoubtedly at that time the railways practiced discrimination," he wrote.

> Perhaps they may argue that the colored population was small and there was protestation for the white employees. But I think the real reason is that the former C.N.R. lines had all white employees and could not harbor the thought of mixed rooms. There was certainly discrimination on everyone's part, Government, railways, unions and employees.[255]

The time was ripe, he concluded, for a merger of the two seniority lists, but that would mean that porter jobs that were traditionally exclusive to members of group two, Black workers, would have to be opened up to other white workers.

Blum issued his report, in which he put forth a compromise between Williams and the executive of the Canadian Brotherhood of Railway Employees. The officials were not anxious to perpetuate discrimination against the porters, especially in light of F.E.P. legislation, but the railway practices as captured in the collective agreement since the 1920s allowed for systemic discrimination against porters. "The Company, as well as other Canadian and North American railways, has in the past practiced a policy of racial discrimination in regard to the employment of Negro applicants and in regard to the promotion of Negro employees to supervisory positions," the report stated. "The enactment of the Canada Fair Employment Practices Act in 1953 prohibited the practice of railway racial discriminatory employment policies."

But the report also pointed to another change in the railway company and its practices. "Employment in the Sleeping, Dining and Parlor Car Department of the Canadian National Railway appears to be declining. Group One (Dining Car Employees and sleeping car conductors) appears to contain no Negro members at present though there is evidence that at least one Negro was hired for a Group one position since 1953. Group Two contains some white members."[256]

The solution, Blum argued, was to amalgamate the seniority list of the two groups, creating one unit for all workers regardless of race or ethnicity. Opponents to the recommendation demanded a referendum for union members. Williams, who denounced the report as biased in favour of the union, would not accept the findings. According to a *Winnipeg Free Press* report on September 25, 1961, Williams labeled the report "a 'whitewash and a carbon copy' to suit the trade union hierarchy involved." He wanted the report to call for the immediate promotion of porters to conductors, and he argued that Canadian National Railway had already "shown its goodwill in this matter by promoting Negroes despite the brotherhood's attitude."[257]

The union called a membership referendum on the recommendation for integration. A surprising 77 percent of the membership voted in favour, though this proved an improper indication of real support, which was much, much higher. Expecting the white and largely anti-Black union members to vote against integration, Williams led the sleeping porters, who accounted for 40 percent of membership, to abstain from voting. To their surprise, they still won integration through the vote; the union regulations stipulated that abstaining from a vote was in effect the same as supporting the motion. Subsequently, the union and C.N.R. reached agreement on a new contract and shortly afterwards three porters, including Lee Williams, were promoted to conductors.[258] In marking this milestone, the *Human Rights Review*, a publication of the Civil Liberties of Canada, reported in July 1964 that the "appointment set a precedent for Negro porters and it is hoped that many such promotions, based on seniority and qualification irrespective of race, will follow."[259]

The structure built on the colour line was finally toppling. But by then, railway travel was in a sharp decline across North America, with the glory days of train travel quickly coming to an end. North Americans were turning to the private automobile and airlines as their primary travel mode. The railways were embarking on a further retrenchment of service, which meant fewer jobs were available to Canadian workers regardless of their skin colour. In addition, women were vying for in-service jobs on railways.

IN AN ADDRESS TO THE fourth triennial convention of the Brotherhood of Sleeping Car Porters in Montreal on September 10, 1962, Randolph noted that times were changing for the railway and porters across the continent. "The problem of the workers in the United States and the Dominion of Canada is the problem of diminishing jobs," he said. "The problem of dwindling jobs exists on the railroads, on the ships, in mills and in practically all of the production and service industries [....] Few passenger operations on any of the roads have escaped some form of abridgement, thereby reducing the porter and attendant personnel force."

As a result, he said, a number of Pullman districts had been abolished across North America, including those in Calgary and Edmonton, with others "just hanging on by the skin of their teeth. Needless to say that these vast changes are made without regard to the concerns of service to some communities or the future of the workers and their families." Randolph noted that half a century earlier, virtually all intercity travel across North America had been by railway. At the time of his speech, ninety percent of this travel was conducted by car, with much of the remainder by intercity bus and air. Rail travel accounted for only three percent. Over this same period, the amount of freight carried by railways had dropped from almost 100 percent to about 40 percent. The issue of automation, a growing feature on the railways, made matters even worse. "Automation has come to the railroads in the form of diesel engines, radar and electronic railway yards, central traffic control, and long freight trains of 150 to 200 cars without a comparable increase in crews above that when the average train consisted of 30 or 40 cars. Porters and attendants have been hard hit by the technology of coordination, and consolidation, as well as the elimination of passenger train operations."[260]

The bitterness and disappointment were palpable in Randolph's voice and throughout the arena. The capitalist system had moved on, once again creating pools of unemployed Black labour, as it had with the abolition of slavery almost a century earlier. The implications of these changes were clear. At a time when the porters had started to make clear employment gains, the market for their business had fundamentally changed. Many were left questioning whether the recent gains were granted by an industry on its last legs, gains the industry had refused to allow at the high point of train travel when it would have most benefitted the porters. Maybe, he argued, the industry and the societies it served no longer worried about relegating Blacks to a single work category, since there was no longer money to be made by these practices. The industry had squeezed out all the profit they could, the monies withheld from the porters adding to their surpluses.

The airline industry, which had now surpassed the railways in importance, needed a class of workers whose duties were similar to those performed by train porters and conductors. However, the airlines, including Air Canada, which opened for business in 1937, were calling such workers flight attendants and stewardesses.[261] These new jobs were exclusively white and female: if the transportation system had diversified, the process did not appear to have included Black people.

Randolph knew the challenge he and his union members faced. "Can we delegates in this Fourth Triennial Convention and Thirty-seventh anniversary, under the fighting banner of this Brotherhood, permit these giant railway carriers not to understand and realize that the economic costs, upon which they eternally harp, are not limited to the financial and material resources they control?" Randolph asked, hoping to rally one last battle cry.

> There are also human costs; they consist in the porters and attendants, dining car employees and red caps that are displaced; their occupational skills become obsolescent; their families are uprooted from their accustomed homes; and feelings of anxiety and insecurity are created. These, too, must be counted among the full costs of economic change. We take great pains to point out these facts to the railway carriers and the public and our membership, for it is important to recognize them so they may be faced explicitly and shared equitably among individuals, the carriers, and government.[262]

In 1978, the federal government stepped in to save the industry by merging the passenger railway services of the Canadian Pacific and Canadian National Railways to create VIA Rail Canada, with its headquarters in Montreal. The Canadian Brotherhood of Transport and General Workers, the successor of the Canadian Brotherhood of Railway Employees, represented the porters with the Crown Corporation. In 1994, the Brotherhood merged with the Canadian Auto Workers.

By then, stalwarts in the struggle from the 1950s had moved on. Grizzle had grown tired of working with the union and railways and had changed jobs, first to mail carrier and then becoming an Ontario civil servant, and, finally, a Canadian citizenship judge. Sid Blum died a young man in 1969, at the age of forty-three. Blanchette died in 1977. "I lost a very dear friend and co-worker," Grizzle said in a union press release on Blachette's death.[263] Randolph died in 1979 after a brief retirement, and without him, and with train travel declining, the Brotherhood soon entered a death spiral. Lee Williams continued working as a conductor until his retirement.

Canada, however, had become a new country. But this did not mean that the problems that had led the porters to agitate for change had gone away. With their traditional role as porters no longer viable, and still facing higher levels of unemployment than other groups, Black people scattered to find employment wherever they could—a task that remained a challenge even as the changes in immigration policies made it possible to see growing numbers of Black people in Canada, especially on the streets of major cities.

For the next two generations, it was still common in the Black community to celebrate the first people, especially males, to get "good jobs." The work of Black women remained concentrated in the health care and other nurturing professions, primarily as nurses and nursing assistants, and as domestic workers and clerks in the service sector.

Four years after the start of the domestic workers program, the national news agency *Canadian Press* declared the initiative a success. "Caribbean Immigrants are Quickly Integrated," *The Gazette* of Montreal reported on November 17, 1958, the year that two hundred workers arrived. "About 35 of the 80 sent here since the program began are still in the Ottawa area. The others have gone mainly to Toronto and Montreal where there are Negro communities and better job and marriage opportunities," the syndicated report said. "After their year's domestic service, many get work as hospital kitchen help, bookkeepers, stenographers, nurses, nurses aides, store clerks or factory workers. Several have sponsored immigration of their fiancés and have since married."

However, the report quoted a liaison officer with the federal citizenship department who was responsible for helping the workers integrate into Canadian society. While the women were integrating well into the society, Violet P. King said, "they have found it difficult in Ottawa to find employment where their present education is adequate. They themselves feel their color has been a real objection."[264] Despite these difficulties, the officer said, the women intended to remain in Canada.

By 1975, Black activists, most notably Stan Grizzle, were publicly demonstrating for liveable wages and improved citizenship rights, including a direct path to permanent resident status and then citizenship for domestic workers. Activists wanted to unionize the domestic workers, arguing that by joining forces in the Toronto-based Canadian Domestic Employees Association the women could fight for "minimum wages, overtime, paid hospitalization, paid legal holidays at time and a half, a 44-hour work week, paid vacations, unemployment and pension coverage and more."[265] In 1981, the Ontario government brought in regulations to end what the activists described as slave wages for domestics. Domestic employees—cooks, housekeepers, and nannies—were guaranteed a minimum of $568 a month, time off of at least thirty-six consecutive hours weekly, a minimum of two weeks paid vacation annually, and public holidays off or payment in lieu. The employer could deduct a maximum of fifty dollars weekly for room and board.

Too many Black men remained stuck in an unskilled labour pool, taking jobs in factories and the service industry, including hotels and restaurants. In the late 1970s it was still largely unthinkable for Black people to be reporters, media figures, television personalities, actors in mainstream advertisements, police officers, firemen, public accountants, principals at schools, and academics at major universities, with most professions still barring the entry of Black people or severely limiting their numbers.

While the few Black professionals and businesses no longer depended on the custom of an exclusively Black clientele, it was still considered unnatural for them to open certain types of business or to cater to a mainstream clientele. Finding Black judges, probation officers, prison guards, top civil servants, elected politicians—and most of all holders of positions with clout in politics—was still uncommon. Those few who broke into the mainstream were saddled with the extra burden of having to position themselves as mentors—those who would point the way for other Blacks to follow.

The problem for Black people was not a lack of mentors or the need of any more guidance than other groups, but a shortage of jobs for them. Mentoring simply served to cover the old argument that Black people were not socially ready to participate fully in society. Because Black people were still deemed not good enough for most jobs, only the most menial positions were offered to them, even after provincial and federal human rights legislation and commissions forbade such treatment of citizens. Black people generally were excluded and/or marginalized, largely passed over for the bulk of the jobs, their status and pay cheques remaining below the average for a similar position. Black people did continue to excel in sports, whether in track and field or professional baseball and football, in keeping with the long held notion that they were physiologically better-suited for such activities. Hockey was the exception to this rule, and it would take another generation to make a real breakthrough, one that allowed Black hockey players to achieve the dreams denied to so many of their brethren for so long.

Despite the obvious progress, plenty of anecdotal evidence existed that showed that Black professionals maintained a tenuous hold on their jobs. If they were not extremely careful, they could slip from their entry position and never get another chance to climb the career ladder. Common sense wisdom among Black people held that they had to be twice as good or better to qualify over white candidates for jobs and they had to be twice as careful as other workers to keep their jobs because a replacement job of the same status, or even in the same profession, was not likely to come around again. There was also anecdotal evidence that Black professionals of one generation did not often pass on their employment and status to their children, thereby limiting the family's social mobility.

By 2006, Statistics Canada reported that unemployment levels for second- and third-generation children of Black immigrants were at 9.2 percent and 8.6 percent respectively, way above the national average of 4.4 and 4.9 percent. In comparison, whites had a rate of 4.9 percent and 4.1 percent for the same two generations and Asians 5.4 and 4.6 percent, with all other visible minority groups between rates of 8.6 and 4.5 percent for the two generations.[266] In general, despite higher levels of education, younger Black people were faring worse in terms of wealth and status than the previous generations—a fate other minority groups had largely escaped. The notion so popular in early Canada that Black people were unsuited for civil society and could not prosper, whatever conditions were put in place to support them, proved an intractable legacy of Canada's previous identity as White Man's Country. Variations of such discredited thinking still persist in some quarters of the country, the obstinacy of which prevents the true blossoming of equality in Canada.

IN 1971, THE FEDERAL GOVERNMENT finally abandoned the position that Canada was a White Man's Country by announcing itself as the world's first officially multicultural country. The federal government brought in new immigration and citizenship acts in 1976 and 1977, paving the way for Canada to become as demographically diversified as the world itself. On the streets of Canada, especially in major cities, the number of non-white faces quickly increased. West Indian immigrants were standing up as Canadian citizens and demanding full citizenship rights, especially the right to work in any field or calling, even when racial discrimination against them was still an issue.

One of the biggest challenges facing Canada was its international role in fighting discriminatory immigration practices, especially within the British Commonwealth. Prime Minister Diefenbaker joined with the new Commonwealth leaders in the Caribbean, Africa, and Asia to denounce racial segregation, especially the official government policy of apartheid in South Africa. In a radio interview with the CBC on March 7, 1962, after visiting leaders in Ireland and the UK, Diefenbaker suggested—he had been lobbied by the porters on this issue for some time—a clean break with apartheid support. "I have made it very clear that Canadians as a whole unequivocally deplore the practice of apartheid," he said when asked if South Africa should remain a member of the Commonwealth.

> We believe that in a Commonwealth composed of many races and colours, in which an overwhelming majority is of a colour other than white, that the principles of equality without regard to race or any other consideration must be acceptable to all the member nations. With respect to the question of membership, I have made it very clear that, having taken a strong stand against discrimination, a stand that has been mine throughout my life, that had its embodiment in the bill of rights which I introduced in the House of Commons, the question of membership is a problem which all the prime ministers, in light of the discussions that will take place at this Conference will determine, I hope, and the result will be the strengthening of the Commonwealth relations cannot be as strong and as effective for peace as otherwise would be the cases.

Asked specifically if this meant that he would be proposing a declaration against religious and racial discrimination, Diefenbaker answered:

> I believe that a declaration of that kind will ultimately have to be accepted. That will be the objective. It takes many years, of course, to bring these things about. As you know, in Canada it took more than fifteen or twenty years to bring about a national bill of rights. Now in the larger field of world affairs, such a declaration on the part of the Commonwealth nations will not be attained today or even tomorrow but I think that we, as a Commonwealth, should be able to arrive at a declaration representative of these principles which all of us accept in the common interest and in the interest of each of us, and in the interest of mankind as a whole.[267]

But history was moving faster than Diefenbaker anticipated. In large measure in response to Diefenbaker's statement, South Africa decided to withdraw from the Commonwealth in 1961. Even then, porters did not relent in their opposition to apartheid, and under the leadership of Grizzle, even after he had stopped working as porter, the group continued to agitate for sanctions until South Africa formally abandoned apartheid in 1993, with Canada continuing its international role at the forefront of this struggle.[268] Canada had, indeed, changed at home and abroad and in ways championed by the delegates who had visited Ottawa in 1954. But there was still much more work to be done.

BEYOND THE RAILS
The Battle for Black Identity

TOWARD THE END OF 1954, Grizzle formally opened up another front in his battle for the full recognition of Black Canadians. This time he was confronting the board of education of his borough of East York in what is now part of the Greater Toronto municipality. In a letter to the board's business administer, Grizzle wrote to complain about a book, Edith Nesbit's *The Enchanted Castle,* which was part of the public school library system. Grizzle wrote:

> On Page 61 of this book the word *nigger* appears on two occasions. My daughter, who brought this situation to my attention, has been told by me that this word is outmoded, contemptuous and therefore not used in educational institutions, has encountered this word in several library books. I am sure that it is known by you and others of our Board of Education that the use of such terms as nigger is one of the many means of emphasizing and strengthening invidious stereotypes that increase racial and colour prejudice in our country. It is known to you that there is a long record of systematic propaganda aimed at depreciating peoples of African origin by name calling, comic cartoons, black-faced minstrels and by limiting their vocational opportunities.

Grizzle asked that the board remove from the school libraries any book with such terms as nigger or other defamatory words, arguing that such clichés should "be placed in the ashbin."[269] He was supported by his comrade-in-arms Sid Blum, who wrote the board on the same day as

Grizzle protesting against the same book. Blum said that the author of the book was

> exhibiting the worst sort of bad taste when she uses a derogatory term in place of a simple acceptable description. The use of this word in children's books and fairy stories is uncalled for, derogatory and defamatory terms like 'nigger' (and there are other similar words applied to other minority groups) only serve to create harmful attitudes and prejudice towards other members of our society. These attitudes and prejudices can form the foundation for later inter-group friction and discord. Perhaps one of the aims of education in a democratic society is to create in the growing child, a respect for human dignity, consideration of the rights of his fellow man—whatever his race, creed or color. The use of such language, unfortunately, destroys rather than creates respect.[270]

Grizzle wrote to the board of education again, having not received a response to his first letter. "On 16 December last I wrote to you concerning books, available in East York Children's libraries, which contain derogatory terms. I would very much appreciate a reply to the above referred letter."[271] The East York Board of Education asked the public library of Toronto to investigate the matter and to make a report. On January 28, 1954, the chief librarian reported to the board: "The book is now some 50 or 60 years old, and throughout more than half-a-century has been a favourite with children," Chief Librarian C. R. Sanderson wrote. "A boy blackens his face and says to someone 'I'm an nigger', which brings the reply that he is not because his ears are white behind." The librarian suggested that since the author had helped to form the Fabian Society, she would not have been prone to racial discrimination. "We will, however, take one positive action in this matter, and that is we will write the publishers and suggest that in the next reprinting the word be altered."[272]

But Grizzle and his allies had already been having some success at sensitizing mainstream Canada about perceptions of Blacks and other peoples of colour. The previous October, Grizzle was watching the television news on CBC when he heard the general manager of the Toronto Transit Commission (TTC), W. P. Duncan, speaking in a way that offended him. Waiting long enough to consult members of his union, Grizzle shot off a letter to Duncan

> to register a strong protest regarding your reference to Afro-Americans as 'niggers' during an interview over a television program emanating from

Station CBLT, Toronto on the evening of 21 October, 1953. The use of such terms as 'nigger' is but one of the many techniques used to (a) build up stereotypes or (b) create anti climate towards and (c) belittle people who have commited [sic] the unpardonable sin of being black. The members of our organization feel that, in view of the present world wide struggle for the allegiance of the peoples of the world to the various types of government, and, since the major portion of the globe's populace is made up of humans of colour, you, as an eminent public servant—an ambassador of democracy, can ill-afford to continue to use derogatory terms such [as] the one used by you and which [for] some of us reflects the hiring policy of the Toronto Transportation Commission, inasmuch as it is our information that men of colour have been turned away subsequent to applying for jobs as motormen and conductors with the T.T.C.[273]

At the same time, the Joint Labour Committee to Combat Racial Intolerance in Toronto was dispatching its own letter of protest to Duncan.

With pressure ratcheting up, Duncan said in a letter on November 2 to Grizzle that he "regretted that in an unrehearsed television show and under stress of answering a barrage of questions I used an expression which is repugnant to members of the negro race" and promised to avoid using the term in the future. In response to the criticisms Grizzle had made of the transit commission's hiring policy, Duncan said suitable employees were selected without reference to racial origin or religion. "As a matter of fact, we have several men in supervisory positions who are of negro origin."[274] *The Canadian Negro* newspaper blared the news on the front of its November issue: "TTC Denies Charges: 'Will Hire Negroes.'"

That month the Joint Labour Committee to Combat Racial Intolerance was also protesting the Ontario Liquor License Board for refusing to pull the liquor licenses of Toronto's private Mercury Club for not accepting Black members and the William Pitt Hotel in Chatham for not serving Black clients. The coalition's spokesman was Grizzle, who was quoted in the *Toronto Star* on November 20, 1953, and in other provincial news outlets as saying that his members had informed him of three additional hotels in Sudbury that did not serve Black people.

Grizzle called on Ontario premier Leslie Frost to intervene against establishments that "don't want to permit people who have committed the unpardonable sin of being black the right to human dignity."[275] The liquor board investigated and found no merit to the accusations against the two businesses, but a milestone had nevertheless been reached on the highway to justice: businesses could no longer openly discriminate against Blacks and other people of colour. If they did, they risked losing their licences to sell alcohol.

Canadian radio stations were also kept under strict watch by the coalition. A dispute with Toronto station CKEY erupted when one of its news commentators, John Kennedy, and two lawyers from the Canadian Bar Association were discussing civil rights and capital punishment in the United States, and in particular the fact that 775 white Americans had been executed by the state between 1937 and 1950 compared with 1,065 Black Americans, even though the latter accounted for only 10 percent of the population. In an attempt to explain these statistics, Kennedy had remarked, "The Negro, as you know, in the South is rather underprivileged, and he is more or less juvenile in his impulses, and he is a gambler by instinct, and protects himself at all times with his old-fashioned razor, which is used rather liberally when gambling goes against him or he suspects somebody of having loaded dice."[276]

Grizzle was quick to send off a letter to the radio station on behalf of the coalition. "We are confident that it was not your conscious intent to make such a sweeping generalization, in effect categorizing all Southern Negroes as gambling murderers. We trust, too, that you do not really subscribe to the scientifically invalid concept that *any* group of people should be considered 'gamblers by instinct', and 'juvenile in impulses.'"[277] The same letter was sent by the Joint Labour Committee for Human Rights, the Negro Citizenship Association, Canadian Jewish Congress, the *Canadian Negro* newspaper, and the Reverend Noel Gonsalves, a minister of the First Baptist Church, to the radio station.

A bigger battle over books used in the school system arose two years later when, as part of a wider protest across Canada, Grizzle wrote the Toronto Board of Education asking for the removal of the book *Little Black Sambo* from Toronto-area schools. At the same time, Lee Williams of the Canadian Brotherhood of Railway Employees, working through the Winnipeg Labour Council, wrote to that city's school board superintendent, Dr. W. C. Lorimer, asking for the same book to be banned.

This was one occasion when the porters at the two national railways openly cooperated on an issue that roiled their community. Several Black intellectuals across Canada, including Dan Hill, had joined the protest against the book and against calling Black people Sambos. "In these days of international tension and strife," Hill wrote, "it seems imperative that educators assume their proper responsibility in the area of human relations: to instill in Canada's future citizens a real respect for the dignity of all human beings, regardless of nationality, race or religion. Stories such as *Little Black Sambo* can only detract from that effort."[278]

Grizzle wrote the Board on January 30, 1956, on behalf of the Toronto division of the Brotherhood and the Toronto Joint Labour Committee.

We feel that the adjective 'black' as used in the title *Little Black Sambo* as descriptive emphasizes pigmentation and tends to overplay physical differences instead of merely denoting a group. The Sambo in the title *Little Black Sambo*, is a carryover from the physical slavery days of Negroes in the United States of America and as such breathes ridicule, disrespect and contempt. We would conclude by saying that the *Little Black Sambo* stories are an affront to human dignity and such should be placed in the ashbin of forgotten stories.[279]

On February 2, 1956, members of a committee of Negro citizens of Toronto appeared before the board of education to argue against the book's continued use in schools. Not only should *Little Black Sambo* be banned, the committee argued, but so should books that used such terms as "half-breeds" when referring to the Métis people. The brief stated that a "continuing awareness by teachers and boards of education of such distorted attitudes towards Canadian history and toward other people can help engender in our children constructive, patriotic attitudes towards our own past and the eventual integration of all national groupings in all aspects of life in the neighbourhood, community and nation."[280]

On February 6, 1956, the Toronto board wrote Grizzle informing him that it had adopted the resolution "that the book *Little Black Sambo* be withdrawn from use in the classroom."[281] Other ethnic communities such as the Jews, Italians, and the Japanese would launch similar efforts to ban derogatory ethnic slurs. "Don't use the word 'Jap,'" said one of the pamphlets issued in this campaign. "It is derogatory in the same sense that 'kike,' 'wop,' 'chink,' and 'nigger,' are derogatory [...] They are a shameful remnant from an earlier era when our country was made up of many unassimilated immigrant groups. But that era is gone, and we are all Canadians proud of our backgrounds and entitled to dignity."[282] It would be more acceptable to refer to them as Japanese-Canadians, the campaign suggested, thereby helping the formalization of the hyphenated identity associated with an officially multicultural Canada, where Canadians may choose to denote a particular ethnicity by attaching a hyphenate to the universal Canadian identity.

ON APRIL 11, 1958, GRIZZLE opened a new front in the battle against discriminatory language, this time in a letter to the editor of *CCF News*. The newspaper representing that political party had published a letter to the editor in which Grizzle claimed the writer "told a distasteful story of a Negro and two niggers. While it is true that across the top of the CCF News editorial page there appears the following words: 'You can say what you like,' the corollary of which is not to abbreviate the rights of others should be maintained uppermost in the [letter writer's] mind." However, there was the important question of where "the rights of one individual end and where the other individual's rights begin. This is the price of freedom which in part is a belief in the essential importance of the person and the supremacy of a society which respects and safeguard the dignity of the individual." Grizzle said that by using the word niggers, "which carries with it contempt and ridicule for Negroes, the writer was contributing to robbing the Negro people of respect and the right to human dignity. I also note that the word 'Negro' is spelled with a small 'n' on one occasion although the term identifies one of the great races of mankind and as such should be capitalized."[283]

At the same time, Donald Moore was battling with the queen's printer in Ottawa—the federal government publisher—about the same issue. In a letter dated February 28, 1955, Moore questioned why the publisher was spelling Negro with a lower case "n" in *Hansard*, the official publication of parliamentary debates. "It has now become the accepted practice with leading newspapers, magazines and periodicals in Canada and the United States to use capital 'N" when using the word Negro. It has been such a long while since I have seen this departure from common usage, that the appearance of the common 'n' in Government publications seems quite glaring."[284]

After much discussion, including the opposition CCF Party's in support of Moore, the publishers decided not to change its spelling. Even then Moore did not let up. In the following months he would send letters of protest to various magazines, newspapers, and government agencies asking them to capitalize the first letter in Negro. "And still the battles rages on," Moore said in his memoirs. "Negroes today don't worry about degrading the word with a common 'n'. They themselves joined in the degrading process by rejecting the word Negro and using the adjective black."[285]

Grizzle recognized the social importance of Black people asserting themselves in prominent roles, especially to fight negative stereotypes. At the height of the struggle for fair employment practices legislation in Ontario, Grizzle argued for a leadership role for Black people. He made this point in a letter to Alex Maxwell, the executive secretary of the Toronto Labour Committee for Human Rights, on May 29, 1958, when the committee was preparing a brief to submit to the government:

> The Federation of Labour should give serious consideration to the inclusion in the aforementioned brief of a matter concerning the appointment of a Negro to the Anti-Discrimination Commission of Ontario and also to the related Citizen's Advisory Group. The inclusion of a person of colour to each of the aforementioned bodies we feel to be reasonable and sound inasmuch as it is established that a large proportion of the persons discriminated against because of race, creed, colour, national origin and/or ancestry have been Negroes. The inclusion of said person of high visibility on each of these two bodies as mentioned would provide a balance of forces in the handling of issues. Naturally, the person of color appointed to these bodies should have experience in the handling of fair practices programs in the areas of administration and education. We cannot stress too strongly our desire to see that the Ontario Anti-Discrimination Commission and the Citizen's Advisory Body are truly representative of those groups of people who suffered the most from racial and/or religious discrimination.[286]

The government established its Ontario Human Rights Commission in 1962 under the leadership of Dan Hill, who was made the first full-time director, and eventually its first full-time commissioner, in 1971.

But perhaps one of the biggest fights was waged against minstrel shows and the use of white actors blackening their complexions with polish or burnt cork. This coincided with the issuing of an official statement in 1951 by the NAACP against race typing in the theatre by portraying Black people as inferior, lazy, dumb, immoral, vicious, dishonest, superstitious, clowning, cowardly, and overly emotional. Ironically, some of the main targets of the protest against minstrelsy were religious institutions that hosted such shows on a regular basis. At a meeting to kick off the 1956 celebration of Brotherhood Week, in which the major religious denominations celebrated a common human dignity and brotherhood, Grizzle and Moore condemned the churches that hosted minstrel shows in their auditoriums. "Although they are not sponsored by the churches the shows are the type of entertainment that brings about a laugh from one party at the expense of another," Moore was quoted as saying in the *Telegram* newspaper on February 20, 1956. It quoted Grizzle as saying that by caricaturing Black people as slaphappy, indolent, dice-shooting buffoons "that would not be any more objectionable than similar caricature of other races if this caricature were balanced by other views of the Negro [...] if it were part of a context. But standing alone, it cannot fail to belittle the Negro and help perpetuate the stereotypes cherished in the minds of many white people."

Grizzle used the opportunity to explain his dream of brotherhood for all of Canada, raising points that would eventually enter Canada's official multicultural policies. "We have here in Canada," he said,

> representatives of all the major divisions of mankind, all the principal religions and all the political philosophies, and out of this mixture leavened by the yeast of freedom and competition we have forged ahead to a high position amongst the community of nations. Now if we are to maintain this position we must continue to set for the world an example of lofty idealism demonstrated by the practical application of brotherhood in our day-to-day activities. Such application can be made a reality by an occasion such as this, which is dedicated to the proposition of improving human relations.

Invoking the argument of Du Bois at the NAACP, Grizzle said, "It is agreed that the theatre is an important instrument in the propaganda field. A farce belittling the Negro, even though it may have been conceived as pure entertainment, may be effective anti-Negro propaganda. If, as some feel, Negroes are hypersensitive, this is not without good reason."[287] Despite these protestations, the churches continued to host the minstrel shows.

On May 15, 1961, Grizzle wrote the leaders of the Beaver Clue Class at the Westmoreland United Church in Toronto to protest the minstrel shows it was mounting. "We strongly object to minstrel shows because this form of entertainment never puts the people of African descent in a favourable light," Grizzle wrote on behalf of his members.

> It portrays him as a clown rather than an intelligent human being with rational thoughts and progressive ideals—thus perpetuating the stereotypes cherished in the minds of many white people. Minstrel shows are

objectionable to many Negroes as well as to many sensitive white people since they are for the most part taken out of the context of Negro life in the United States of America in the unpleasant early days—thus painting an unbalanced picture of the Negro—which is harmful.[288]

As part of its programming to mark the festive season, CHCH TV in Hamilton, Ontario, broadcast a show in 1962 in which a member of a choir masqueraded in black face while singing songs made popular by Al Jolson, the American entertainer who controversially blackened his face, especially when singing African American songs. Daniel Brathwaite, describing himself as a Negro working in the field of human relations, was offended and wrote to the television station on January 15, 1962, condemning the show. "The black-faced minstrel appearing on TV or in any other form in our society is an affront to the Negro people and an anachronism in our modern day thinking. I sincerely hope your television station, which has consistently produced good programs, will refrain from exhibiting black-face minstrels which is a source of race prejudice and represents a sick society."[289] Eight days later the station's production manager, J. O. Burghardt, wrote a classic brush-off to Braithwaite, thanking him for his letter but promising to do little about it.

THE EPICENTRE FOR THE DEBATES about language and culture in the world of the porters was the West Indian community in Harlem, and specifically in the Frederick Douglass Book Center that was one of the noted establishments of the community. It attracted Black people from around the world for its unmatched collection of books on the Black experience, its conversations with pan-Africanist writers and intellectuals, and for its lectures and workshops. Few Canadian porters visiting New York or laid over in the city didn't visit the Center. They took away from it not only the most recent books, pamphlets and magazines on Black causes but engaged while there in the philosophical discourses that made the center so popular. Canadian Pacific Railway porter Leonard Johnson and his wife Gwendolyn would try to recreate a similar centre in Toronto by establishing Third World Books and Crafts on Bathurst Street, which was open between 1967 and 2000. Working on the railway and minding the store in his off time, Johnson, an active member of Grizzle's division of the Brotherhood of Sleeping Car Porters, made the business one of the foremost places in North America to hunt for Black literature and crafts.

A series of lectures was given at the Frederick Douglass Book Center in 1960 by one of the resident intellects of the community, the Barbados-born

Richard Moore, in which he argued that Black people the world over should stop calling themselves Negroes because the name was demeaning. The idea for the lectures had belonged to the primate of the leading Black church in New York, Archbishop Reginald Barrow. He suggested that the lectures address "the impertinent and arrogant reference in an English magazine to a very distinguished American as a 'negro' and a 'native'." Barbados-born Barrow was a founding member of African Orthodox Church, often called the Garveyite church or a Black consciousness religion, and was the father of the future Barbadian prime minister Errol Barrow, who led the island to political independence in 1966. The lectures were popularized throughout the Black diasapora and were eventually expanded and published in the book *The Name Negro: Its Origin and Evil Use*, thereby kicking off a movement in the United States that led to the adoption of the descriptor Afro-American and then African-American. "So it is hoped, therefore," Moore said in the 1960 foreword to the book,

> that this (denunciation) will conduce to the adoption of the proper names: *African* for the native people of Africa, *Afro-American* for people of African ancestry in the United States, and similar names for people of like origin elsewhere, denoting the connection with land, history and culture as well as their present national identity.
>
> If a significant contribution shall thus be made to improve the regard for and the condition of my people, and thus to aid the establishment of mutual respect, amicable relations, and peace and concord among mankind the purpose of these lectures and essays will have been successfully and fully achieved.[290]

By giving up the Negro ascription, they were choosing to identify primarily with specific countries and citizenship.

But throughout it all, these former Negroes, even when preferring a primary national identity, still maintained the pan-Africanist identities and commitments forged in a shared global experience, accepting collective identities and histories that transcended specific nation states. In this regard, many of them still identified with a transnational Black descriptor and also as people of colour, especially in a neo-racial and neocolonial world still polarized between black and white as racialized status symbols.

Grizzle argued that one of the most visible sites for the incorporation of these changes was in the arts—in a people of a given nation telling stories to themselves about themselves as part of a nation. Especially in Canada and the United States, writers and the work that once was classified as simply Negro became African American or Canadian while retaining a cosmopolitan Black classification. Porters and their supporters, especially those who were members of the US-based National Association for the Advancement of Colored People, were conversant with the argument that how Black people were portrayed mattered. They were familiar with the arguments of writers like W. E. B. Du Bois, head of the NAACP and the founding editor of its newsletter *The Crisis*. "We can go on the stage; we can be just as funny as white Americans wish us to be; we can play all the sordid parts that America likes to assign to Negroes; but for anything else there is still small place for us," Du Bois wrote, calling for a better deal for Black people artistically. "And so I might go on. But let me sum up with this: Suppose the only Negro who has survived some centuries hence was the Negro painted by white Americans in the novels and essays they have written. What would people in a hundred years say of black Americans? Now turn it around. Suppose you were to write a story and put in it the kind of people you know and like and imagine. You might get it published and you might not. And the 'might not' is still far bigger than the 'might.' The white publishers catering to white folks would say, 'It is not interesting'—to white folk, naturally not. They want Uncle Toms, Topsies, good 'darkies' and clowns."

In language that still resonates to this day in multicultural Canada, Du Bois argued that the Black artist writing out of a Black consciousness must be able to speak about truth and beauty as he perceived them—the same way that other artists have done historically.

> First of all, he has used the truth—not for the sake of truth, not as a scientist seeking truth, but as one upon whom truth eternally thrusts itself as the highest handmaid of imagination, as the one great vehicle of universal understanding. Again artists have used goodness—goodness in all its aspects of justice, honor, and right—not for an ethical sanction but as the one true method of gaining sympathy and human interest. The apostle of beauty thus becomes the apostle of truth and right not by choice but by inner and outer compulsion. Free he is but his freedom is ever bounded by truth and justice; and slavery only dogs him when he is denied the right to tell the truth or recognize an ideal of justice.[291]

In pluralistic societies, such as those of North America, Du Bois' universal judgment and soul could only be a plural one, could only be multicultural, to adequately capture the spirit of all peoples and their times. Indeed, Du Bois, towards the end of his life in 1963, had come to understand the unintended outcome of his prophesy, for instead of seeing unfurl a literature that universally erased differences between Blacks and whites, he had found to his chagrin that this colour line was still very much intact, even if for reasons he had not fully realized at the time. Du Bois had argued that there is a strong propagandistic element to the arts, with different artists proselyting from different perspectives, a point that had been taken up by porters and their allies in the Black community when they conceived of Canada as essentially a brotherhood of humanity while maintaining pride in their Blackness. As intellectual historian Richard H. King has suggested, people like the porters would have been conscious of the changes underway in North America, and that Canada and its people were perceived as a unity that was still marked by differences—where despite those differences, citizens were all equal.[292]

Much of this early Black writing was part of the process of signalling the arrival of peoples of African ancestry into the modern nation-state. Often these early works were held up as mirrors to attempt to reflect whether or not this integration had worked. Even in the midst of their struggles for initial recognition, the porters and their allies had anticipated when the dialectic would shift and what was once categorized as Negro, African or Black writing would be perceived as simply multicultural, one of the inherent and necessary elements in a literature or art that is as multicultural as Canada itself. Instead of the literatures of Canada being reconciled into a labelless, universalist literature, distinctively Canadian literature would be noted for the way every group expresses its Canadianness and how they come together imaginatively and in a narrative—about a shared past, present and future—that is *genuinely* multicultural. Black literature would be just as much about the Canadian aesthetic as that of any other group—though it would be grounded in a specific Black tradition. The dreams of a new world carried in the minds of Black people would be authentically Canadian and would be offered as realistic alternatives for the construction of the country's future.

Activists remained vigilant in the struggle to ensure Black people in Canada were portrayed with dignity in both the works of others and in their own increasing creative output. When looking back on these times, it is a struggle that even now many porters, long retired, know to be only partially won.

IT WAS A TOUGH BUT GOOD LIFE, Jackie States recalls in retirement. Most of his years on the trains were spent in the era that began with the amalgamation of the passenger services of Canadian National Railway and Canadian Pacific Railway in 1978. "Amalgamation was good," says States. "You could bid for all jobs and get better pay. It makes you wonder about the opportunities that so many people missed working on the train before my time."

States began his career in the linen service for Canadian National Railway and rose through the ranks to become the first Canadian Black station manager, one of the most prestigious jobs on the rails. Along the way he served in administrative positions, including conductor, inspector, and trainer of on-board staff. It all started for him as a teenager, when someone told him the CNR was hiring. This was in the 1960s, when jobs were not plentiful for young Black men in Nova Scotia. Coming from a farm outside Halifax, States thought the best he could do was land menial work in the federal civil service, and he had nothing to lose by applying at the railway. So he went to the Halifax office, filled in some forms, and interviewed. Though he was only sixteen years old and management asked him for proof of age showing he was at least seventeen, he was hired anyway and always found an excuse for not delivering his birth certificate. Management eventually stopped asking and he continued to work, taking soiled linen off the trains and packing new linen before delivering it to the platform. When he heard there were openings for porters, he used his inside track to claim one of the jobs that were still exclusively held by Black people. After two weeks of training, he was coupled with a senior porter for a cross-country trip that tested how he would perform. After that, he regularly worked trips from Halifax to Montreal and all the way to Vancouver. One of the most memorable was when he served Robert Stanfield, former premier of his native province and then federal Opposition leader. Stanfield was travelling between Halifax and Ottawa by way of Montreal. "We fed him and took care of him," States recalled. "He said he enjoyed the meal, that the service was good and he gave me a five-dollar silver coin as a tip. I still have it."

CONCLUSION
A Multicultural Brotherhood Fulfilling a Dream

AMONG STANLEY GRIZZLE'S PAPERS IN the Canadian Archive a speech stands out. It was by Canadian Minister of State for Multiculturalism Norman Cafik to the Third Canadian Conference on Multiculturalism in Ottawa on October 28, 1978. It was titled *Multiculturalism—A Canadian Reality*. The 18-page document is tucked away among folders of speeches and various media clippings and documents on the topic of Brotherhood, the philosophy of what was at the time called social fraternity by the many people advocating for social acceptance and recognition of a common humanity among diverse groups.[293] After Cafik addressed the conference the rate of change in Canada with regards to issues of diversity and equality seemed to increase. Two years prior, Parliament had passed a new immigration act that removed ethnicity as a criteria for admission to the country, replacing it with a liberal points system based on ability, merit and the country's manpower needs at a given time. The Negro Citizenship Association had argued for this change for many years, although there was still some concern about whether or not the new policy was being implemented evenhandedly for Black applicants. Parliament passed a new citizenship act the following year, in 1977, which radically transformed how new immigrants, both in terms of timeline and procedures, could become Canadian citizens. Cafik's speech was primarily reflecting on how all of these prior changes coalesced around a central idea and issue: multiculturalism. Change had not come easily.

Seven years have just passed since the announcement by the Prime Minister of Canada, the Right Honourable Pierre Elliott Trudeau, of the

Government of Canada's commitment to a policy of multiculturalism for Canada. Although multiculturalism is a Canadian reality it is still a largely misunderstood and unknown reality. In my numerous trips across Canada I have been told that multiculturalism is divisive. I have been admonished because some perceive multiculturalism to be equated to official multilingualism. I have been informed that I was helping create cultural ghettoes and solitudes. Some have even told me that multiculturalism is only for the immigrants not for Canadians. Nothing can be further from the truth.[294]

On the morning of October 8, 1971, Liberal Prime Minister Pierre Trudeau had stood in the House of Commons to announce this dramatic change for Canada and Canadians. In an ironic twist that appeared to have escaped observers since that date, Trudeau's speech was given in the presence of the prime minister of Malaysia, Tun Abdul Razak, who under previous immigration criteria would have been deemed an Asiatic and therefore from a group of people long considered undesirable for admission to Canada. Moments before the speech Razak had been welcomed to the House as a distinguished visitor by the speaker. As Razak bowed to the parliamentarians' applause, social activists like Moore and Grizzle who had fought so long for a new immigration policy must have smiled at the advances that had been made, and at the irony underlining such pageantry.

Trudeau's historic announcement would mark the official end of the tragic experiment of trying to carve a European state out of North American Aboriginal lands, keeping it as a preserve exclusively for Europeans, as White Man's Country. It was one of the few times in history that such a development had occurred in a settler-colonial state without bloodshed and the collapse of government institutions. In the parlance of historians and social scientists alike Canada was about to become the world's first postmodern state, a homeland that existed independently of a particular ethnicity, that would indeed offer a home for all ethnicities the world over. In his speech Cafik would gesture with pride to the international plaudits that celebrated Canada for taking such a unique and bold step, urging others to join the country. Trudeau's speech would also firmly signal as policy the ending of Canada's colonial history. The defence of Canada as White Man's Country had led it into a social and moral dead end, such as had been predicted by Grizzle, Donald Moore and so many Black people going back to the days of Mary Ann Shadd and Lord Simcoe. This was the final necessary acknowledgement that the new country Canada was becoming would not be based on the mistakes of the old.

The final reports of the 1963 Royal Commission on Bilingualism and Biculturalism, which has been established at the time to discover ways to revitalize the flagging Canadian confederation, had acknowledged the failures of the more closed policies of previous generations. As he addressed Parliament and the Canadian people at large, Trudeau acknowledged the wisdom of the recommendation by the commission that the Canada of old could no longer continue. In a final report on Canadian culture the commissioners had argued that instead of finding as they'd hoped that Canada was bicultural—in effect culturally and separately French and English—they discovered that the country was indeed made up of a multiplicity of cultures, including those of the Aboriginal peoples. For the country to have a future these other cultures needed to be acknowledged alongside the English and French as equally Canadian. "It is the view of the royal commission, Trudeau said:

> shared by the government and, I am sure, by all Canadians, that there cannot be one cultural policy for Canadians of British and French origin, another for the original peoples and yet a third for all others. For although there are two official languages, there is no official culture, nor does any ethnic group take precedence over any other. No citizen or group of citizens is other than Canadian, and all should be treated fairly. The royal commission was guided by the belief that adherence to one's ethnic group is influenced not so much by one's origin or mother tongue as by one's sense of the group's "collective will to exist." The government shares this belief.

With this pronouncement, Trudeau officially and finally turned Canada away from the influential positions espoused by Robert Knox and others. In their place, Trudeau argued that no ethnic or racial group was *naturally* suited to Canada. Canadian identity and citizenship was, rather, predicated on one's actions, and the common commitment and willingness of different people to live together in harmony. Canada, by this reasoning, had to be constructed day by day through civic interactions, a position that had been previously and vociferously espoused by the intellectuals among the sleeping car porters throughout the hemisphere, as well as with the likes of US civil rights leader Martin Luther King Jr. and the new leaders of the independent nation-states in the Caribbean. Trudeau was a regular visitor, like Diefenbaker before him, for reasons of both business and pleasure, to the Caribbean, and he had met the new leaders of the former British possessions of Barbados, Jamaica and Guyana while studying with them at the London School of Economics in the wake of the Second World War. It is notable that in his memoirs he chose to include a photograph of former Jamaican prime minister Michael Manley, which offers an indication of their close friendship. As Trudeau explained to Parliament:

> A policy of multiculturalism within a bilingual framework commends itself to the government as the most suitable means of assuring the cultural freedom of Canadians. Such a policy should help to break down discriminatory attitudes and cultural jealousies. National unity if it is to mean anything in the deeply personal sense, must be founded on confidence in one's own individual identity; out of this can grow respect for that of others and a willingness to share ideas, attitudes and assumptions. A vigorous policy of multiculturalism will help create this initial confidence. It can form the base of a society which is based on fair play for all. The government will support and encourage the various cultures and ethnic groups that give structure and vitality to our society. They will be encouraged to share their cultural expressions and values with other Canadians and so contribute to a richer life for us all.

Trudeau was announcing a re-birth for Canada, one that would effectively call for the rewriting of the narrative of what is Canada and who was a Canadian. It was for this reason that he ended his speech by emphasizing the new roles the existing cultural agencies would have to undertake to make this new vision a reality. Government institutions like the Department of Citizenship and Immigration, the CBC, the National Film Board and the National Museum of Man (now named the Canadian Museum), among others, would all be required to contribute to this new narrative of Canada and thereby help engender unity among Canadians. "These programmes will be revised, broadened and reactivated," Trudeau said, "and they will receive the additional funds that may be required." The Canadian government would also provide support to the publishing and printing sectors to help tell this story, and it would extend financial support for the Canadian National Archives and public library.

> I wish to emphasize the view of the government that a policy of multiculturalism within a bilingual framework is basically the conscious support of individual freedom of choice. We are free to be ourselves. But this cannot be left to chance. It must be fostered and pursued actively. If freedom of choice is in danger for some ethnic groups, it is in danger for all. It is the policy of this government to eliminate any such danger and to "safeguard" this freedom.[295]

Not a parliamentary voice was raised in opposition. The Tory Leader of the Opposition Robert Stanfield supported Trudeau for his "excellent words," adding "I am sure this declaration by the government of the principle of preserving and enhancing the many cultural traditions which exist within our country will be most welcome. I think it is about time this government finally admitted that the cultural identity of Canada is a pretty complex thing." Switching to French, Stanfield added, "I wish to state immediately, Mr. Speaker, that the emphasis we have given to multiculturalism in no way constitutes an attack on the basic duality of our country. What we want is justice for all Canadians, and recognition of the cultural diversity of the country."[296]

David Lewis, the leader of the House's third party, the New Democrats, also supported Trudeau: "The most striking wealth of our country is the fact that it has been founded by two distinct groups having two distinct languages well known throughout the world. However, another wealth is also important, since we find in Canada some representatives of almost all the cultures in the world. I say that they must be proud of these two enriching aspects of our country."

But while on the surface the opposition leaders appeared to be speaking similarly to Trudeau, they were imagining and even communicating something fundamentally different. Was Canada starting anew as a single and indivisible nation state with no official culture and with two official languages? Were Canadians creating a new nation from the heteronomy of different peoples and cultures, jettisoning the ethnocentric approaches and narratives that had earlier framed what was known as Canada's history? Or was it still to be the same old country, founded by two distinct peoples with their distinct cultures and languages, with these distinct peoples continuing to enjoy privileged positions in the Canadian hierarchy of cultures? Was the Canadian history of the past to be adapted to include the stories and histories of primarily non-anglophone and non-francophone characters? Was this new Canada to be marked by the equality of different peoples living together as common citizens, everyone with exactly the same rights and privileges, or would it continue to be essentially two nations within one country, with other groups merely "included" in the national scheme and each ultimately having to choose which of the two founding nations they needed to give allegiance?

Whatever the celebratory civility within the commons, these questions and others quickly sparked national public debate. Opponents in Quebec branded multiculturalism as selling out to immigrants and undermining a distinct French role and identity in the country, an argument that would be used in favour of Quebec separation. Pointedly, the Quebec government would announce in response to the national policy of multiculturalism its own policy of interculturalism based on the centrality of the French language and culture and arguing for assimilationist tendencies within its provincial borders. Aboriginal critics argued that their cultures and histories were not well enough recognized and that they were often merely lumped in with non-European immigrants and cultures. Others questioned the dismissal of the avowed Christian underpinning of the state; some cynically branded multiculturalism as a sop by the party in power to attract and keep the immigrant vote. Still others raised the spectre, since it would now be acceptable for so many languages to be openly spoken, of Canada descending into chaos and illiteracy.

It was against this background that Minister Cafik made his presentation, reminding his listeners that multiculturalism had not begun in 1971. Its roots went back far, far longer and deeper:

> The Prime Minister (Trudeau) did not create a multicultural society that year—we have always had one. In the days before the arrival of the first French explorers our Native population was composed of numerous distinct linguistic and cultural groups. Those cultures have been alive in Canada for 100 years before the federal Government enunciated the policy of a multiculturalism. The government was not trying to create a multicultural society—we are living in one. Multiculturalism is a pragmatic policy based on the realities of Canada. Multiculturalism is a vital key to our national unity [...] The Dimensions of human freedom have been expanded by the implementation of this policy. We recognize that when someone comes from abroad to become one of our citizens, they are free to retain their cultural background, and their values. They can do that here by virtue of the freedom offered to all individuals within our land.

In this respect, multiculturalism was always organic—some would say natural—to Canada. What was new was that since 1971 Canadians had begun to truly recognize themselves for what they were, and what they always had been: a pluralistic society.

But what did all this mean in practical, or as the minister had said, pragmatic terms? Diversity would be the order of the day. Cafik argued:

> One of my jobs is to ensure that every Canadian is given an equal opportunity to be of service to their country. The Government of Canada makes appointments to the judiciary, to advisory councils and to numerous boards and agencies. When the Cabinet approves those order-in-council appointments,

I must have an impact on behalf of all the ethnocultural communities to ensure that all are represented. Now that's important for a multiplicity of reasons. The representation of various cultural backgrounds makes those bodies function better than they would if they didn't have that input, because each one of us as a Canadian is unique. We are unique because we are created as individual human beings and because of the input of our parents, the cultural background and diversity that we have inherited. That has given each of us an opportunity to make a unique contribution. If our boards, bodies and agencies do not reflect the cultural diversity of this nation, then they will be less workable and less valuable to the Canadian well-being. That's the first reason. The second reason is that all of us react instinctively against appointments if they provide equal opportunity for all men and women.[297]

The clear implication of Cafik's speech was that for multiculturalism to work the entire state had to be radically restructured.[298]

TWENTY YEARS BEFORE CAFIK EXPLAINED how multiculturalism would reshape Canadian citizenship, the Canadian director for the Brotherhood of Sleeping Car Porters A. R. Blanchette gave a talk in Toronto titled *The Brotherhood, is it Attainable?* Delivered on March 23, 1958, to mark Railwayman's Day, the annual event to honour those who worked on the railways, this talk was also about daily life in a society like Canada and whether or not it would ever be possible for diverse people to live together in peace and harmony. Making use of the cadence and rhetorical riffs of a Negro Baptist minister, which was second nature to Blanchette as a lay minister, he reminded his audience of what had been achieved through common brotherhood:

The record of the socio-economic improvements in the lot of the porter-employees of the Canadian Railways, through the past some thirty or forty years, bears eloquent testimony to the vision, faith, courage and unity of purpose of the patriarchs and pioneers among the porters of our racial persuasion who, in the authentic voice of suffering, sacrifice and struggle, set their hands and wills to the task of integrating themselves and their fellow-porters in the Organized Labour Movement of North America. Imbued with the idealism of Brotherhoods, and charged with the conviction that Organization is the instrument, alone, by which workers can throw off industrial dictatorship, and win respect for their rights, these noble pioneers formed Porter-Brotherhood, with national and international affiliations, and thereby drove monarchy from the railroads of Canada and the United States of America, and laid the foundation of Industrial Democracy and Economic Citizenship for the Sleeping Car Porters. These Brothers built the bridge over which hundreds of Sleeping Car Porters and their families, through the years, have ensured the right to earn Bread with Freedom. Be it said to the credit of those venerables that their signal contribution to the advancement and promotion of the cause of this confraternity of Sleeping Car Porters reflects their devotion and consecration to the idealism of True Brotherhood.

This True Brotherhood, Blachette explained, was captured in a love of other human beings and in striving for what he called the perfection of man— making human beings better largely by improving their social conditions. But this could only occur in a society that recognized the human dignity of everyone.

"There is a great difference between love for people you never saw, and may never see," Blanchette said, "and for those with whom you mingle in close relations. There are some persons, whose souls glow with compassion-ate affections for the Hindus, the Japanese, the Chinese, who yet utterly fail in loving their nearest neighbor, those who jostle against them in business, in pew, in church aisle, in society." Blanchette continued with a scathing denunciation of what he called the Western democracies and of their accep-tance and even condoning, especially in the years immediately following the end of the Second World War, of oppression:

The concept of True Brotherhood is not reflected in the policies of the so-called Western Democracies, notwithstanding the nomenclature, where men are discriminated against on the basis of race, colour, creed, national ori-gin and ancestry, rather than being considered on the basis of merit, worth, ability and creativity of the individual. Racial and religious Discrimination have no place in a democratic society. The idealism of Brotherhood does not characterize the ideologies that postulate and promote Bigotry, Hatred, and the doctrine of the superiority or inferiority of any given race. True Brotherhood does not hold with the repugnant policy of British Colonialism in South Africa and in the Islands of the Caribbean; is totally inconsistent with the philosophy of Russian Communism and Totalitarian Imperialism; and indicts the practice of Jim Crow and Segregation in the Southern States of America, and the subtle discrimination in employment, housing, restaurants and places of amusement against Minority Groups in the Dominion of Canada and the Canadian Government's warped immigration policy in respect to West Indians of colour. True Brotherhood stands aghast, in moral indignation at the fact that the Chief Executive of the strongest nation in the world, the so-called "Land of the Free and Home of the Brave", could, a year or so ago, to use his own words, "shudder at the crimes and terror in Hungary", and at the same time could not find a single word to rebuke the mobs that were running wild in Alabama (terrorizing Black people). True Brotherhood is the very antithesis of Anti-Semitism, Anti-Catholicism and Negrophobia; rather, True Brotherhood promulgates and extols the Dignity of Man, and his fundamental and inalienable Human Rights from the beginning of Time.[299]

Four years later it was Grizzle's turn to publicly offer his views on brotherhood as an expression of human dignity. On February 18, 1962, he spoke at St. Luke's United Church in Toronto at a service to mark the beginning of Brotherhood Week by the Council of Christians and Jews. "If all men are brothers, then all men regardless of race, creed, colour, national origin and ancestry are equal before the law," he said. "And if all men are equal before the law—then it is a logical and inevitable conclusion that all men are entitled to equal treatment." Dignity was a God-given attribute found in all human beings and, by extension, freedom and equality of treatment was recognition of this God-given gift as well. Dignity was expressed through the rights and daily living of citizens and how they treat one another.

But such was not the case in Canada, Grizzle argued. This could be clearly seen with the Canadian Indian Act, which "provides for maintaining of reservations for the very first citizens of this country thus depriving our Indians of property rights and concomitantly subjecting them to lower educational and health standards. This is a shameful situation to put it mildly." It also wasn't the case in Toronto where a survey by the Toronto Labour Committee for Human Rights found "that some 50 per cent (of) housing, apartment summer resort owners and operators denied Jews and Negroes accommodation because of the sound of their name and colour of skin." And true brotherhood was not expressed in the Canadian immigration policies that excluded Black immigrants and other peoples of colour solely in an attempt to keep Canada white. And it was not the case, Grizzle argued, in Canada's treatment of Japanese and Chinese immigrants and in the stereotypical way some people were depicted and called racist names.

The foregoing instances of discrimination account (for) race, colour, national origin and so on—some of which have been perpetuated by governments—particularly, are strong forces for the nourishing (of) prejudice because persons knowledgeable of official policy towards people of colour get the impression that government (approves), is enough to convince them that these coloured people are not quite as good as whites.

We place a stigma of inferiority on our Indians by pictorializing them as fierce warriors riding wild horses, wearing feather bonnets, living in tee-pees of buffalo hides, and nearly always losing in battle to the white men.

Have you noticed that too many Italian sounding names are associated with crimes on television and radio? Yes, these are some of our ways of nourishing prejudice. Along with the Amos & Andy Shows and Minstrel Shows which put the black man in the unfavourable light of an unintelligent, clowning, dancing, crap-shooting buffoon incapable of rational thoughts and progressive ideals—thus not to be associated with.[300]

This limitation of the roles which a person of colour is permitted to fill is true of the entertainment field generally, (even) [...]to the legitimate stage. And (this situation) so incensed Mr. Percy Rodriguez, Canada's leading Negro actor, that he was quoted a year ago by the *Toronto Daily Star* as saying "that there is a lack of imagination in casting. It's just that if there isn't a part in a play for a C.P.R. porter (railway) you don't hear from them.

Apropos this type-casting subject, I had a personal experience last summer which I should relate to you. Having been invited to participate on a program on CBL-TV (Toronto local CBC station) along with the Secretary to the Ontario Premier's office for the purpose of discussing Ontario fair practices legislation—I decided to conduct a test for my own information by telling 10 persons (white) all under 50 years of age—so I thought—that I would be appearing on a TV show on a given date. Six of the 10 persons enquired as to whether I would be singing or dancing on the show. This I submit evidences the images that too many white persons have of people of high visibility.[301]

By keeping these issues of how all Canadian were depicted before the public, Grizzle and his allies were tackling an issue that Black intellectuals had faced for decades: how can historically disadvantaged groups feel accepted as genuine members of their societies? This was the issue at the heart of the struggle by Black intellectuals throughout the hemisphere. The porters in the vanguard of this struggle knew that how people were perceived mattered; that how they were recognized for their humanity and dignity was a first step in according them full citizenship. Not only must they be citizens by law, carrying passports, voting and paying taxes, they must be imagined as such—as typically Canadian in all aspects of life, as naturally Canadian as any other claimant.

With their emphatic emphasis on the importance of a society united in common brotherhood, the porters not only helped rewrite the mythology of who Nature intended to be Canadian and what is naturally Canada, but also the perceptions of peoples excluded from such consideration because of inheritances that included, among others, African ancestry. As one would expect, language was a key aspect of these struggles, resulting in changes in how we used words and which words should be used. Later generations, continuing the porters' struggle, would abandon, for example, the term Negro as a commonly accepted descriptor of all people with Black skin or African ancestry. As a term of aboriginality, Negro fell out of service as people from this group began to assert their peculiar citizenship

ON APRIL 17, 1982, PRIME Minister Trudeau was putting in place what he hoped would be the final piece that would make Canada genuinely a multicultural country. This time he was marking the repatriation of the Canadian constitution with an amending formula, but just as importantly with a Charter of Rights and Freedoms. Speaking at the proclamation ceremony in Ottawa, he noted:

> I speak of a Canada where men and women of Aboriginal ancestry, of French and British heritage, of the diverse cultures of the world, demonstrate the will to share this land in peace, in justice, and with mutual respect. I speak of a Canada which is proud of, and strengthened by its essential bilingual destiny, a Canada whose people believe in sharing and in mutual support, and not in building regional barriers. I speak of a country where every person is free to fulfill himself or herself to the utmost, unhindered by the arbitrary actions of governments. The Canadian ideal which we have tried to live, with varying degrees of success and failure for a hundred years, is really an act of defiance against the history of mankind. Had this country been founded upon a less noble vision, or had our forefathers surrendered to the difficulties of building this nation, Canada would have been torn apart long ago. It should not surprise us, therefore, that even now we sometimes feel the pull of those old reflexes of mutual fear and distrust.[302]

As Trudeau explained, "The Canada we are building lies beyond the horizon of such fears. Yet it is not, for all that, an unreal country, forgetful of the hearts of men and women. We know that justice and generosity can flourish only in an atmosphere of trust." The charter would offer protection: for individuals and minority groups against the tyranny of a majority and for French-speaking Canadians, Aboriginal peoples and new Canadians against the fear of injustice. The charter would recognize Canada as a multicultural society that upholds the rights of women and peoples with disabilities, among others. But there was one thing the constitution and the charter could not do: give the country a heart and the kind of good will that was generally associated with the notion of brotherhood, although Trudeau did not use that word. Instead he said:

> It must however be recognized that no Constitution, no Charter of Rights and Freedoms, no sharing of powers can be a substitute for the willingness to share the risks and grandeur of the Canadian adventure. Without that collective act of the will, our Constitution would be a dead letter, and our country would wither away. It is true that our will to live together has sometimes appeared to be in deep hibernation; but it is there nevertheless, alive and tenacious, in the hearts of Canadians of every province and territory. I wish simply that the bringing home of our Constitution marks the end of a long winter, the breaking up of the ice-jams and the beginning of a new spring. For what we are celebrating today is not so much the completion of our task, but the renewal of our hope—not so much an ending, but a fresh beginning.

A new beginning: such was a dream of the sleeping car porters and the members of the Negro Citizenship Association who rallied under the notions of brotherhood and the creation of a new citizenship—often with the two ideals amounting to the same dream. By the time of their deaths both Moore and Grizzle were welcoming the changes in Canada even while cautioning that much was left to be done to ensure that all Canadians received full recognition and treatment as citizens. As a citizenship judge, Grizzle had the pleasure of administering the oath of citizenship to hundreds of people from all parts of the world. Such is the legacy, working individually and collectively, that he and the rest of the porters gave all Canadians.

AFTERWORD
Appreciating the Legacy

By THE TIME I ARRIVED in Canada in 1979 much of the proverbial heavy lifting that would make life better for a generation of Black immigrants like me had been completed. And even though there was much still to be done, the generation of stalwarts that had fought to make it possible for someone like me to enter the country had passed on a legacy many recipients did not fully appreciate. In my own case, I was able to do what had been denied to many Black people in the era before my arrival, without so much as a second thought. So many of those Black people from an earlier time, who had come from afar for an education or to get started on a new or better life, may have also wanted to be a journalist and an author and to be recognized over a lifetime's work as a public intellectual and an academic not only in Canada but in the United States, thereby achieving much of the dream that had propelled me out of the Caribbean as a young man. Perhaps it was for this reason that, even after seeing Stanley Grizzle at various events around Toronto and after developing a lasting friendship with Billy Downey in Halifax, and even after I covered railway matters as a transportation reporter for Canadian national newspapers for years, I never fully appreciated the many contributions of the sleeping car porters, nor understood their slow and hard-won transformation of Canada. It is perhaps one of the problems of both history and human understanding that it is only when one places one's own life in direct relation to others who've not had your opportunities to fully develop and enjoy human dignity that their own stories, perversely, gather their true power. Such, in any case, is my own relation to that of the sleeping car porters. It is only now, so well versed in the history of their collective struggle, that I can both easily and properly appreciate that nagging question posed by the US poet Langston Hughes in the midst of the continent-wide struggles by porters: "What happens to a dream deferred? / Does it dry up / like a raisin in the sun?"[303] Worse: what happens when it is absolutely denied, stillborn, as dead as a man who passed a civil service exam but instead of getting the inside administrative job he cherished is sent to a farm to raise Minorca hens, if only because they are Black like him?

Fortunately, those Black activists did not simply consider one question by asking another and then another in an interminable discourse among themselves. They actually did something to bring about change. And this change is most evident in the faces of so many young Canadians whose grandparents came from parts of the globe that would have meant that they were excluded from even the possibility of immigrating to Canada. It is evident in the mixing of ethnicities from all over the world, with nary a care for racial or ethnic purity. What a liberated generation. And Canada is the place where this is happening, unnoticed and without alarm. Urban centres boast the best and most diverse of cuisines in restaurants offering combinations of dishes and styles of cooking—Sino-West Indian-Filipino cuisine recently captured my eye in Scarborough, Ontario—that only a uniquely modern place like Canada could produce. For there is so much life to celebrate in such indiscriminate mixing.

In Canada it is now possible for Cabinet ministers to hail from every part of world—to appear in Parliament in their distinctive cultural wear— and yet to be unquestionably Canadian. It is possible for descendants from parts of the globe previously limited to immigration quotas of less than 200 people annually to rise up to lead a national political party and to dream of becoming prime minister, and for this to be considered routine. For such living is the breadth and depth of citizenship. And as Canada piles up milestones for how it has survived as a nation-state, it owes a deep debt of gratitude to a special group of its citizens for making it the country it has become. The sleeping car porters and their allies successfully placed Canada on a very different track. By challenging Canada to become both modern and different, they have taken us to places that Canadians would otherwise never have known. But their struggle is not yet over, not even remotely, if only because those to whom are bequeathed such a rich legacy are now all Black, every last one, and this country, after all, is still Canada.

ENDNOTES

1 Stephen Leacock, *Frenzied Fiction* (New York: John Lane Company, 1917), 95.
2 Wilfrid Laurier, "Speech at Canadian Club" (1904), in *Canada's Prime Ministers, 1867–1994: Biographies and Anecdotes* (Ottawa: National Archives of Canada, 1994), 40.
3 House of Commons, *Debates*, 12th Parl, 5th Sess, Vol. 2 (18 March 1915), 1201.
4 This decline was officially attributed to Black people returning to the United States at the end of the American Civil War, and shows a sharp outflow at a time when 15,000–16,000 entered Canada between 1850 and 1860. See Royal Comission on Bilingualism and Biculturalism, *Report of the Royal Commission on Bilingualism and Biculturalism*, Vol. 4: *The Cultural Contribution of Other Ethnic Groups* (Ottawa: Queen's Publisher of Canada, 1970), 21. However, there is growing evidence that, with support for the Southern Confederacy still strong in Canada after the American Civil War, Blacks were leaving because they were already beginning to feel unwelcome in the new Canada that, similar to the US South, was a Confederacy.
5 One percent figure was the magic figure social scientists of the day considered to be the ideal absorption rate for maintaining social peace and avoiding social indigestion from trying to assimilate outsiders. This view is still very much in vogue in Canadian immigration policy, which maintains an annual absorption rate of one percent or less for new immigrants. Indeed, in 1993, Laurier's successor as leader of the Liberal Party, Jean Chrétien, scored political points during the federal election by committing, in his party's election manifesto known as the Red Book, to an annual immigration intake of one percent—a commitment the party did not meet over three mandates, but which was never officially removed from the party's platform even under subsequent leadership.
6 Mary A. Shadd, *A Plea for Emigration, Or, Notes of Canada West: In its Moral, Social and Political Aspect: with Suggestions Respecting Mexico, West Indies, and Vancouver Island for the Information of Colored Emigrants* (Detroit: George W. Pattison, 1852), 2–3.
7 George Spring Merriman, *The Negro and the Nation: A History of American Slavery and Enfranchisement* (New York: Henry Holt and Company, 1906), 3.
8 Martin Luther King Jr., "Letter from a Birmingham Jail," *Liberation: An Independent Monthly*, Vol. 8, no. 4 (June 1963), 13.
9 Merriman, *The Negro and the Nation*, 3.
10 Duncan Campbell Scott, *John Graves Simcoe* (Toronto: Morang & Co., 1906), 89–91.
11 Ibid.
12 Robin W. Winks, *Canadian-West Indian Union: A Forty-Year Minuet*, Commonwealth Papers (London: The Athlone Press, 1968), 9.

13 Harold Adams, Michael Tynes, and Thornton Williams, conversation with author, Halifax, NS., Summer 2017.

14 Elombe Mottley, telephone conversation with author, Summer 2017.

15 Bromley Armstrong with Sheldon Taylor, *Bromley: Tireless Champion for Just Causes: Memoirs of Bromley L. Armstrong* (Pickering: Vitabu Publishing, 2000), 47.

16 Armstrong with Taylor, *Bromley: Tireless Champion for Just Causes*, 72.

17 Herb Carnegie, *A Fly in a Pail of Milk: The Herb Carnegie Story,* (Oakville: Mosaic Press, 1997), 191–196.

18 Carnegie, *A Fly in a Pail of Milk*, 74–75.

19 Carnegie, *A Fly in a Pail of Milk*, 113.

20 Lincoln M. Alexander with Herbert Shoveller, *"Go to School, You're a Little Black Boy": The Honourable Lincoln M. Alexander, a Memoir* (Toronto: Dundurn Press, 2006), 17–18.

21 Alexander with Shoveller, *"Go to School, You're a Little Black Boy"*, 19, 25.

22 Adams, Tynes, and Williams, interview.

23 Ibid.

24 James Watson, interview by Patrick Brode, tape recording, Windsor, Ont., December 1989, Osgoode Society Oral History Programme, Archives of Ontario, Toronto.

25 Dorothy W. Williams, *The Road to Now: A History of Blacks in Montreal* (Montreal: Véhicule Press, 1997), 34.

26 Article, George F. Brown, *Courier Magazine,* October 31, 1953, Stanley G. Grizzle fonds, R-12294, LAC.

27 Carter G. Woodson, "The Migration of the Talented Tenth," in *The Portable Harlem Renaissance Reader*, ed. David Levering Lewis (New York: Penguin, 1994), 7–8.

28 House of Commons, *Debates*, 12th Parl., 1st Sess, Vol. 1 (18 January 1912), 1413.

29 House of Commons, Standing Committee on Railways and Shipping, *Journals*, 14th Parl, 3rd Sess, Vol. 61, App. 5 (26 June 1924), 234.

30 Conciliation Report, Industrial Disputes Investigation Act, December 1926, Stanley G. Grizzle fonds, R-12294, LAC.

31 Ibid.

32 Memorandum, Canadian Brotherhood of Railway Employees to Canadian National Railway, 17 December 1926, Stanley G. Grizzle fonds, R-12294, LAC.

33 Canadian Pacific Railway, "Employee Statement," Stanley G. Grizzle fonds, R-12294, LAC.

34 Pierre Berton, *The Last Spike: The Great Railway, 1881-1885* (Toronto: Anchor Canada, 2001).

35 Canadian Pacific Railway, *Handbook for Train Porters*, 1921, Canadian Pacific Railway Fonds, EXPORAIL, the Canadian Railway Museum, Saint-Constance.

36 John Harewood, conversation with author, Ottawa, Summer 2017.

37 Circular, Canadian Pacific Railway to Employees, 1946, Canadian Pacific Railway Fonds, EXPORAIL, the Canadian Railway Museum, Saint-Constance.

38 Pocketcard, Canadian Pacific Railway, "Canadian Pacific Railway Company Sleeping Car Service–Helpful Hints for Porters," Canadian Pacific Railway Fonds, EXPORAIL, the Canadian Railway Museum, Saint-Constance.

39 Circular, Canadian Pacific Railway, "Instructions to Sleeping Car Conductors and Porters relative to handling Linen and other Car Equipment," 1 February 1914, Canadian Pacific Railway Fonds, EXPORAIL, the Canadian Railway Museum, Saint-Constance.

40 "A Long Run," *Manitoba Daily Free Press*, 12 September 1891.

41 House of Commons, Special Committee on Railway Act, *Journals*, 12th Parl, 7th Sess, Vol. 61, App. 1 (8 May 1917), 155.

42 Ibid, 153.

43 "A Long Run," *Manitoba Daily Free Press*, 12 September 1891.

44 House of Commons, *Debates*, 8th Parl, 3rd Sess, Vol. 2 (6 June 1898), 7213–7214.

45 C. L. Dellums, *C.L. Dellums: International President of the Brotherhood of Sleeping Car Porters and Civil Rights Leader*, transcript of oral history conducted by Joyce Hendersen (1973), Earl Warren Oral History Project, Bancroft Library, UC Berkeley, Berkeley, 5, 80.

46 Ibid, 13–15.

47 Harry Gairey, *A Black Man's Toronto 1914-1980: The Reminiscences of Harry Gairey*, ed. Donna Hill (Toronto: Multicultural History Society of Ontario, 1981), 7–8.

48 Letter, Sir A.E. Kemp to Lieutenant-Colonel Frederic Lum Wanklyn, 10 May 1917, Canadian Pacific Railway Fonds, EXPORAIL, the Canadian Railway Museum, Saint-Constance.

49 Douglas N.W. Smith, "Farewell to the Ottawa-Toronto Overnight Train," *Canadian Rail* 409, (March–April, 1989), 51–53.

50 Letter, Sir A.E. Kemp to Lieutenant-Colonel Frederic Lum Wanklyn, 10 May 1917, Canadian Pacific Railway Fonds, EXPORAIL, the Canadian Railway Museum, Saint-Constance.

51 Letter, Lieutenant-Colonel Frederic Lum Wanklyn to Sir A.E. Kemp, 11 May 1917, Canadian Pacific Railway Fonds, EXPORAIL, the Canadian Railway Museum, Saint-Constance.

52 Letter, Sir A.E. Kemp to Lieutenant-Colonel Frederic Lum Wanklyn, 29 June 1917, Canadian Pacific Railway Fonds, EXPORAIL, the Canadian Railway Museum, Saint-Constance.

53 Letter, Lieutenant-Colonel Frederic Lum Wanklyn to Sir A.E. Kemp, 30 June 1917, Canadian Pacific Railway Fonds, EXPORAIL, the Canadian Railway Museum, Saint-Constance.

54 Letter, Ernest Russell to A. Philip Randolph, 4 May 1939, Stanley G. Grizzle fonds, R-12294, LAC.

55 Letter, A. Philip Randolph to Ernest Russell, 10 May 1939, Stanley G. Grizzle fonds, R-12294, LAC.

56 Letter, Ernest Russell to A. Philip Randolph, 1 June 1939, Stanley G. Grizzle fonds, R-12294, LAC.

57 Letter, A. Philip Randolph to Ernest Russell, 7 June 1939, Stanley G. Grizzle fonds, R-12294, LAC.

58 Letter, Ernest Russell to A. Philip Randolph, 22 June 1939, Stanley G. Grizzle fonds, R-12294, LAC.

59 Membership form, Canadian Association for the Advancement of Coloured People, 1945, Stanley G. Grizzle fonds, R-12294, LAC.

60 Unpublished writings, Stanley Grizzle, 1945, Stanley G. Grizzle fonds, R-12294, LAC.

61 Editorial, *Globe and Mail*, 7 July 1956.

62 Winks, *Canadian-West Indian Union*, 7.

63 "The wisest among my race understand that the agitation of questions of social equality is the extremest of folly," noted Negro intellectual Booker T. Washington had claimed in his much publicized *The Atlanta Exposition Address*, at the turn of the century, "and that progress in the enjoyment of all privileges that will come to us must be the result of severe and constant struggle rather than artificial forcing. No race that has anything to contribute to the markets of the world is long in any degree ostracized. It is important and right that all privileges of the law be ours, but it is vastly more important that we be prepared for the exercises of these privileges." See Booker T. Washington, "The Atlanta Exposition Address" (1895), *I am Because We Are: Readings in Africana Philosophy*, ed. Jonathan Scott Lee (Amherst/Boston: University of Massachusetts Press, 2016), 343. Other intellectuals went even further in recommending a separation of Blacks and whites as the only solution. Martin Delaney was one of the earliest to suggest this when he argued, "this we conceive to be all-important—of paramount consideration, and shall endeavor to show the most advantageous locality; and premise the recommendation, with the strictest advice against countenance whatever, to the emigration scheme of the so called Republic of Liberia." See Martin R. Delany, "The Condition, Elevation, Emigration, and Destiny of Colored People of the United States" (1852), in *Reflections: An Anthology of African American Philosophy*,

ed. James A Montmarquet and William H. Hardy (Belmont: Wadsworth Cengage Learning, 2000), 81. And perhaps most typical of this view was the advocacy by Marcus Garvey and his followers the world over that Black people in the Americas should return home to Africa.

64 Robert Knox, *Races of Men: A Fragment* (Philadelphia: Lea & Blanchard, 1850), 38–39.

65 Ibid, 44.

66 Ibid, 47.

67 Ibid, 52, 54.

68 Ibid, 43.

69 W.D. Scott, "Letter to Shipping Agents" (1944) in *Viola Desmond's Canada: A History of Blacks and Racial Segregation in the Promised Land*, Graham Reynolds with Wanda Robson (Halifax: Fernwood Publishing, 2016), 127.

70 Madison Grant, *Passing of the Great Race: or, The Racial Basis of European History*, (New York: Charles Scribner's Sons, 1922), 18. This is the thing that would automatically classify someone like American President Barack Obama—and so many children in multicultural Canada—as Black just like his father, rather than white like his mother.

71 William Graham Sumner, *Folkways: A Study of the Sociological Importance of Usages, Manners, Customs, Mores and Morals* (Boston: Ginn and Company, 1906), 12.

72 Letter, Stanley Grizzle to Donald Moore, 2 April 1954, Stanley G. Grizzle fonds, R-12294, LAC.

73 Donald Moore, *Don Moore: An Autobiography* (Toronto: Williams-Walker Publisher Inc., 1985).

74 Armstrong with Taylor. *Bromley, Tireless Champion for Just Causes*, 109–110.

75 Among their gifts to Canada were two notable sons: Dan, who became an internationally acclaimed musician and author, and Lawrence (Larry), a much-praised Canadian author of fiction and non-fiction with international acclaim of his own.

76 Drafted Brief, Negro Citizenship Association, 1954, Donald Willa Moore fonds, Fond 431, City of Toronto Archives. The Canadian government would confirm, in 1969, that the Immigration Act of 1923 stripped Black West Indians of their right to be identified as British Subjects. "Negroes also suffered from discriminatory measures in 1923, when it was decided that only citizens of Commonwealth countries with predominantly white populations would be considered British Subjects," the government said in a report on the cultural and ethnic composition the country. See Royal Commission on Bilingualism and Biculturalism, Report, 28.

77 Drafted Brief, Negro Citizenship Association, 1954, Stanley G. Grizzle fonds, R-12294, LAC.

78 Article, *Daily Mercury*, 19 October 1953.

79 Drafted Brief, Negro Citizenship Association, 1954, Stanley G. Grizzle fonds, R-12294, LAC.

80 Brief, National Committee on Racial Tolerance of the Canadian Congress of Labour to Milton Green, 27 May 1952, Stanley G. Grizzle fonds, R-12294, LAC.

81 Ibid.

82 Immigration Act, "Order-in-Council P.C. 695" (21 March 1931), RG2-A-1-a, Vol. 1479, PC 1931-695, LAC.

83 Canada, *Statutes of Canada: An Act Respecting Immigration Act, 1910*, Ottawa, SC 9-10 Edward VIII, Chapter 27, No. 39, LAC.

84 Letter, Stanley Grizzle to Louis St. Laurent, 26 April 1954, Stanley G. Grizzle fonds, R-12294, LAC.

85 Stanley Grizzle with John Cooper, *My Name's Not George: The Story of the Brotherhood of Sleeping Car Porters in Canada* (Toronto: Umbrella Press, 1998), 97.

86 The following telegram was sent to Randolph and his committee the day before the March on Washington. "The undersigned Canadian organizations which have for years carried the battle for equality, regardless of race, creed or color, hail your gallant struggle for complete

equality and full citizenship of the American Negro. We express our solidarity with your march on Washington composed of citizens of all races and colors and hope that your aim will be fully achieved and your struggle completely vindicated. Abraham Lincoln's famous dictum that freedom is indivisible has an ever-wider application today as the struggle for freedom is universal. Your achievement of freedom and equality for the American Negro is essential to the struggle for freedom and equality the world over. Its delay could only bring turmoil and bitter discouragement to all those who are fighting on the frontier of freedom on all continents of the globe. We join with you in fervent hope that August 28th, 1963 will mark a great milestone in the broadening and extension of human dignity, freedom and equality everywhere. Signed: Montreal Committee for Human rights, Gérard Rancourt, president; Quebec Federation of Labour, Roger Provost, president; Montreal Labour Council, Louis Laberge, president, Jewish Labour Committee of Canada, M. Rubinstein, president." The telegram was circulated to all members of the National Committee on Human Rights for the Canadian Labour Congress by David Orlikow, the committee's associate secretary.

87   Gairey, *A Black Man's Toronto 1914-1980*.

88   Introductory Remarks, Donald Moore, 27 April 1954, Stanley G. Grizzle fonds, R-12294, LAC.

89   Paul Andrew Evans, "The Least Possible Fuss and Publicity" in *The Politics of Immigration in Postwar Canada, 1945-1963*. UWSpace.http://hdl.handle.net/10012/13700, fn p.119 (accessed December 8, 2018).

90   Moore, *Don Moore*, 107.

91   House of Commons, *Debates*, 11th Parl, 3rd Sess, Vol. 3 (9 March 1911), 4931.

92   W.E.B. Du Bois, *The Souls of Black Folk* (New York: Signet Classics, Penguin Group, 2002), 17.

93   Colin A. Thomson, *Blacks in Deep Snow: Black Pioneers in Canada*. (Don Mills: J.M. Dent & Sons Ltd, 1979), 83.

94   Du Bois, *The Souls of Black Folk*, 7. For emphasis, Du Bois had stated the same sentiment in the very first words of the book as an address to the reader. Du Bois wrote in his "Forethought": "Herein lies buried many things, which if read with patience may show the strange meaning of being black here at the dawning of the Twentieth Century. This meaning is not without interest to you, Gentle Reader, for the problem of the Twentieth Century is the problem of the color line."

95   Sarah-Jane Mathieu, *North of the Color Line: Migration and Black Resistance in Canada, 1870–1955* (Chapel Hill: University of North Carolina Press, 2010), 15.

96   Wilbur Henry Seibert, *The Underground Railroad from Slavery to Freedom* (New York: The MacMillan Company, 1899), 197. This was possibly Captain Hiram Chapman, who was a well known transporter of slaves to freedom across Lake Erie during this period.

97   House of Commons, *Debates*, 11th Parl, 3rd Sess, Vol. 3 (9 March 1911), 4930.

98   Ralph Ellison, *Invisible Man* (New York: Random House, 1947), 388.

99   House of Commons, *Debates*, 11th Parl, 3rd Sess, Vol. 4 (23 March 1911), 5941–5942.

100 Ibid, 5942–5944.

101 House of Commons, *Debates*, 11th Parl, 3rd Sess, Vol. 4 (3 April 1911), 6524.

102 Thomson, *Blacks in Deep Snow*, 77.

103 Ibid, 6524–6525.

104 Thomson, *Blacks in Deep Snow*, 80–81.

105 House of Commons, *Debates*, 11th Parl, 3rd Sess, Vol. 4 (23 March 1911), 5944–5945.

106 House of Commons, *Debates*, 11th Parl, 3rd Sess, Vol. 3 (22 March 1911), 5912.

107 House of Commons, *Debates*, 11th Parl, 3rd Sess, Vol. 4 (23 March 1911), 5945–5946.

108 Robert A. Huttenbeck, *Racism and Empire: White Settlers and Colonial Immigrants in the British Self-Governing Colonies, 1830–1910* (Ithaca: Cornell University Press, 1976), 177.

109 House of Commons, *Debates*, 20th Parl, 2nd Sess, Vol. 1 (9 April 1946), 608–609.

110 House of Commons, *Debates*, 20th Parl, 2nd Sess, Vol. 1 (9 April 1946), 700.

111 House of Commons, *Debates*, 20th Parl, 3rd Sess, Vol. 5 (19 June 1947), 4354.

112 House of Commons, *Debates*, 20th Parl, 3rd Sess, Vol. 5 (20 June 1947), 4417.

113 House of Commons, *Debates*, 20th Parl, 3rd Sess, Vol. 5 (25 June 1947), 4615.

114 Editorial, *Winnipeg Free Press*, 3 October 1945.

115 House of Commons, *Debates*, 19th Parl, 5th Sess, Vol. 3 (16 May 1944), 2971.

116 Unpublished manuscript, Stanley G. Grizzle fonds, R-12294, LAC.

117 Editorial, *Winnipeg Free Press*, 3 October 1945.

118 House of Commons, *Debates*, 21st Parl, 7th Sess, Vol. 4 (24 April 1953), 4351.

119 Brief, Canadian Congress of Labour to Government of Canada, 1952, Stanley G. Grizzle fonds, R-12294, LAC.

120 UN General Assembly, *Universal Declaration of Human Rights*, 10 Decemeber 1948, 217A (111), http://www.un.org/en/universal-declaration-human-rights/ (accessed August 3, 2017).

121 Union memoranda, Stanley G. Grizzle fonds, R-12294, LAC.

122 Letter, A. Philip Randolph to A.R. Blanchette, 28 December 1955, Stanley G. Grizzle fonds, R-12294, LAC.

123 Letter, Walter Harris to Stanley Grizzle, 20 May 1952, Stanley G. Grizzle fonds, R-12294, LAC.

124 Letter, J.W. Pickersgill to Donald Moore, 13 February 1955, Stanley G. Grizzle fonds, R-12294, LAC.

125 Ian R. G. Spencer, *British Immigration Policy Since 1939: The Making of Multi-Racial Britain* (London: Taylor and Frances, 1997), 53.

126 House of Commons, *Debates*, 13th Parl, 5th Sess, Vol. 1 (10 March 1921), 776.

127 UK House of Commons, *County Court Case, Lambeth (Judge's Remarks)*, Vol. 535 (13 December 1954), 72.

128 Article, *Toronto Star*, 14 December 1954.

129 George Pearkes, remarks at press conference, Ottawa, 1957, Stanley G. Grizzle fonds, R-12294, LAC.

130 Spencer, *British Immigration Policy Since 1939*, 54.

131 Canada, Department of Citizenship and Immigration, *Are You Thinking of Emigrating to Canada?* (Ottawa: Queen's Publisher, 1954).

132 Robert A. Huttenback, *Racism and Empire: White Settlers and Colored Immigrants in the British Self-Governing Colonies, 1830–1910* (Ithaca: Cornell University Press, 1976), 177.

133 Canada, *Statutes of Canada, An Act Respecting Immigration, 1910*, Ottawa: SC 9-10, Edward VII, Chapter 27, No. 39, LAC.

134 Imperial Conference, *Imperial Conference, 1926: Summary of Proceedings* (Ottawa: Queen's Publisher, 1926), 35.

135 See Cecil Foster, *Blackness and Modernity: The Colour of Humanity and the Quest for Freedom* (Montreal: McGill University Press, 2007), 1–86. A good example of this are the Black trade unions in Britain, whose members are not only those with black skin but all people facing social inequalities based on not being white or European.

136 Imperial Conference, Imperial Conference, 1926, 35.

137 Charles A. McCurdy, "Thoughts Arising out of the Imperial Economic Conference, 1926," *The Contemporary Review*, (1 July 1926), 690–696.

138 Ibid.

139 See Secretary of State for the Colonies, *West India Royal Commission Report* (London: His Majesty Stationery Office, 1945). This report is often called the Moyne Commission Report on the West Indies. Lord Moyne headed the commission after an outbreak of violence and other forms of social unrest in the British West Indies between 1933 and 1939. The report recommended self-government for the colonies, but stopped short of recommend-

ing full political independent as some of political leaders and trade unionists in the region were advocating.

140 Colonial Office, *British Dependencies in the Caribbean and North Atlantic* 1939–52 (London: Her Majesty's Stationery Office, 1952), 6–7.

141 Introductory Remarks, Donald Moore, 27 April 1954, Stanley G. Grizzle fonds, R-12294, LAC.

142 Spencer, *British Immigration Policy Since 1939*, 50, 52.

143 Ibid, 23.

144 "Color Bar at Gate? A Question in Britain," *Globe and Mail*, 6 December 1954.

145 House of Commons, *Debates*, 21st Parl, 7th Sess, Vol. 4 (24 April 1953), 4351.

146 Armstrong with Taylor, *Bromley: Tireless Champion for Just Causes*, 104–105.

147 In typical fashion, Grizzle wrote the dean of medicine at Howard University in Washington on April 12, 1954: "I am active in Civil Rights and Human Rights Organizations here in Toronto and we are interested in getting the answers to the following questions: Do Negroes or whites coming from the West Indies or Italy have any difficulty with meeting the climatic conditions of the northern US? Which group has the most difficulty in meeting the climatic change Negroes or whites?" Harold B. Jordan, administrative assistant in the university's School of Medicine, responded on May 12, 1954: "In our opinion, it is doubtful whether any scientific research has been done to validate the premise that races have difficulty in adapting themselves to radical changes in climate. I might point out that it was a Mr. Matthew Henson, a Negro, who accompanied Commander Peary to the North Pole, and that for centuries the Nordics have colonized and settled in tropical areas throughout the world." Grizzle also wrote to the dean of medicine at McGill University in Montreal, the School of Hygiene at the University of Toronto, and the federal director of research at the Department of Health and Welfare. In their replies, none offered any evidence to support the government's claims. See Stanley Grizzle fonds, R-12294, Library and Archives Canada.

148 House of Commons, *Debates*, 21st Parl, 7th Sess, Vol. 4 (24 April 1953), 4351–4352.

149 Ibid, 4352–4353.

150 Ibid, 4354–4355.

151 Ibid, 4356–4357.

152 Senate, Standing Committee on Immigration and Labour, *Proceedings of the Standing Committee on Immigration and Labour* (Ottawa: Queen's Publisher, 1946), 208.

153 Editorial, *Toronto Star*, 16 February 1955.

154 Introductory Remarks, Donald Moore, 27 April 1954, Stanley G. Grizzle fonds, R-12294, LAC.

155 Remarks, Ottawa Delegation, 27 April 1954, Stanley G. Grizzle fonds, R-12294, LAC.

156 Ibid.

157 House of Commons, *Debates*, 20th Parl, 3rd Sess, Vol. 3 (1 May 1947), 2644–2646.

158 Remarks, Ottawa Delegation, 27 April 1954, Stanley G. Grizzle fonds, R-12294, LAC.

159 Letter, A. Philip Randolph to Stanley Grizzle, 13 January 1954, Stanley G. Grizzle fonds, R-12294, LAC.

160 James Eayrs, *Northern Approaches: Canada and the Search for Peace* (Toronto: Macmillan, 1961), 58.

161 Moore, *Don Moore*.

162 Gordon Milling, "What about Our Social Policy?" *Comment On: Immigration* 2, no. 9, (September 1952).

163 Austin Clarke, *'Membering*. (Toronto: Dundurn Press, 2015), 24.

164 Ibid, 24–25.

165 M. G. Smith, *The Plural Society in the British West Indies*, (Berkeley: University of California Press, 1965/74), 5, 7–8.

166 C. S. Salmon, *The Caribbean Confederation* (London: Cassell & Company, Limited, 1888), 3.

167 Ibid, 3–4.
168 W. A. Domingo, "Gift of Black Tropics," in *The Portable Harlem Renaissance Reader*, ed. David Levering Lewis (New York: Penguin Books, 1995), 11–12.
169 Louis S. Meikle, *Confederation of the British West Indies versus Annexation to the United States of America* (New York: Negro University Press, 1969), 6.
170 Ibid, 47–48.
171 Ibid, 58–60.
172 Ibid, 16.
173 John C. Walter, "West Indian Immigrants: Those Arrogant Bastards," *Contributions in Black Studies* 5, no. 3 (2008).
174 Winston James, *Holding Aloft the Banner of Ethiopia: Caribbean Radicalism in Early Twentieth-Century America* (London: Verso, 1999), 1.
175 Sir Grantley Adams, "Challenge of the West Indies" (speech, Toronto, 23 October 1958), Barbados Labour Party, www.blp.org.bb/wp-content/uploads/2016/12/Challenge-of-the-West-Indies—Sir-Grantley-Adams-1958.pdf.
176 Norman Manley, "Speech at Mount Allison Summer Institute" (1957) in *Canada and the West Indies: Speeches by Sir Grantley Adams, Professor Alexander Brady and Others*, ed. P.A. Lockwood (Sackville: Mount Allison University Publication, 1957), 24–26.
177 Martin Luther King Jr., "The American Dream," (1965) in *A Knock at Midnight: Inspiration from the Great Sermons of Reverend Martin Luthor King Sr.*, eds. Clayborne Carson and Peter Holloran (New York: Warner Books Inc., 1998).
178 Moore, *Don Moore.*
179 Gairey, *A Black Man's Toronto 1914-1980.*
180 Letter, Gordon Milling to Kalman Kaplansky, 2 March 1953, Kalmen Kaplansky fonds, MG30-A53, R5491-0-8-E, LAC.
181 Article, *Globe and Mail*, 2 May 1954.
182 Article, *Toronto Star*, 10 July 1954.
183 Editorial, *Globe and Mail*, 8 December 1955.
184 Article, *Toronto Star*, 15 June 1957.
185 Letter, Donald Moore to Wilberforce Maxwell, 28 January 1956, Stanley G. Grizzle fonds, R-12294, LAC.
186 Letter, Ethel Brown-Owen to Department of Citizenship and Immigration, 1954, Stanley G. Grizzle fonds, R-12294, LAC.
187 Letter, Department of Citizenship and Immigration to Ethel Brown-Owen, 12 January 1955, Stanley G. Grizzle fonds, R-12294, LAC.
188 Petition, Canadian Congress of Labour to Government of Canada, 1956, Stanley G. Grizzle fonds, R-12294, LAC.
189 Letter, Stanley Grizzle to Gordon Cushing, 21 March 1956, Stanley G. Grizzle fonds, R-12294, LAC.
190 Letter, A. Philip Randolph to A.R. Blanchette, 1956, Stanley G. Grizzle fonds, R-12294, LAC.
191 Letter, A.R. Blanchette to A. Philip Randolph, 15 March, 1956, Stanley G. Grizzle fonds, R-12294, LAC.
192 Resolution, Ontario Federation of Labour, February 1955, Stanley G. Grizzle fonds, R-12294, LAC.
193 Letter, C.E.S. Smith to Stanley Grizzle, 27 February 1956, Stanley G. Grizzle fonds, R-12294, LAC.
194 Letter, Stanley Grizzle to A.R. Blanchette, 12 March 1956, Stanley G. Grizzle fonds, R-12294, LAC.
195 Article, *Globe and Mail*, 6 July 1957.
196 Article, *Globe and Mail*, 7 August 1957.

197 Article, *Toronto Star*, 15 June 1957.

198 Article, *Toronto Star*, 25 October 1959.

199 Canadian Pacific Railway, *Employee Handbook*, 1921, Canadian Pacific Railway Fonds, EXPORAIL, the Canadian Railway Museum, Saint-Constance.

200 Ibid.

201 Statement, James Ewing to Canadian Pacific Railway, December 1954, Canadian Pacific Railway Fonds, EXPORAIL, the Canadian Railway Museum, Saint-Constance.

202 Supervisory Write-up, S. Gilmore to Canadian Pacific Railway, December 1954, Canadian Pacific Railway Fonds, EXPORAIL, the Canadian Railway Museum, Saint-Constance

203 Statement, James Ewing to Canadian Pacific Railway, December 1954, Canadian Pacific Railway Fonds, EXPORAIL, the Canadian Railway Museum, Saint-Constance.

204 Circular, Division of Night Watch, Canadian Pacific Railway, 1938.

205 Ibid.

206 Canadian Pacific Railway, *Employee Handbook*, 1921, Canadian Pacific Railway Fonds, EXPORAIL, the Canadian Railway Museum, Saint-Constance.

207 Canadian Pacific Railway, *Employee Handbook*, 1964, Canadian Pacific Railway Fonds, EXPORAIL, the Canadian Railway Museum, Saint-Constance.

208 Canadian Pacific Railway, *Employee Handbook*, 1921.

209 Canadian Pacific Railway, *Employee Handbook*, 1964.

210 Gairey, *A Black Man's Toronto 1914–1980*, 34-35.

211 Brief, British West Indies Federation to John Diefenbaker, 1959, Stanley G. Grizzle fonds, R-12294, LAC.

212 Brief, Canadian Free Enterprise Committee, "Re: Fair Employment Practice," 1952, George Alexander Drew fonds, Mg 32 C 3, Vol. 182, File 35, LAC.

213 Ibid. It is noticeable that the long list of minorities included groups that are now considered to be white, an indication of how fluid this descriptor as an authentic Canadian has become. But in its day, these descriptors mattered.

214 Ibid.

215 Subcommittee of the Committee on Education and Labour, *Fair Employment Act: Hearings on S. 2048, A Bill to Prohibit Discrimination in Employment Because of Race, Creed, Colour, National Origin or Ancestry*, 78th Congress, 2nd Sess (Washington: United States Government Printing Offices, 1944).

216 House of Representatives, *Congressional Record*, 90th Congress, Vol. 90, Pt. 4 (26 May 1944), 5053-5054.

217 Subcommittee of the Committee on Education and Labour, *Fair Employment Act: Hearings on S. 2048, A Bill to Prohibit Discrimination in Employment Because of Race, Creed, Colour, National Origin or Ancestry*, 78th Congress, 2nd Sess (Washington: United States Government Printing Offices, 1944).

218 Letter, A.R. Blanchette to Bennie Smith, 25 October, 1952, Stanley G. Grizzle fonds, R-12294, LAC.

219 House of Commons, *Debates*, 21st Parl, 7th Sess, Vol. 4 (13 April 1953), 3762.

220 Ibid, 3778.

221 House of Commons, *Debates*, 22nd Parl, 1st Sess, Vol. 6 (26 June 1954), 6816.

222 Ibid, 6821–6822.

223 Ibid, 6826.

224 Memorandum, C.E.S. Smith to Laval Fortier, 1954, in Bromley Armstrong with Sheldon Taylor, Bromley: Tireless Champion for Just Causes (Pickering: Vitabu Publishing, 2000), 113.

225 Resolution, Negro Citizenship Association to Louis St. Laurent, 7 March 1955, Stanley G. Grizzle fonds, R-12294, LAC.

226 Letter, Bromley Armstrong to Toronto District Trades and Labour Council, March 1955, Stanley G. Grizzle fonds, R-12294, LAC.

227 House of Commons, *Debates*, 22nd Parl, 2nd Sess, Vol. 2 (15 February 1955), 1171.

228 Letter, W.W . Dawson to Donald Moore, 6 October 1955, Stanley G. Grizzle fonds, R-12294, LAC.

229 Letter, John K. Crutcher to M.M. Maclean, 21 May 1954, Stanley G. Grizzle fonds, R-12294, LAC.

230 Ibid.

231 Letter, Stanley Grizzle to M.M. Maclean, November 1954, Stanley G. Grizzle fonds, R-12294, LAC.

232 Letter, Bennie Smith to Stanley Grizzle, 10 November 1954, Stanley G. Grizzle fonds, R-12294, LAC.

233 Letter, A. Philip Randolph to Stanley Grizzle, 9 November 1954, Stanley G. Grizzle fonds, R-12294, LAC.

234 Letter, Stanley Grizzle to A. Philip Randolph, 13 November 1954, Stanley G. Grizzle fonds, R-12294, LAC.

235 Letter, Sid Blum to Stanley Grizzle, 1 December 1954, Stanley G. Grizzle fonds, R-12294, LAC.

236 Letter, John K. Crutcher to M.M. Maclean, 25 June 1954, Stanley G. Grizzle fonds, R-12294, LAC.

237 Letter, Stanley Grizzle to Brotherhood of Sleeping Car Porters Head Office, 30 April 1955, Stanley G. Grizzle fonds, R-12294, LAC.

238 "Pullman Company will Hire Negro Conductors!" *Pittsburgh Courier*, 22 May 1954.

239 "C.P.R. Promotes Negro Porters to Conductors," *Toronto Telegram*, 2 May 1956.

240 Letter, A. Philip Randolph to Stanley Grizzle, 29 March 1955, Stanley G. Grizzle fonds, R-12294, LAC.

241 Letter, Sid Blum to Stanley Grizzle, 15 March 1956, Stanley G. Grizzle fonds, R-12294, LAC.

242 Letter, V.I. Petgrave to Michael Starr, 7 April 1958, Stanley G. Grizzle fonds, R-12294, LAC.

243 Letter, Bernard Wilson to V.I. Petgrave, December 1958, Stanley G. Grizzle fonds, R-12294, LAC.

244 Letter, Sid Blum to Leo Gaskin, 7 March 1956, Stanley G. Grizzle fonds, R-12294, LAC.

245 Letter, Sid Blum to Stanley Grizzle, 18 November 1955, Stanley G. Grizzle fonds, R-12294, LAC.

246 Letter, Sid Blum to Kalman Kaplansky, 30 November 1955, Kalmen Kaplansky fonds, MG30-A53, R5491-0-8-E, LAC.

247 Letter, Sid Blum to Kalman Kaplansky, December 1955, Kalmen Kaplansky fonds, MG30-A53, R5491-0-8-E, LAC.

248 "Sleeping Car Porters Accuse Railway Firm," *Winnipeg Free Press*, April 26, 1961.

249 Letter, Lee Williams to John Diefenbaker, 1 August 1957, Stanley G. Grizzle fonds, R-12294, LAC.

250 Ibid.

251 Letter, M.M. Maclean to W.J. Smith, 27 September 1957, Stanley G. Grizzle fonds, R-12294, LAC.

252 Memorandum, Ministry of Labour to Brotherhood of Sleeping Car Porters, 4 October 1957, Stanley G. Grizzle fonds, R-12294, LAC.

253 Letter, Lee Williams to Claude Jondoin, 4 October 1957, Stanley G. Grizzle fonds, R-12294, LAC.

254 Letter, D.I. Fenton to Sid Blum, 24 May 1961, Stanley G. Grizzle fonds, R-12294, LAC.

255 Letter, A. Kamarowsky to Sid Blum, 24 May 1961, Stanley G. Grizzle fonds, R-12294, LAC.

256 Report, Sid Blum to Lee Williams and Canadian Brotherhood of Railway Employees, 1961, Stanley G. Grizzle fonds, R-12294, LAC.

257 Article, *Winnipeg Free Press*, 25 September 1961.

258 The others were McKinley Crawford and Lawrence A. Lewsey.

259 *Human Rights Review*, Civil Liberties of Canada (July 1964).

260 A. Philip Randolph, "Address to Triennial Convention of the Sleeping Car Porters," (speech, Montreal, 10 September 1962), Stanley G. Grizzle fonds, R-12294, LAC.

261 As Trans-Canada Airlines, Air Canada started as a subsidiary of Canadian National Railway. In 1948, Canadian Pacific Railways started a domestic rival, Canadian Pacific Airline.

262 A. Philip Randolph, "Address to Triennial Convention of the Sleeping Car Porters," (speech, Montreal, 10 September 1962), Stanley G. Grizzle fonds, R-12294, LAC.

263 Press Release, Brotherhood of Train Car Porters, 1977, Stanley G. Grizzle fonds, R-12294, LAC.

264 "Caribbean Immigrants are Quickly Integrated," *The Gazette*, 17 November 1958.

265 Flyer, Canadian Domestic Employees Association, 1975, Stanley G. Grizzle fonds, R-12294, LAC.

266 Statistics Canada, "Employment and unemployment rates of the second- and the third-and-higher-generation Canadians aged 25 to 54, May 2006," *Statistics Canada 2006 Census*, accessed December 23, 2017, http://www.statcan.gc.ca/pub/11f0019m/2011331/t012-eng.htm.

267 John Diefenbaker, interview, CBC, 7 March 1962.

268 Even then Grizzle and fellow activists in the Black communities across Canada did not relent in their opposition to apartheid. Well into the 1990s they were members of, among others, the Canadian Coalition to Close the Apartheid Embassy, Canadian Peace Congress, and The Committee for the Freedom Ride Against Apartheid to fight for Canadians to break all ties with apartheid South Africa, including leading a popular boycott of South African wines and fruits. Grizzle was also a leading member of Toronto-based The Biko-Rodney-Malcolm Coalition around the same time. One of the BRM Coalition's demonstrations against apartheid was held outside the South African Consulate in Toronto on September 12, 1985, in memory of the murdered Civil Rights icon Steve Biko, at which Grizzle was a main speaker along with guests from South Africa. In 1989, Grizzle received a letter from Secretary of State for External Affairs, Joe Clark, recognizing his participating in the international fight against apartheid. The letter reiterated the Canadian government's commitment to a peaceful dismantling of apartheid in South Africa. Clark said: "Apartheid is an unconscionable and systemic denial of human dignity."

269 Letter, Stanley Grizzle to East York Board of Education, 16 December 1954, Stanley G. Grizzle fonds, R-12294, LAC.

270 Letter, Sid Blum to East York Board of Education, Stanley G. Grizzle fonds, R-12294, LAC.

271 Letter, Stanley Grizzle to East York Board of Education, January 1954, Stanley G. Grizzle fonds, R-12294, LAC.

272 Letter, C.R. Sanderson to Stanley Grizzle, 28 January 1954, Stanley G. Grizzle fonds, R-12294, LAC.

273 Letter, Stanley Grizzle to W.P. Duncan, October 1953, Stanley G. Grizzle fonds, R-12294, LAC.

274 Letter, W.P. Duncan to Stanley Grizzle, 2 November 1953, Stanley G. Grizzle fonds, R-12294, LAC.

275 Article, *Toronto Star*, 20 November 1953.

276 John Kennedy, "Civil Rights and Capital Punishment in the United States," interview, CKEY.

277 Letter, Stanley Grizzle to CKEY, Stanley G. Grizzle fonds, R-12294, LAC.

278 Letter, Dan Hill to Toronto Board of Education, 1956, Stanley G. Grizzle fonds, R-12294, LAC.

279 Letter, Stanley Grizzle to Toronto Board of Education, 30 January 1956, Stanley G. Grizzle fonds, R-12294, LAC.

280 Brief, Negro Citizens of Toronto Presentation to Toronto Board of Education, 2 February 1956, Stanley G. Grizzle fonds, R-12294, LAC.

281 Letter, Toronto Board of Education to Stanley Grizzle, 6 February 1956, Stanley G. Grizzle fonds, R-12294, LAC.

282 Pamphlet, Japanese Canadian Citizen Association, "Please Don't!," Stanley G. Grizzle fonds, R-12294, LAC.

283 Stanley Grizzle, "Letter to the Editor," *CCF News,* 11 April 1958.

284 Letter, Donald Moore to Queen's Printer, 28 February 1955, Stanley G. Grizzle fonds, R-12294, LAC.

285 Moore, *Don Moore,* 121–138.

286 Letter, Stanley Grizzle to Alex Maxwell, 29 May 1958, Stanley G. Grizzle fonds, R-12294, LAC.

287 Article, *Toronto Telegram,* 20 February 1956.

288 Letter, Stanley Grizzle to Westmoreland United Church, 15 May 1961, Stanley G. Grizzle fonds, R-12294, LAC.

289 Letter, Daniel Braithwaite to CHCH TV, 15 January 1962, Stanley G. Grizzle fonds, R-12294, LAC.

290 Richard Moore, *The name 'Negro': Its Origin and Evil Use* (Baltimore: Black Classic Press, 1960), 31–32.

291 W. E. B. Dubois, "Criteria of Negro Art," in *The Portable Harlem Renaissance Reader,* ed. David Levering Lewis (New York: Penguin Books, 1994), 100–102.

292 Richard H. King, *Race, Culture, and the Intellectuals, 1940–1970* (Washington: Woodrow Wilson Center Press, 2004), 8.

293 Among the papers is a document titled "What is Brotherhood," written by Peter E. Terzick and distributed by the New York-based Jewish Labor Committee. It lists six possible definitions of Brotherhood, giving as the final one that "it is not life. It is more than that. It is that which gives meaning to life and makes it worth living. That is brotherhood." See Stanley Grizzle fonds, R-12294, Library and Archives Canada.

294 Norman Cafik, "Multiculturalism—A Canadian Reality" (speech to Third Canadian Conference on Multiculturalism, Ottawa, 28 October 1978), Stanley G. Grizzle fonds, R-12294, LAC.

295 House of Commons, *Debates,* 28th Parl, 3rd Sess, Vol. 8 (8 October 1971), 8545–8546.

296 Ibid, 8546–8547.

297 Cafik, "Multiculturalism—A Canadian Reality," speech.

298 See Cecil Foster, *Genuine Multiculturalism: The Tragedy and Comedy of Diversity.* (Montreal: McGill University Press, 2014).

299 A.R. Blanchette, "The Brotherhood, Is It Attainable?" (speech, Toronto, 23 March 1958), Stanley G. Grizzle fonds, R-12294, LAC.

300 A popular minstrel show first on radio and then television from 1928 to 1960. Set in Harlem NY as the capital of Black America, at the outset the show was written and acted by the two same white men in black face as bumbling, never-do-good Black fools. In the 1950s when it moved to television as well, the main roles were played stereotypically by Black actors. The show was strongly criticized by members of the black communities across North America.

301 Stanley Grizzle, (speech to St. Luke's United Church, Toronto, 18 February 1962), Stanley G. Grizzle fonds, R-12294, LAC.

302 Pierre Elliott Trudeau, *Remarks by the Prime Minister at the Proclamation Ceremony on April 17, 1982* (Ottawa: Office of the Prime Minister, 1982), 7.

303 Langston Hughes, "Harlem," in *Selected Poems of Langston Hughes* (New York: Random House Inc., 1994), 426.

INDEX

ACKNOWLEDGMENTS

MANY PEOPLE CONTRIBUTED TO THE making of this book, going back especially to the 1980s-90s when I was a transportation reporter at the *Globe and Mail* Report on Business and the *Financial Post.* Among them are the porters who in interviews gave so generously of their time, memories and hospitality. Edward William (Billy) Downey, to whom I dedicate the book, spent 40 years on the trains and was one of the first Black Canadians to rise up through the ranks as a Canadian porter. He was a dear friend and much that I know about the life of porters came from the many conversations I had with him, particularly when for a year starting in the fall of 2008 four of us—Billy, his brother Graham who was one of the first Black aldermen in Halifax, their life-long friend Mike Tynes, and me—would meet for lunch on Saturdays at Jim's Restaurant overlooking the scenic Bedford Basin in Halifax. I hope that in my writing I do him justice. Rest in peace, my friend.

Special thanks are owed to a number of people for their research help. These include archivist Mylène Bélanger at Exporail, the Canadian Railway Museum, archivist Amy Putnam (Diefenbaker Papers, University of Saskatchewan) and various unnamed archivists at Concordia University in Montreal, the Canadian Archives in Ottawa, and the Sleeping Car Porters Museum in Chicago. Glendora Cooper, retired librarian at the University at Buffalo, SUNY deserves special thanks as does historian Patrick Brode in Windsor for generously sharing some of his research with me.

But most of all, I offer special thanks to Biblioasis, especially to publisher Dan Wells and editor Janice Zawerbny, and to all their associates. They had the foresight to imagine what this book could be and then the steady guiding hands to make the book a reality. If there are any errors or omissions, they are mine.

For allowing me time to think and write this book, I thank my colleagues and students in the Department of Transnational Studies at SUNY at the University at Buffalo, especially students in my graduate classes on transnationalism and on diversity, inclusion and cultural awareness.

I thank my family for support, especially my wife Sharon for always providing love, inspiration and advice, and my grandchildren for always giving me great joy.